JOURNEY TO JUSTICE

JOURNEY
TO
JUSTICE

JOHNNIE L. COCHRAN, JR.

WITH TIM RUTTEN

ONE WORLD
BALLANTINE BOOKS • NEW YORK

My story is first of all the story of an American family. I dedicate this book to my beloved, late mother, Hattie B. Cochran; to my wise and supportive father, Johnnie L. Cochran, Sr.; to my dear wife, Dale Mason Cochran; and to my wonderful children, Melodie, Tiffany, and Jonathan, who are our family's hope and treasure.

I dedicate this book as well to all those clients who have paid me the compliment of trusting me with the defense of their constitutional rights. As my parents gave me life, so those clients have given me purpose. I have done what I can to keep faith with them all.

The differences between black folk and white folk are not blood or color, and the ties that bind us are deeper than those that separate us. The common road of hope which we all have traveled has brought us into a stronger kinship than any words, laws, or legal claims.

—*12 Million Black Voices*, Richard Wright

We all came here on different ships but we are all in the same boat together now.

—Jesse Jackson

Let's not run and hide, let's acknowledge the divide. Let's work together to make things better.

—*Bridging the Divide*, Johnnie L. Cochran, Jr., 1995

CONTENTS

Introduction   3

1. Gifts of the Spirit   7

2. In the Glow of the Golden Dream   23

3. A Wider World   45

4. A Soul Divided   71

5. A Wanderer in the Wilderness   94

6. My Brother's Keeper   128

7. Jonah and the Whale   142

8. "He Was Our Pride and Joy"   164

9. All That Glitters   196

CONTENTS

10. "Does He Need Your Help?"   225

11. Thirty Pieces of Silver   247

12. "By Their Fruits Shall Ye Know Them"   270

13. "And David Took a Stone"   301

14. From Seeds of Doubt, Justice Flowers   322

15. A Duty of Conversation   358

JOURNEY TO JUSTICE

INTRODUCTION

I T WAS A SWELTERING DAY IN EARLY SEPTEMBER 1972. I
was thirty-four years old; I had tried and won ten murder cases
in a row; I had my confidence: I was on a roll.

Then I agreed to defend Geronimo Pratt. Geronimo was innocent. We were friends. I never had cared about a client as deeply
as I did him. And now I was on my way to visit Pratt in the
prison where the state of California intended to keep him for the
rest of his life.

What happened? What went wrong?

As I was driving north out of San Francisco on that sweltering
day, Pratt's trial was still fresh in my mind. As I headed for San
Quentin, I replayed it over and over in my head. Most of all, I
recalled the moment less than two months before when Judge
Kathleen Parker's bailiff had intoned the familiar "All rise" and
we stood to hear the jury's verdict.

Pratt's trial on charges of murder, robbery, and aggravated
assault had been hard fought but no more difficult than many
others I had won over the years. Still, I was inordinately tense as

Judge Parker scanned the verdicts, then handed them to her clerk to be read. From the start, an indescribable undercurrent had surged beneath the surface of the Pratt case. Like an underground river, dark and hidden, it had silently eaten away at the very foundations of my confidence in the integrity of the criminal justice system.

My client, the leader of the Black Panther Party's Los Angeles office, had insisted from the start that his case "was about something else. They're out to get me, Cochran," he said over and over, "and they're going to do whatever they have to do." But I was an experienced attorney. I dealt in facts, not conspiratorial fantasies. With all they had on their minds in those turbulent years, it seemed somehow improbable to me that federal, state, and local authorities would plot secretly together to persecute a single Vietnam veteran whose worst fault was a taste for hyperbolic revolutionary jargon.

But as Geronimo and I stood shoulder to shoulder to hear his fate pronounced, why was my stomach heaving?

"The defendant will face the jury," Judge Parker instructed, and Geronimo and I turned as if in harness. I scanned the jurors' faces. They did not return my gaze.

"We the jury in the above action find the defendant . . ."

I had done my best. But suddenly—for perhaps the first time—I wondered if it really had been enough.

". . . guilty, as charged, of the crime of murder."

A few weeks later, on August 29, Judge Parker denied without comment my motion for a new trial and sentenced Geronimo Pratt to life in prison. In the days that followed, there were rumors and whispers, glimmers of dark secrets. I had begun to learn things, though not nearly as much as I intended to know. One of us, indeed, had been living in a fantasy world. But it wasn't my client.

I had come to San Quentin, in part, to tell Geronimo that. The guard who escorted me to the three-by-five-foot cubicle set aside for visiting lawyers and their clients smiled chillingly as he opened the door. This, he informed me, was the very room in which George Jackson had been handed a gun by his lawyer shortly before his fatal escape attempt. Pratt was in solitary confinement, where he would remain for the next eight years, and they brought him to me chained hand and foot. He wore a white jumpsuit with a huge black X stenciled on its back.

"Cochran," he said matter-of-factly, "this thing on my back is a target. When I walk back across that yard, if I fall down they will shoot and kill me."

We sat across from each other at a wooden table, a metal screen between us. We talked for hours without ceasing. Then the walls of that tiny room began to close in on me. I felt suddenly desperate, as if I might be going mad. It was time to go. We rose and put our hands together against the screen.

"Don't forget me, Cochran," he said.

"I won't," I promised.

And I never have. Driving back toward San Francisco, I approached the Golden Gate Bridge, and, all at once, its storied beauty seemed somehow forbidding and tragic, part of another world in which people lived happily and unburdened. If I was to keep my promise to Geronimo Pratt, if I was to complete this journey to justice on which I had embarked, I would need more strength than I ever had imagined.

I knew just where to find it. As I have so many times in my life, I recalled the words of the Prophet Isaiah: "But they that wait upon the Lord shall renew their strength; they shall mount up with wings as eagles; they shall run, and not be weary; and they shall walk, and not faint."

That's the thing about roots. They nourish you, and a man who has them always knows where he stands. My own roots run through the rich, black earth of my family's love, across the continent and back nearly sixty years to a clapboard house on a red dirt hill in Shreveport, Louisiana, and to the Little Union Baptist Church where I first heard the voices that have been with me ever since. . . .

1

Gifts of the Spirit

O**N OCTOBER 2, 1937, IN SHREVEPORT'S CHARITY HOS**-pital, my mother—Hattie B. Cochran—delivered me into a world where your food was always fried and everyone you knew was black and a Baptist. I was named for my father, Johnnie L. Cochran, Sr., and, over the next three years, my mother bore him two daughters, Pearl and Martha Jean, whom we've always called "Jean."

We children didn't know it, but we were poor. The Great Depression still had its hands around the throats of Louisiana's working folk, and Jim Crow's iron heel remained firmly planted on the necks of black men and women throughout the South. But the particular world my earnest and enterprising parents built for us was as secure as any palace, so filled with warmth and affection that, looking back through the years, what I recall is its bounty.

But most of all I remember the Sundays. Now, some will insist that after nearly six decades, a man's memory grows selective; I prefer to think that it retains essential truths. So I can say with some confidence that during my childhood in Shreveport, the sun always shone on Sunday and that, whatever the season, it was hot.

When my sisters and I were small, we played in the yard but were careful not to disturb the vegetable garden my mother tended in a vacant lot beside our single-story, white clapboard house. The three-bedroom dwelling, with its covered front porch, was located in Shreveport's Lakeside section, a bit more than a block from the Little Union Baptist Church.

Our Sunday started early. It was a day of rest from work, but not from activity—at least not in the Cochran house, which Jesus may have had in mind when he told his disciples that "the sabbath was made for man, and not man for the sabbath."

My parents, my sisters, and I shared our rented home with my father's mother, Hannah Cochran—whom we all called "Big Auntie"—and my father's cousin, Arthur Lee, along with his widowed mother, Aunt Easter, whose nourishing hugs, kisses, and words of encouragement were nearly as sustaining as my mother's marvelous cooking.

We always arrived early for church, which began at 11 A.M. Between rising and then, there were eight baths to get and your Sunday-go-to-meeting clothes to don—suits and ties for the men, dresses, hats, and heels for the women, short pants and a white shirt and dark tie for me. No less important, there was one of my mother's unforgettable breakfasts to enjoy.

Even though there were two other women in the house, my mother did most of the cooking. By the time the rest of us sat down to breakfast, she had already started the greens and other slow-cooked dishes destined for Sunday dinner. In the meantime, the breakfast table was groaning with grits, eggs, and bacon, sausage, or ham. Best of all were the biscuits she made each day from scratch. I can still taste them, swimming in real butter and crowned with fresh fruit preserves, which had been put up by my maternal grandmother, who lived in the country not far away. All of it was washed down with tall glasses of milk—whole milk. Like so many women educated in an era when malnutrition was still widespread in the South, my mother had a respect for calcium that bordered on reverence. She also had a country girl's shrewd appreciation for traditional remedies and periodically would serve my sisters and me small helpings of dirt from her garden. Multivitamins were unheard of in my mother's world, but generations of experience had taught rural Southern women who'd never heard of the periodic table of the elements that the red earth nourishing their crops was rich in trace minerals, which would help their children flourish. Our mother was proud of the fact that her family ate a balanced diet, and if the meals she fed us were partly responsible for my later struggle with high cholesterol, they also get the credit for the strong teeth my sisters and I still enjoy.

But man, as the Scriptures tell us, does not live by bread—nor even biscuits—alone. And the bright center of our Sundays was down the block in the sanctuary of the Little Union Baptist Church, where my grandmother, Big Auntie, who was also known as "Sugar," sang in the choir and my father, despite his youth, was already a deacon. We always walked to services as a family, and on the way we would meet friends and exchange hellos. Like our house, the church was a clapboard building, white and set back from the street. Inside were a double row of pews and, at the front, the pulpit behind which the white-robed choir stood on risers. There were uniformed ushers, and you always waited for them to seat you. It was hot inside, but the air was always in motion, propelled this way and that by dozens of ladies vainly attempting to cool themselves with the paper fans

9

provided, as their inscription proclaimed, courtesy of the Pierre Street Funeral Home.

Our father sat apart with the other deacons, but I hardly noticed since my eyes, like those of the rest of the congregation, were riveted on the diminutive man who bestrode Little Union's pulpit like a colossus. Ceasar Arthur Walter Clark—known to his flock as C.A.W. Clark—was a stern little figure, barely five-foot-five, with a mustache as neat and tiny as the man himself. He always wore a black robe when he delivered the message, which occupied about a third of each week's three-hour service. No matter how warm the day, when C.A.W. Clark preached, no head nodded, no eyes wandered in search of distraction. He never used a note, because he had committed the Bible to memory and the Scriptures were alive on his tongue. He always began his message with this familiar invocation: "And let the people of the Lord say Amen."

When our pastor evoked the poetry of the Psalms, his melodic voice was sweet as honey; and when he spoke the words of the Prophets, he proclaimed them in the accents of thunder. His rhythmic cadence brought the Scriptures to life, made it a living thing whose force penetrated the flesh, caressing the soul and bringing chorus after chorus of shouted praise from the faithful. The congregation felt it in their bones when he talked of trials and tribulations. His message of faith, hope, and redemption touched us in a healing way, renewing and revitalizing us for another long, hard week ahead. Heads nodded and paper fans stirred the heated air as he talked of a merciful God who answered prayers, a compassionate God who might not always come when you wanted him but who always came on time.

The long sleeves of his black robe fluttered as he put a quiver in his voice while talking about heaven and hell, how we know that our actions have consequences, how we reap what we sow, how we must repent, how we must take our sins to God the Father.

In the end, Pastor Clark always found his way back to the concept of faith, of relying on the Holy Spirit, of putting our changing hand in God's unchanging hand, of trusting in his Holy Word. Here he paused, then quoted James 2:17: "Faith, if it hath not works, is dead." Ofttimes someone in one of the back rows would give off a low moan as the Spirit came over him. I understood what Pastor Clark was saying: A good Christian can't just say he believes in the Holy Word; he must not only talk the talk of the Saved but walk the walk of the Righteous. And, somehow, whatever path Pastor Clark took through the Word, it always led back to John 3:16: "For God so loved the world, that he gave his only begotten Son, that whosoever believeth in him should not perish, but have ever-lasting life."

By the time he got to that point, Pastor Clark had most of the congregation on their feet, and he wouldn't quit until everybody was up—the women standing, waving their hands and shouting, and the men murmuring, "Amen" and "Tell it, Doctor Clark." My parents were quiet, serious, deeply religious people. My father would stand with the other deacons, but he never made a sound, though his face—normally so sedately composed—would reveal how moved he was. Our mother, a small, demure woman whose outward sweetness belied her resolve, never shouted either, but tears would roll down her cheeks.

At about that time, an exhausted C.A.W. Clark would wrap it up and a couple of the deacons would come forward and drape a dark cape over his perspiration-soaked shoulders. I recall being fascinated not only by what I had heard but also by what I had seen. Through the breadth of his learning, the depth of his conviction, and the artfulness of his rhetoric, this man had moved us. He held us all in the palm of his hand. It was, as I would come to realize in later years, much more than just a performance. Mere eloquence without conviction is hollow; conviction that does not find a voice is too often impotent.

After the sermon there was always singing. We all were proud of my grandmother's role in the choir, which performed so beautifully. The lyrics to their hymns were as familiar as our own names: "Amazing grace, how sweet the sound . . . Even me, Lord . . . On an old rugged cross on a hill far away, on an old rugged cross . . . emblem of suffering and shame." Nowadays, I think of the words to "The Old Rugged Cross" more than I used to. For it seems to me that the notion of goodness and mercy transforming the worst imaginable "suffering and shame" into an act of redemption is a powerful reproach to the mean-spirited direction our American society has taken. A memory I've carried with me since my childhood is C. A. W. Clark's description of the terrible day on which Jesus was crucified, how his own cross was placed atop a hill between those of two common thieves. The one thief mocked Christ. But the other—Dismas, "the good thief"—repented of his former life and rebuked his partner in crime for reviling a blameless man. I can still hear the breathless wonder in C. A. W. Clark's voice as he recited to us from memory the Savior's response: "And Jesus said unto him, 'Verily I say unto thee, Today shalt thou be with me in paradise.' " There he was, a repentant thief, and his salvation had been announced by the Savior himself. No one else in history can make that claim— neither judge nor juror, nor prosecutor nor lawmaker, no matter how exalted his station. And when I hear such people dismiss the very concept of rehabilitation as an absurdity, I find myself wishing they'd had just one hot Sunday's benefit of C. A. W. Clark's preaching.

After the service, we'd all gather briefly in front of the church, waiting for the Reverend Clark to join us. "That was a powerful, powerful message," my father would say to him. For my part, I always looked forward to our pastor's handshake, and, young as I was, I remember being impressed that, though he was a little man, his grip was as strong as his preaching.

Then it was back down the street to our own house for my mother's lavish Sunday dinner. There was always fried chicken, rice, gravy, and freshly baked corn bread, along with greens—mustard, collard, or turnip—with yams or macaroni and cheese or fresh corn shaved from the cob and served cream style. Frequently, my mother also fixed okra, which she'd sometimes cook up with tomatoes and black-eyed peas to serve over the rice. On the table were pitchers of lemonade and Kool-Aid; there was no alcohol in our devout household. And always—perhaps best of all—there was dessert: peach cobbler in season, deep-dish apple pie, or, if we were lucky, my mother's famous three-layer pineapple coconut cake.

But before we took a bite of anything, all eight of us stood, joined hands, and prayed. We said the Lord's Prayer, we asked God to protect us all. This, we felt, was our world, and we loved it and couldn't imagine it without each other. There was affection and laughter around our table, but always something more. For at its head sat my father, who, though he was still in his mid-twenties, already had acquired the combination of deep reflection and concern for others that led people in our community to seek his counsel. His abiding faith was a kind of birthright, but in high school he also had come to love the Greek philosophers and to share their fondness for aphorisms. He has composed his own ever since, and, even when we were small, he would share them with us.

"Always recognize that all human endeavors are imperfect and incomplete," he would advise us during those Sunday dinners. "Perfection demands continuous study, growth, progress, and change."

He used to tell us to "thank God, for no power on earth can

successfully challenge or defeat the truth. Good deeds enhance the worth of each individual. Evil deeds destroy or bankrupt the lives of all who engage in them."

My mother, less poetic perhaps but no less convinced of what was right for us, simply would remind my sisters and me again and again to "always be the best that you can be." Another of her favorite sayings was that "truth crushed to earth, will rise again." You didn't fib to a woman like that, not even about small things.

My father, who set the tone for our Sundays—and upon whose advice I have relied ever since—was born to a share-cropping couple on a cotton plantation in the Caspiana township of Louisiana's Caddo Parish. His father, Alonzo, was an ambitious man who married a woman named Hannah from a similarly get-ahead family "over across the bayou." Alonzo's family name was Crockrum, but he changed it to Cochran, which he thought more suitable to his family's progress. "Lonnie Cochran," as he was known, farmed a six-acre plot on a plantation that was owned by four brothers, white men named Will, Lee, Trigg, and Charles Hutchinson. They advanced their tenants seed and implements and—after deducting the cost of those things plus rent for their unpainted, unheated cabins without electricity or running water—let the farmers keep a share of the proceeds from the cotton crop they'd planted, tended, harvested, and baled. That payment, however, was made in scrip, which could be redeemed only in a general store owned by the Hutchinsons.

Cash, therefore, was a rare commodity in the Cochran cabin. But, somehow, Lonnie managed to scrape together enough to buy books for the son in whom he invested so much hope. While Lonnie and Hannah tended their crops, they sometimes left their precious only child in the care of his great-grandfather, David Brown, whose wife Patsy had died earlier. Both had been born in the 1830s. Their own lives had encompassed not only the awful darkness of slavery but also the great good morning of emancipation and the long, tragic twilight of legal discrimination that followed. African American history was a living tradition in the Cochran household and to my future father, the studious young man who was called "Boy C" by the folks around him. His own father constantly reminded him, "I never had a chance. So I want you to make an impression wherever you go, on every level."

Alonzo—by all accounts a stern taskmaster—did all he could to ensure that his son did not disappoint him. He insisted my father follow a regimen that would guarantee that he could compete with anyone. After a full day in school, my father would help in the fields, then use what was left of the daylight for reading. When supper was finished, he would pore over his books by kerosene lamplight. By his early teens, he had exhausted the local parish's educational possibilities and was sent twenty miles north to Shreveport to live with his mother's younger sister Lucille and her husband, the dapper Aristide Albert, who claimed descent from Prince Albert of pipe tobacco fame. My father was surrounded by other relatives who had migrated there in the intervening years. Shreveport was the nearest town with a secondary school—segregated, of course—that would accept blacks or Negroes (as we were called then): Central Colored High.

To the faculty's amazement, this sharecropper's son passed his entrance examinations with such high marks that he was admitted to the tenth grade. He quickly became his class's top student and a champion debater whose eloquence earned him the admiring nickname "Demosthenes." It was a fateful conjunction—the man and the nickname—for the original Demosthenes was known not only for his eloquence, statesmanship, and flair for conciliation, attributes my father seems to have enjoyed from birth, but also for his striking concept of a decent social order. He was once asked when Athens, a democracy, would achieve justice. "There will be justice in Athens," he replied, "when those who are not injured are as outraged as those who are."

My father's social values, though never stridently expressed, were more or less defined by that sentiment. I remember him telling my sisters and me that "good and evil can never, ever live peacefully together. The apparent success of evil depends on the refusal of the forces of good to engage in battle to overcome evil with good."

He had to return home twice each year to help with the spring planting and fall harvest, but my father flourished at Central Colored High, graduating at the top of his class with every reason to believe that he would fulfill his father's lifetime wish and achieve the unthinkable—go on to college. At that point, however, the ulcers that had made Alonzo's life a misery flared virulently. They began to bleed. The local doctors operated and botched the job. Alonzo died. It was a mistake, the doctors said. But in Louisiana, in 1935, mistakes were of no consequence; like the maltreatment of a black patient, they simply were put behind you.

Unless, of course, you were Alonzo's grieving wife, Hannah, and his stunned son, Johnnie. Alonzo had a crop planted when he passed away, which meant his family had to make good on the debt he owed the Hutchinson brothers for seed, implements, and rent. So my father deferred his dreams of college and went home to bring in his parents' crop. He picked four hundred pounds of cotton a day that fall and harvested seventeen full bales, enough to settle his family's affairs forever in Caddo Parish.

That year, my father took Hannah back to Shreveport, where he and his cousin Arthur Lee, who by then also was supporting his widowed mother, pooled their funds and rented a house. My father was eighteen and a high school graduate. Besides caring for the crops, my father was also a Sunday school superintendent and a church deacon. Despite the hardship of losing his father, my father's strong faith in God helped him provide for the financial needs of his family, something he has managed to do for his whole life. But the only job he could secure at eighteen was as a delivery boy for Walgreen's drugstore on Texas Avenue, across the street from Charity Hospital, where I would one day be born.

Not long thereafter, my father and Arthur Lee also went together and bought an old car, ostensibly to help them get to work and make quicker deliveries. That old car had seen better days, but my father and Arthur Lee loved it. No matter how many times that car broke down, Arthur Lee, always a quick one with a joke or story, would make everyone forget the inconvenience and go about fixing it. Like the rest of the family, Arthur Lee was unfailingly optimistic.

My father loved that car for good reason. It also made possible what soon became a weekly ritual in my father's life. During his years at Central Colored High, he had met and fallen in love with a delicate, quiet young woman named Hattie Bass, whose fierce ambition and deep religious convictions matched his own. After graduation she had returned to her parents' farm about ten miles outside Shreveport at a place called Robson and Forbings. Every Sunday, after church, my father would drive down there to continue their courtship. Early in 1937, two years after Alonzo died, my parents were married. Their wedding pictures show Hattie as a petite brown beauty. Throughout Hattie Cochran's life, everyone commented on the loveliness of her features, her high cheekbones, and, what the photo doesn't reveal, the reddish tones of her flawless skin. Hattie believed in dreams; on the eve of her wedding, she dreamed she would have four children, and ultimately she did. She not only believed in dreams, she had an unswerving faith in her God and in her family's ability to set goals and attain them. She passed that ability to envision a future on to me. She and my father would remain together until her death in 1991, fifty-three years later.

Soon after his marriage, my father took up what became his life's occupation—selling insurance. In those days, the five largest black-owned businesses in the country were all insurance companies. If you weren't a doctor or a lawyer and felt no call to the cloth, selling insurance—particularly in the South—was a black man's best shot at the middle class. My father sold for the Louisiana Industrial Life Insurance Company, and, despite his firm's attractive rates, easy terms, and willingness to serve a community the white-owned insurance companies tried their best to ignore, it wasn't easy. Times were hard, money was tight, and some blacks retained a visceral suspicion of a company owned by other blacks. My father used to sum up the problem with the story of a black man who got together the money to start his own ice company, which seemed like a sure thing in an era before refrigeration, when every household needed a daily delivery of the stuff. His prices were lower than his competitor's and his deliveries more frequent. But most of his black neighbors still bought their ice from a white-owned company. Finally, the black owner confronted one of those neighbors:

"Why don't you buy from me?" he asked in exasperation.

"Well," his neighbor replied thoughtfully, "I'd like to, but everyone knows the white man's ice is colder."

What my father always loved about the insurance business was the room it made not only for his entrepreneurial spirit but also for his love of helping those around him. This latter side of his personality was nourished by C.A.W. Clark's weekly messages; the former was reinforced on those Sundays when we didn't head straight home after church for dinner. Instead, we'd all pile into the car and drive out to my mother's family farm.

My maternal grandparents, Emmanuel and Cloteal—whom we called "Little Auntie"—Bass, owned their own land on Route One, Box 396, Robson and Forbings. The road to their place ran back from the highway, through thick stands of pines and fields of bamboo and sugarcane. Emmanuel was legendary, both as an entrepreneur, growing the largest watermelon crop in Caddo Parish, and as a civic and religious leader. He acted as a counselor for his family as well as for other farmers in the area. Emmanuel and Cloteal grew vegetables and fruit for sale, but most of Emmanuel's income came from his work as a tree surgeon on a nearby state-run pecan station. There, his skill at grafting had made him a valuable part in the ongoing effort to develop more productive strains of that staple Southern tree crop. His thrift and the steady income derived from his skill had made Emmanuel Bass truly master of his own house, and my father studied his example with interest.

But what I treasured most about my mother's parents were our idyllic Sunday afternoons in the country with them. I can still see their house coming into view through the trees. My mother's brother Arthur had been badly burned in a childhood accident, and his injuries had left him so crippled he seldom left the farm. He was always waiting for us, the first to spot our car and begin waving. Then there were hugs and kisses from our grandfather and Little Auntie and handshakes from my other maternal uncles, Ladell and Henry. It was like coming home all over again. Even the food was the same, though out there Little Auntie did the cooking and we knew just how fresh the chicken was since, soon after we arrived, my grandfather would wring the neck of a fryer or two from his flock. As I recall, we always ate outdoors under the trees. And we talked, mainly about church since it was Sunday. The drive home through pitch-dark, tree-shrouded country roads was always a memorable end to the excursion.

Most Sundays, however, we remained at home, and, at 6 P.M., we were back at Little Union for the Baptist Youth Training Program meeting. It was a Bible study class conducted by C. A. W. Clark, and that man knew his Bible. In between dinner and the class and afterward, our family would sit out on our covered front porch, where it was cooler. We'd talk among ourselves and with the neighbors, who always dropped by for a chat. I was somewhat precocious—"smart" as my admiring female relations called it—and began reading at the age of three. Those quiet Sunday moments were a great time to sit in Big Auntie's dark wooden rocker and thumb through one of my boyhood favorites, *The Encyclopædia Britannica*, which encompassed a world at which a Shreveport boy could only wonder. I suppose it was then, eyeing the full-color maps of all nations, that my desire to see as much of the world as I could began. Sometimes, I'd stretch out to read on my bed or on the bedroom's cool pine floorboards. Sometimes, when the house would fill with visiting cousins or neighbors, I'd find a quiet moment on the screened-in service porch at the back of the house or under one of the trees in the yard. But wherever I was, I had a book with me.

On the warmest afternoons—after dinner and before the evening meeting at Little Union—my father would make ice cream out on the service porch. As I got older, he would let me turn the crank as he added ice and salt. Later, I would negotiate with my sisters over which of us would get to lick the cold ambrosia off the dasher.

Sundays were for church and family. On Saturday, our parents sometimes permitted us to go to the movies. I didn't know it at the time, but blacks didn't have free access to Shreveport's segregated theaters. You simply recognized this fact and you sat in the balcony and not down on the lower floor. I never thought to ask, "Why can't I go down there?" I was among family and friends, and that was enough. In those days, the only white person I really knew was the young daughter of the family for whom Big Auntie did housework during the week. That girl and I would sometimes play together. But even after I started first grade at the segregated West Shreveport Elementary School, I didn't stop to wonder why there were no children like her in my class. Movies and playmates, however, were for other days, not the Sabbath.

It always was a special treat when our relatives joined us for Sunday dinner. And, to me, none was more welcome than my aunt Lucille, whom we called "Lucinda," and her husband, that dazzlingly handsome Creole gentleman named Aristide Albert. Uncle Aristide ran on the railroad; he was a Pullman porter on the Sunset Limited that traveled between New Orleans and San Francisco. It was to that unimaginably far-off place that he had taken his bride and bought her a big, three-story frame house on California Street. Aunt Lucinda and Uncle Aristide's visits were a special treat for a curious boy whose world extended no further than Robson and Forbings, ten miles down the road. I knew my father and grandfather and their work; I knew the minister at Little Union; I had a passing familiarity with the men who delivered our milk and ice. Beyond that, in those days of few films and no television, the world was a hazy place. Uncle Aristide was full of firsthand stories of people and places across the continent.

Aunt Lucinda was full of advice for my father. By late 1942, the Second World War was a fact of life, even in Shreveport. With a wife, three young children, and a mother to support, military service was out of the question for Johnnie L. Cochran, Sr. Still, he wanted to do his part, and, just as the matter came to preoccupy him, Aunt Lucinda came home to visit. In California, she told my father on one of those long, hot Sunday evenings, there were jobs going begging in what had come to be called "the war effort." My father would sit quietly, holding his chin between his thumb and forefinger, listening to Aunt Lucinda talk about how in the shipyards on the West Coast, black men and white men worked side by side at the same job for the same wages. My father recalled Alonzo's stern reminders that "a man always has to be going for something better." And, in Louisiana, my father thought, a man who wants to do that usually has to pack his bag and get to stepping. Late one Sunday night, my mother had another of her dreams: She saw palm trees and a house with a green front lawn for her family.

That's how we came to San Francisco.

2

In the Glow of the Golden Dream

IN SEPTEMBER OF 1943, MY FATHER SET OFF WEST TO scout the promised land. As usual, he'd thought the whole thing through and made careful plans. By previous arrangement, Uncle Joe Fuller, Big Auntie's brother, came to stay with us in Shreveport. He slept out back on the screened-in service porch and provided us all with the good-humored but reassuring masculine presence deemed essential in well-brought-up Louisiana circles of the day. His tenure, however, was short-lived. Within a matter of weeks, my father had found work as a pipe fitter with Bethlehem Steel in the Alameda Naval Shipyards. Plans were made for us to join him immediately. It was an exciting time but a sad one: Hannah Cochran, the sharecropper's wife, the scholar's mother, my loving grandmother, announced she would remain behind. Shreveport was her home. It contained her memories, her church, and its members. My father was worried and disappointed but, as always, accommodating of her wishes. He arranged for her to continue living in the white frame house down the street from the Little Union Baptist Church, though the quiet that settled over the place must have seemed as strange to her as her absence did to us.

To accompany Mother on our transcontinental journey, my father chose my great-aunt Mary, a big, forbidding woman nearly six feet tall. We children thought her implacable and dreaded her tongue; the problem wasn't just that she brooked no "nonsense" but that her notion of "nonsense" covered a wide, wide territory. My earliest memories of Aunt Mary are of the times she would join us on the walks home from church. High spirits, she felt, must always give way to decorum. "You children are *not* going to run in those good clothes," she would say in a tone so final that it admitted no appeal.

In the fall of 1943—about the time I turned six—mother, Aunt Mary, Pearl, Jean, and I, along with a few suitcase and enough home-cooked food to last four days, boarded the Southern Pacific and said good-bye to Shreveport. At the first stop, little Pearl wondered plaintively if we "were there."

"Not yet," my mother said soothingly.

Aunt Mary, rustling among our parcels, pursed her lips over such nonsense and stiffly informed us that we were only in Marshall, Texas.

Pearl began to sniffle.

"A little while longer, sugar," our mother said consolingly.

"Sugar?" I asked. "But that's what everybody calls Big Auntie"— whom I already missed. "I don't think Pearl is sugar. I think Pearl is just Pearl."

Mother only sighed, but Aunt Mary sternly admonished me "not to dispute your mother's word." Moreover, I was "not going to run around this train" and I was "going to sit up straight." I was beginning to realize that we had left Louisiana behind but not its ways.

We ate our lunch. Soon, the train began to move again. I sat, as instructed, on Aunt Mary's lap and seemed to fall into a kind of dream, lulled by the click of the wheels on the rails and her softly hummed rendition of "Amazing Grace." Before I knew it, we were in California—the land of the free and the home of the gold.

When the Japanese bombed Pearl Harbor and America entered the war, there were fewer than ten million people in all of California, which was still primarily an agricultural state and a transshipment point for the raw materials of the West. It also was an overwhelmingly white state, most of whose policy makers and law enforcement officers—whatever their political affiliations—were traditionally hostile to the Asian, Latino, and, at the time, relatively small number of African American minorities. During the previous decade, the state had been convulsed by bitter labor strife. The big farmers and shippers, along with their allies in government and law enforcement, had responded harshly. Just a few short years before we arrived, a series of agricultural strikes up and down California had culminated in the prosecution and conviction for "conspiracy to commit criminal syndicalism" of Caroline Decker, Pat Chambers, and six other leaders of the Communist-led Cannery and Agricultural Workers Industrial Union. Meanwhile, Harry Bridges, the longshoremen's leader, had repeatedly shut down the West Coast with a series of bitterly fought strikes.

The war changed all that. California's heavy industries—ship and aircraft building, steel, munitions—burgeoned. Agricultural production went into high gear. For the moment, there was labor peace. Economic necessity overwhelmed prejudice, as California's employers sought workers wherever they could find them. Rural blacks and poor whites from the South and plains states streamed into the shipyards and aircraft factories. Mexican immigrants by the thousands trekked north to tend and harvest the crops of the great Central and Coachella valleys. Together, they and their progeny one day would reshape the face of the Golden State. And not least among these ambitious, tireless newcomers were Hattie and Johnnie L. Cochran, Sr., and their three young children.

But first, our family would have to rebuild its own life. Like Moses' firstborn, Gershom, we were "strangers in a strange land." We didn't stay that way for long, though. By the time we arrived, our father was already hard at work reshaping the contours of our future. For a time, we all lived with my Aunt Lucinda. San Francisco was bulging at the seams, and there was an acute housing shortage throughout the Bay Area. But my father, who by then was working two shifts at the shipyard and taking a correspondence course in drafting by night, somehow had contrived to get us on the list for government housing in Alameda. Within a short time, we were at home in our own furnished three-bedroom apartment in a housing project near the shipyard. In those wartime days, no stigma was attached to living in public housing. It was our first experience in an integrated neighborhood. African Americans, working-class whites, Latinos, and others lived side by side. There were Catholics, Jews, other kinds of Protestants, and folks whose faith you could only guess at, all living in about as much harmony as neighbors anywhere. That was a novel experience. But, for us, there also was a touch of home. My father's cousin Amanda Pierre, her husband, Burton, and their son, O.C., who was just my age, had preceded us on the Southern Pacific. They, too, had listened to Uncle Aristide's stories and had decided their future was in the West. With Aunt Lucinda and the Pierres nearby, we quickly resumed our close-knit family life. Daddy even found a church,

Beth Eden Baptist in Oakland, and somehow the time to resume a deacon's duties.

Those were little touches of Louisiana, but, like our housing, school was something new and exciting. In Alameda's up-to-date, integrated schools, I began to excel, skipping the second grade entirely. Like Lonnie before him, my dad was ambitious for his son. He was proud of my achievements but always anxious for me to do better. At the end of my fourth-grade year, I'd racked up twenty-seven A's and three B's. The A's were duly praised, but each and every one of the B's—in penmanship, art, and music appreciation—was discussed at length and a program for improvement was laid out. "Progress demands continuous study and growth," my father would remind me. "Always be the best that you can be," my mother would add.

In those days, we didn't have to look far for a model of academic diligence. Tired as he was from his work in the shipyard, my father spent most evenings studying. His frustration over his own aborted school career never sapped his belief in unceasing self-improvement. He was always engrossed in his correspondence courses, the Bible, or his writing, which by then included religious and philosophical poetry. At the dinner table, he spoke to us frequently about the overriding importance of education and simply took it for granted that I would attend college. Whenever he would make that point—and he did so more often as the years went on—my mother invariably would interject, "And the girls, too." Ultimately, all three of us would graduate from the University of California at Los Angeles. In her own quiet way, my mother was every bit as strong as her husband.

Like any small child, I took my parents' strength for granted. In Alameda I began to appreciate it and to develop a sense of just how valuable it was to all of us. On one level, my understanding of all this was simplistic. I can still see my dad trudging home from an exhausting twelve-hour day in the shipyard. I would dash to meet him, and, as I grew older, he would allow me to relieve him of his toolbox. It was so heavy I could barely lift it, yet it had been his constant companion through all those weary hours. Once in the house, he would sit and unlace the high, steel-toed boots he wore in the shipyard. As I carried them to the closet for him, I remember wondering how anyone could even stand in them, let alone walk to and from his job. But no day was ever so grinding that he was too tired to greet his wife tenderly, to speak at length with his three active children, and—after dinner—to turn to his newspapers, magazines, and books. My father neither drank nor smoked; religion and his family were his principal pleasures, with sports a distant but constant third.

No matter how difficult the moment, he and my mother treated each other with unfailing affection and respect. They set a powerful example, and we children deviated from it at our peril. Like nearly all parents of their generation, my mother and father were firm believers in corporal punishment. Discipline in our family never was arbitrary, but it was swiftly and sometimes painfully administered. The task usually fell to Mother, who, despite her physical delicacy, was a formidable figure when she had a switch in hand. My father, always the conciliator, preferred long talks, particularly when the miscreant was one of my sisters. On the rare occasions he did spank us, he actually would say, "This is going to hurt me more than it hurts you." At the time, I thought it was the only foolish thing my dad had ever said to me. Years later, when I became a father, I found out that he'd been right, even about that.

Daddy also had a flair for dramatic instruction. Once, while we were living in Alameda, I let a disagreement with my mother escalate to the point of disrespect. As I recall, my complaint had something to do with the unfairness of compelling me to come inside from play before the streetlights went on. I don't remember exactly what I said, though it couldn't have been too bad since in our household profanity was a vice ranked only a bit below alcohol and tobacco. Still, my insurrection was enough to provoke my father's intervention. Since I no longer would listen to my parents or speak to them respectfully, he announced, there was nothing left to do but take me to reform school. I was in shock, which quickly turned to fear as my parents methodically collected my toothbrush, pajamas, and other belongings and placed them in a brown paper shopping bag. My father handed me my pitiful "luggage," picked up his car keys, and ordered me to follow him for the ride to my new home. I tried to maintain my composure as he grimly led me down the steps to the curb, where our car was parked. As the door slammed behind me, I looked out the car window to where Pearl and Jean stood, hugging each other tightly, expressions of horror twisting their little faces into masks of misery.

"You could be next," I mouthed through the glass, and, with that, all three of us exploded into tears. Sobbing, I begged for a second chance, and my father solemnly agreed. After a suitable—equally tearful—apology to my mother, I was allowed to "unpack" and move back into my room. I don't remember ever talking back to either of my parents again.

As I grew older, I came to share my father's love for sports, and it was there I found my first role models outside the tightly drawn circle of family and church. Nothing brought our neighbors together quite like a heavyweight title fight, and the man who then held the crown was the fighter against whom all future champions would be measured, Joe Louis. He was called the "Brown Bomber," and he was one of us. He had redeemed our country's honor by knocking out the "Nazi" contender Max Schmeling in the first round in 1938. And, through the subsequent years, he defended his crown against all comers. On the night in 1941 when he fought the great Billy Conn in New York's Polo Grounds, everyone in our household bent over the radio, bodies tense, gazes distant, as we "watched" the fight through the announcer's rapid-fire description.

My father and I clenched our own fists as the announcer told us, "Louis lands a left and another left and a right. . . ." Like men in houses all around us, we ducked involuntarily when we heard, "Conn lands a crashing right hand." It was a tough fight all the way, which made Louis's victory even sweeter when it came. Afterward, we went out on the stoop and discussed every blow in every round with our neighbors. We were proud that Joe Louis, the champion of the world, the man who had snatched the crown from under the shadow of Nazi tyranny, was an American. And, in the Cochran household, we were proud that he also was a black man. We never boasted of it, but we never forgot it either.

There was something else I never forgot about Joe Louis. His grammar was fractured and—compared to my father—he was inarticulate. Yet, no matter how great his victory, he never forgot the place from which he came or the people he came from. He always remembered and spoke unself-consciously about the neighborhood in Detroit where he'd once hauled blocks of ice for a living. After every fight, Louis would thank the people who'd helped him and send his greetings back to "the guys" in the pool hall in his hometown. He was talented, tough, and gracious, and he was my hero.

So, too, was Jackie Robinson. In those years, baseball was my passion. As the war wound down in 1945, my father had more time for us. When he came home from work, he no longer was bone-weary, and he frequently would join my cousin O.C. and me for a game of catch. There were no major-league clubs on the

West Coast in those years. But on the weekends, Dad and O.C.'s dad, Burton Pierre, would take us out to Emeryville, where the Oakland Oaks fielded one of the Pacific Coast League's memorable teams. Casey Stengel was the manager, and Billy Martin was on second base. They had a home-run-hitting catcher named Ernie Lombardi, and Joe DiMaggio's brothers, Vince and Dom, were on the roster.

One summer, my dad even sent me to baseball camp, where I learned to slide and to bunt. That also was the year we eagerly awaited each evening's newspapers for the news of Jackie Robinson. Boxing's color line had been broken more than a generation before by the incomparable Jack Johnson. But until Jackie got his chance, America's national pastime remained lily-white. Just as Joe Louis had redeemed America's honor by keeping the heavyweight crown out of the hands of goose-stepping killers, so we all were counting on Jackie to redeem America's game from the shadow of its own injustice. So, wherever they came from, Alameda's blacks rooted for the Brooklyn Dodgers that summer of 1947 and disdained the St. Louis Cardinals for their overt bigotry against our hero. I still recall how thrilled we all were when Jackie was named the National League's Most Valuable Player in 1949. But I also remember that my father and his friends frequently talked about how Jackie Robinson wasn't even the best player in the Negro Leagues.

In those days, I was as full of questions as my father was of answers, and I asked him to explain to me why, if Jackie was not the best player in the Negro League, he was the first to make it to the majors. It was because, my dad explained, Jackie was the best able to "handle it." Looking back, I can only admire the wisdom and subtlety my father displayed during those conversations. On the one hand, he was implicitly preparing me for the hard fact that the bar was always going to be at least a little higher for a black man, whatever his natural talents. On the other hand, holding up Jackie Robinson's example gave my dad another opportunity to repeat his favorite message: "Your horizons are unlimited. But you must be disciplined and hardworking to attain them. Never forget, though, that you can attain them." Nowadays, they call that self-esteem, and it was one of our parents' most precious gifts to us.

Our years in Alameda, though happy ones, were also marked by the first family tragedy I can remember. In late 1943, Uncle Aristide died in an accident. Somewhere in Utah, as his beloved Sunset Limited highballed toward San Francisco, he fell from the train. We never learned how it happened; it just did. We all missed his sophisticated gaiety and his stories. But his savings and the pension from the Pullman porters' union left Aunt Lucinda comfortably fixed. Always a pillar of strength, Aunt Lucinda was not content to let others do for her. She continued to work as a practical nurse until she was ninety. Both Aristide's and Lucinda's efforts were a notable legacy in a community where—even in the best of times—economic insecurity was accounted simply a fact of life.

Our own family's economic prospects were also on the rise. Late in the war, seeing her neighbors flush with cash from their shipyard jobs, my mother had begun selling Avon cosmetic products. Then, just as the shipyards began to scale back after V-J Day, my father was recruited by Golden State Mutual, California's leading black-owned insurance company. The state's African American population was swelling with discharged servicemen and additional waves of job-seeking newcomers from the rural South. Experienced insurance agents, who knew the field and the market, were in great demand. As usual, Dad made the most of his opportunity. Within a short time, he became Golden State's top-selling agent in the Bay Area and the company offered him a promotion to manager of its San Diego area office. We were proud of Daddy, but the prospect of living in San Diego filled us with trepidation. I didn't want to go, and neither did anyone else but Dad. We had no family there, and it seemed as far away from Alameda as San Francisco had from Shreveport. Moreover, the Pierres had recently moved to a house in Oakland. Mother had never forgotten her dream of a palm-shaded home of her own. There was little chance of that in San Diego. But my father stood by my grandfather Lonnie's axiom: "A man always has to be going for something better." And my mother, as always, stood by my father.

So, in the fall of 1948, we packed up the family Chrysler, made our unhappy farewells to family and friends, and set off south for San Diego.

Daddy had assured us all that "the weather in San Diego is great." He was right about that, but the same couldn't be said for our living conditions. We moved into a tiny, two-bedroom apartment on Ocean View Boulevard from which, despite its optimistic name, you could not see the sea. To my mother's chagrin, on the day we moved in there wasn't a stick of furniture in the place except the double bed in which all five of us slept that night. Still, before we retired for the night, my mother somehow contrived to put together our favorite supper—fried chicken, rice, gravy, creamed corn, and greens. We'd come a long way, but with our family around us and our mother's cooking before us, we were home.

Somehow, though, I never settled into San Diego. In those days, the odor of fish belched from the bayside canneries and hung over our neighborhood like a cloud. On the days when they weren't processing their malodorous catch, the canneries emitted the smell of sulfur. The streets were filled with sailors, big white men in whiter uniforms who, unlike the folks I'd met before, never smiled at small black boys, however friendly and polite they were.

My school, Logan Elementary, was integrated and excellent, and I soon found my place at the top of the class. But Sundays were still the highlight of our week. Sometimes, we would drive up to Los Angeles, where some of mother's people had settled in Watts in a house just off 103rd Street. Watts at that time was something new under the sun, a black suburb, and the people who lived there were proud of it. On Sunday afternoons, Uncle Ladell, my wonderful aunt Janie, Cousin Leamon, and Cousin Cloteal, now a beautician, would take us window-shopping "downtown" on 103rd Street. Our mother would make sure we were dressed in our best and would warn us to act like we "had good sense." Cousin Cloteal would chime in: "Now be on your best behavior. We're in downtown Watts." Today, when that name has become virtually synonymous with deprivation and self-destruction, it all seems like a long time ago and very, very far away.

Most Sundays, we stayed in San Diego, where we attended Bethel Baptist Church. It was there, at the age of eleven, that I finally joined the church. A Baptist doesn't join the church just because he or she attends services. Joining requires a personal commitment. My parents had never pressured me to take that step, and I had no plans to do so on that particular Sunday, when the Reverend Charles Hampton, our colorful pastor, took the pulpit. I don't recall everything the Reverend Hampton said that day, but I do remember that when he quoted John 3:16— "For God so loved the world, that he gave his only begotten Son"—his words merged into those of C.A.W. Clark and lit a fire in my heart that burns to this very moment. At the conclusion of his message, I gave my life to Christ, accepting him as my Savior and agreeing to do my best to live from that day on according to his teachings. I've sometimes failed to live up to that agreement, but I've never regretted it.

When I look back on that Sunday, I realize the profound contract made on that day between the Lord and myself, a willingness to offer my life in its totality to someone larger than myself. From the age of eleven onward, there has been a serenity, a sense of purpose to my life from knowing the Lord has a divine plan for me. I do not fight that heavenly design. I only seek to fulfill it as every good Christian must.

THE YEAR WAS 1949. SERIOUS FILMS ABOUT BLACK people and the race problem appeared on the screen, movies that depicted us as little more than an afterthought: *Lost Boundaries*, *Pinky*, *Home of the Brave*, and *Intruder in the Dust*. Both of my heroes were in the news. Joe Louis retired as world heavyweight boxing champion in 1949 after holding the title for more than eleven years. Also, Jackie Robinson, the National League's MVP, won the league's batting crown that year, with an average of .342.

Meanwhile, my father's career was thriving, and he was asked to come to Los Angeles, where Golden State Mutual was headquartered, and to take over one of the local district offices. In the fall of 1949, just days before the start of the school year, we packed the Chrysler again and headed back north, to the city that has been my home ever since.

Our move to Los Angeles precipitated one of the few real disagreements between our parents that I can remember. My father, a thrifty man with neither vice nor expensive hobby, had managed to put aside $5,000. He proposed to use that money to buy a small apartment court in which we would occupy one unit, while the rest were rented out for income. It was a sensible enough plan, but my mother felt she had deferred her dream of home ownership long enough. She dug in her heels. She insisted.

She won. Five thousand dollars was a considerable down payment in 1949, and, along with the promise of a mortgage loan from Golden State, it secured my parents a house on West Twenty-eighth Street, a prestigious address among members of the city's small but growing black middle class. My mother's dream house was a white, single-story, wood-framed structure. It had a large front lawn and a big backyard with a spreading avocado tree, which was better than a palm tree since it gave not only shade but also fruit. And, just to let you know that you really were in Los Angeles, there was a three-car garage. It all suited Mother admirably, and I can still remember the sound of her humming as she happily watered her new front lawn.

In fact, our neighborhood was the geographic vanguard of the city's growing and increasingly prosperous African American community. In Los Angeles, as in America as a whole, your material progress is often gauged by how far west you've moved. By the time we arrived, Main Street was the black community's dividing line: If you lived east of Main, "you weren't doing so well"; west of Main, where we had located, "you were doing all right and hoping to do better." To the south, there was Watts, while our northern horizon extended to the Uptown Theatre on Western Avenue, just below Olympic. To the west, there was the manicured prosperity of the Crenshaw district with its sprawling craftsman-style mansions and chic shops.

At the time I didn't know it, but these divisions were neither accidental nor purely economic. Los Angeles was a city of restrictive real estate covenants, which prohibited the sale of houses in most neighborhoods to nonwhites or, often, Jews. Those restrictions were not only written into many deeds, they also were physically enforced by the Los Angeles Police Department, whose commanders believed that "keeping a lid" on the city's Latino and African American populations was as much a part of their job as arresting criminals. Homes in our neighborhood, for example, had became available to black buyers in large part because many of the area's previous residents—first-generation Japanese Americans, or Nisei—had lost their houses and businesses during the long years of their imprisonment in the internment camps during the Second World War.

The vile injustice inflicted on these innocent people had been approved not only by a great president, Franklin D. Roosevelt, but also by the governor of California, Earl Warren, the nation's future chief justice. It had even been ratified by the federal courts in a decision—*Korematsu v. United States*—that stands in a line of judicial infamies stretching back through *Plessy v. Ferguson* all the way to *Dred Scott v. Sandford*. That we newcomers were the beneficiaries of another people's misfortune was only dimly known to even the adults among us, if at all.

The memory of our Nisei predecessors lingered in the handful of shop windows that still bore Japanese characters and in the neighborhood's carefully tended gardens.

The black community into which we had moved was a vibrant, optimistic, increasingly self-confident place. Just around the corner, at Adams and Western, was the gleaming, up-to-date new headquarters of my father's employer, Golden State Mutual Life Insurance Company. The building was a focal point of community pride, offering regular tours and a cafeteria that was open to the public. It was so well appointed and the food was so good that it quickly became a favorite lunch spot for local business and professional men.

My father's own district office was first on 111th and Avalon and later on Central Avenue, right next to the *Los Angeles Sentinel*, then, as now, the city's leading African American newspaper. Central Avenue was sometimes called the "Harlem of the West," site of a thriving artistic and cabaret scene that attracted people of all colors from all over the city. Scores of young white musicians—some of them future jazz greats like Chet Baker and Gerry Mulligan—came to Central Avenue to learn from such reigning local masters as Dexter Gordon and Wardell Gray. There was something about bebop's searching style that matched the restless, improvisational quality of life in Los Angeles at the century's midpoint.

But however well they captured the spirit of the time, jazz clubs weren't a part of our strict and strictly religious household. We'd quickly found and joined a suitable church, Second Baptist, the city's leading black congregation and headquarters to the local chapter of the NAACP. My father's activities, however, were never overtly political. He continued to devote himself to his family, the church, his expanding business, and, though he also joined the NAACP, to the local chapter of the YMCA. The immediate benefits of the personal contact and direct action on behalf of others there suited his sense of Christian obligation better than contentious abstractions like political organizing.

Along with our family's weekly trips to Second Baptist, we began to make regular Friday-night visits to another local attraction, the Crenshaw Shopping Center, America's very first shopping mall, located at the corner of Crenshaw and Santa Barbara, now called Martin Luther King Boulevard. We always went as a family, and, in those days, we were just window-shopping, but it was my first glimpse of some of the things hard work could buy.

For my part, I quickly found a place for myself at Mount Vernon Junior High School. It was my fourth school in California, and, like the others, it was completely integrated, though there were only about twenty blacks in a student body of about 1,500. Almost immediately, I made two fast friends from among the other pupils. One was Don Buford, who shared my love of baseball and later went on to play for the Baltimore Orioles and is still employed by that organization. The other was Ted Alexander, who ultimately earned his doctorate and became assistant superintendent of the Los Angeles Unified School District, the nation's second largest. Teddy, Don, and I would walk to school together and became so close that our mothers took turns cooking breakfast for all of us in a kind of rotation. Mount Vernon, with its diverse student body drawn from ambitious, upwardly mobile, middle-class families, was the most challenging of the schools I'd attended. But I quickly rose to the top of my class and, like my dad before me, began to show a flair for discussion and debate. I also met my first Jewish friend, though our association ended under circumstances that have troubled me more as the years go on. Her name was Elaine Kuznitz, and she may have been one of the brightest pupils in our class. I often walked her home from school, and she introduced me to her parents, who were warm and welcoming people. Then, one day, Ted showed me a copy of the *Herald*, the local Hearst newspaper. On the front page was an article about Elaine's parents.

"Did you know her folks are two of the leading communists around here?" Ted demanded. "They're Reds, man!"

According to the very uncomplimentary article, Elaine's mother and father were officials in the local party chapter. It would be years before I would hear the word "McCarthyism" or learn of the Red-baiting Hearst press's role in propagating it. But the Cochran household was nearly as steeped in conventional American patriotism as it was in Baptist piety. I liked Elaine, but it was hard to know what to say about her parents' being part of a "foreign conspiracy" against the country whose flag we saluted every morning. Our friendship became strained and eventually petered out. Young people make mistakes. That was one of mine.

Other intimations of the perils beyond our tightly drawn

family circle were beginning to make themselves known to me. Every summer, we went back to Louisiana to see Big Auntie and our other relatives. At first, we'd take the train, and what I recall most about those trips was my gnawing suspicion that Texas was endless. You'd go to sleep clacking through Texas, and, no matter how long you slept, when you woke up you were still in Texas. Sometime after our move to Los Angeles, however, we began to drive back to Shreveport. Suddenly, Texas began to take on another, more sinister character. I remember how my mother would become visibly tense and watchful as we crossed into the state. Over and over, she would caution us to behave ourselves, to speak to the people we met only when spoken to. "If anything happens," she would warn us, "keep quiet. Leave it to your daddy."

At first I was puzzled by her apprehension. Then I learned. We had stopped, and I—ignoring Mother's repeated demands to "stay close"—went looking for a rest room. Outside the door of the first one I located, I found myself staring up into the chilly eyes of a large white man in a cowboy hat.

"Boy, can't you read?" he said in a voice dripping with unfamiliar contempt. Before I could reply, my mother bustled into sight and hustled me away. It was then that I noticed there were two sets of rest rooms—one labeled "White" and one labeled "Colored." It was my first personal encounter with racial discrimination, and later, in the car, my father and I discussed it carefully and at length. I don't recall everything he said to me, but I will never forget his closing admonition: "Watch and remember," he said to me in what I understood even then to be a solemn charge.

I did not understand the color line or Jim Crow in the way that I do now as an adult. I did not understand why we sat in the back of the bus or in the balcony. Or searched with anxious eyes for signs that read FOR COLORED or FOR WHITES. Neither Jim

Crow nor white faces frightened me. I was too young. I accepted these inequities as we all did. It was a way of life.

In 1951, I also learned a lesson about the fragility of life itself. One late night there on West Twenty-eight Street, the pain my mother had had for some time in her lower abdomen became unbearable. My father, his children in tow, rushed her to the hospital, where we were met by Dr. Leroy Weeks, one of Los Angeles' pioneering black physicians, who quickly determined that Mother's appendix had burst. Our father took Pearl, Jean, and me to the hospital waiting area and quietly told us to "sit still" while he went to make the necessary arrangements. I sat frozen, elbows on knees, chin in hands, virtually numb with fear. Finally, our father rejoined us. Mother was having an operation, he explained, and then he lapsed into silence, pulling at his chin. I know now that he must have been thinking of his dad, Lonnie, and the tragedy that had changed his own life forever so many years before.

"Will Mother be all right?" I kept asking my father, who sometimes said nothing, only staring into space. My alarm was magnified because this sudden illness had come over her in the middle of the night. Our family never thought about illness because nobody had ever been sick. Nobody ever went to the doctor or to the hospital. For my mother to go to the hospital, she really had to be seriously ill.

Mother came through the operation but quickly developed severe peritonitis. For weeks, she hovered between life and death. I recall that time as kind of an interminable twilight. Each day, I returned home from school and there was no one there to urge me to start my homework, no one to say, "You leave those books for now. Wash your hands and get ready for dinner."

Our father was at Temple Hospital with our mother. Each night, when he returned home, we asked, "Is she coming back today? When is Mother coming home?"

"She's very sick," my father would say, "but we think she's going to get better."

Then we would pray. My father always had been a man of prayer, but in those days I virtually stormed heaven with my petitions. I made a covenant with God. I promised God that if He would return my mother to us, I would do everything for her and with her. God kept his promise and so did I. We were not allowed to visit Mother. After a time, however, she did speak to us by telephone. Her words were brave, but her voice was weak. Finally, two months after her operation, she returned home in a wheelchair. We children decorated the house with a welcoming banner and soaked her nightclothes with our tears. I went to our parents' bedroom and hugged her, holding on as if I couldn't ever let go. And, in a way, I never have.

After that illness, I vowed to make the most of my time with my mother. She was an incredible woman, not big, just a small woman with this great, indomitable will. She was our shoulder to cry on, our sounding board, a dispenser of sage advice, our mother-confessor, our most honest and valued critic, and our staunchest defender. She exhorted us to be our best, and she was a living example of the kind of hard work that being the best entailed. No *"i"* went undotted, no *"t"* went uncrossed in Hattie Cochran's world. Sometimes I would sit with her while she lay in bed and we'd talk about God, life, and not wasting the precious gifts that the Lord had given us. I was reminded of how I'd seen the power of God at work in our lives. I had beseeched Him and He had anwered me. God sent me another reminder of his great power and mercy when my mother again fell ill in 1971. As before, I asked God to give me more time with her. She spent another twenty years with us before she departed this life in October 1991. Sometimes, as a young boy, I would stand with her as she cooked in the kitchen, making these big, tasty meals that she really couldn't enjoy because of the complications from her illness. Amazingly, she never complained or mentioned the great pain that was her constant companion. Sometimes the burden of it would quickly flash across her warm, beautiful face and she'd wince momentarily. If she caught me looking at her, she called me to her, hugged me, and wrapped me in the comfort of her loving arms.

Though our mother never really regained her former strength, she lived on for another forty precious years. In all that time, there was never a night I didn't call her, no matter where I was or what I was doing. I returned from every trip I took with a doll or other special gift for her. I did these things because, in my darkest hours, both God and my mother are always there for me. Even now, I visit her crypt every week, and her good counsel is inscribed on my soul.

Not long after my mother returned from the hospital, my parents and I began to discuss seriously what I would do with my life. Father and Mother had always nourished a private hope that I would study medicine, become a doctor, perhaps even a research scientist discovering new cures for disease. But at Mount Vernon, I had come to prefer words to numbers, and the cut and thrust of debate was much more to my taste than the solitary dedication demanded by life in a laboratory. So, one night at the dinner table, I told my parents that I wanted to be a lawyer. Though I had never met a lawyer or seen one in action, I knew that I wanted to be one. It wasn't as if I sat down with a list of my strengths and characteristics and matched them with possible careers. It was much more intuitive than that. It was like an inner calling. Only later would I see how the law had really chosen me, that I was following my destiny.

As she cleared away the dishes, Mother's disappointment was palpable. "Now, Hattie," my father said, "if he wants to try and become a lawyer, let him. As long as he can do the best that he can, then let him do that."

Mother sighed. She hadn't dreamed of a career in medicine for me, but she still wanted it. "John, just promise me this," she said. "Be the best that you can be."

I didn't know it at the time, but my father was already at work behind the scenes to make sure I wouldn't disappoint her.

3

A Wider World

MY PARENTS' MOST VALUABLE ASSET MAY HAVE BEEN their unshakable conviction that lofty ideals and awesome practicality naturally go hand in hand. The Cochran family did not leave its religion in church on Sunday or let its ambitions fade with the rest of the dinner-table conversation. Even so, I was stunned when, shortly after I graduated from Mount Vernon Junior High, my father came home one evening and announced that I would enroll at Los Angeles High School in the fall.

During the early 1950s, Los Angeles boasted one of the nation's best public school systems, which was organized on a strict geographic basis. Graduates from our junior high, for example, were supposed to go on to Dorsey High, whose student body was drawn mainly from the city's embryonic black middle class and from those working-class Jewish families who recently had made their own westward trek out of the historic Boyle Heights neighborhood east of the Los Angeles River and some Asian students from the Crenshaw area. Dorsey was a fine school, but Los Angeles High was something else entirely. It was situated on the south edge of Hancock Park, one of the city's wealthiest neighborhoods and then home to the old white Anglo-Saxon Protestant elite that had run Los Angeles since before the turn of the century. They were, in a very real sense, the modern city's founding families, and their sprawling mansions arrayed along the neighborhood's tree-lined streets had been built and maintained by "old" land, oil, and railroad money. In those days, Hancock Park was still home to the Van Nuys, Doheny, Banning, Ahmanson, and Huntington families, along with the Chandlers, who not only controlled the *Los Angeles Times* and *Daily Mirror* but also California's Republican Party. Many of the homes abutted the fairways of the Wilshire Country Club, an institution so exclusive that it would not accept actors as members since their profession was regarded as "disreputable" and they may have been Jewish despite their Anglo stage names. Some years later, an exception was made for the cowboy film star Randolph Scott. Most people said it was because he had promised never to make another movie. Others, less kind, said he'd never been an actor anyway.

The board of education ran Los Angeles High with the rigorous standards of a private institution, and many of Hancock Park's residents demonstrated their approval by forgoing prep schools and sending their sons and daughters to their "neighborhood school." There, they rubbed shoulders with the children of the many upwardly mobile, middle-class Jewish families who had settled in the mid-Wilshire neighborhoods to the south and west and with the handful of black and Asian American students who had gained admittance. Together, these students had given Los Angeles High one of the highest academic ratings in the country. And, somehow, my resourceful father had figured a way for me to join them.

When I asked him why, he simply replied, "Look, I want you to have the best."

"But we live in Dorsey's district," I insisted, partly because I was mindful of the friends I would leave behind, partly because I couldn't imagine how he'd arranged it.

Daddy swept both considerations away with one of his discussion-ending declarations: "L.A. High has the reputation as the best public school in Los Angeles," he said. "That's where your mother and I want you to go."

And so I did.

I understood my father's mandate: to strive, to excel, to take full advantage of every educational opportunity offered to me. If I had any doubts about my place among Los Angeles' young intellectual elite, they quickly vanished as I walked onto the school's sprawling campus. I knew I'd do well there. After all, as I looked around me, I saw that the buildings, though more ornate than I was accustomed to, were still school buildings with lockers, desks, and chalkboards. And my fellow students, while maybe turned out a bit more fashionably, were, beneath a veneer of breeding and self-assurance, essentially the same as I was.

Crowned by a soaring clock tower, L.A. High's red-brick and ivy campus looked like a Hollywood set designer's notion of a small New England college. Getting there from West Twenty-eighth Street required changing buses, and, from the start, it seemed to me that I was entering new territory in every sense of the word. My new school not only had a fully equipped library but also an Olympic-sized swimming pool and tennis courts, things I'd never seen on a campus before. There were clubs for every imaginable interest and teams that competed in sports like diving, gymnastics, and fencing. It was 1952, and, like the city around me, I suddenly was intoxicated by the sense of unlimited possibilities.

I had always been a good student, but in L.A. High's unrelentingly competitive atmosphere I blossomed. I discovered I had a flair for languages. I learned to read and speak Spanish fluently and took courses in French and Italian. I learned the formal rules of debate and reveled in the complexities of advanced courses in political science and economics. With more than five hundred students, our freshman class was the largest in the school's history. I was shy in those days. Yet, my shyness didn't prevent me from getting good grades. Although I was never the first one to raise his hand, I was always prepared with the right answer.

Only about 3 percent of L.A. High's students were black, among them my Mount Vernon classmate George F. Jackson, Jr., who would go on to become a distinguished cardiovascular surgeon. Most of my new buddies were white, including actor Dustin Hoffman. Many of my closest friends were fellow members of the Honor Society, which was open to students who ranked in the top 5 percent of their class. A fair number of the club's members were Jewish girls, including Gail Hirson, Cookie Wapner, Judi Glatt, Elaine Fenimore, and Seema Joseph. From them, I learned a whole new set of holy days—Yom Kippur, Rosh Hashanah, Simchas Torah, and Pesach. Our discussions of the Holocaust, in which many of them had lost family members, and of the Jewish people's long struggle for a national home were the beginnings of my lifelong support for the state of Israel. In those years, the little community we formed at L.A. High was as blind to color and ethnicity as any I've ever known, and an extraordinary number of the friendships we formed there have persisted through all the difficulties since.

We Honor Society members often studied together after school, frequently at the nearby home of one of our Hancock Park friends. For a kid from West Twenty-eighth Street, that was another sort of education. Nearly all the houses we visited were vast and elegantly appointed, with sweeping oak and marble staircases. They had paneled libraries. They had rooms for dining, for breakfast, and for the billiards and music that presumably came after or in between. Some even had ballrooms and bowling alleys. In the backyard, they had swimming pools and private tennis courts. One of my classmates had his own archery range, another a basement set up for pistol shooting.

What also surprised me was that my friends' families often didn't say a prayer over their meals. My family always did. If I was eating at a friend's house, I would quietly say grace. I wasn't about to impose on anyone and ask them to join me. Not praying over meals was a small thing, but these families rarely ever talked about God either. It was interesting to see how other people lived, how what was at the center of my life was at the edge of theirs. For my part, I was still quite active in our church as a Sunday school leader and as a speaker at the church youth programs.

My friends and their families lived the sort of life I had previously glimpsed only in the movies. But I was interested rather than dazzled or envious. I came from a community where home ownership and the modicum of security that came with life insurance and the possibility of a pension were accounted as affluence. Suddenly, I was beginning to sense that hard work and success could bring much, much more. Some of my friends' fathers were lawyers. They had fine houses and vacation homes in the mountains and at the beach. They assumed an active role in the city's politics and were respected for it. They took it as a matter of course that every member of their family—from the oldest to the youngest—would live in comfort and security. If I, too, became an attorney, then I saw no reason why all those things shouldn't be within my reach as well.

I think my lifelong love affair with the automobile also began at L.A. High. By the end of my sophomore year, many of my classmates were driving their own cars to school, most of them late-model convertibles. It wasn't just a question of money but of culture. This was, after all, Los Angeles in that most ebullient of tail-finned decades, the 1950s. Our campus was just two blocks south of Wilshire Boulevard, the longest, widest city street in America and the first great processional avenue ever conceived with the automobile in mind. In its sixteen-mile traverse from the heart of downtown to the sands of Santa Monica Bay, Wilshire Boulevard is intersected by 202 other streets. One of those intersections—Wilshire and Westwood—is the single busiest urban crossroad in the world. Just west of our campus was a stretch of Wilshire called—somewhat immodestly, I admit—the "Miracle Mile." With its elaborate, oversized, street-level display windows and concealed parking lots, it was the first luxury shopping district ever designed to cater specifically to customers who came by private car.

Wilshire Boulevard was even named for one of those wondrous, high-minded eccentrics for whom my city is famous—A. Gaylord Wilshire, a socialist land developer and golfer who made a small fortune by breeding a new kind of seedless orange and lost another marketing a magnetic collar he claimed could restore gray hair to its original color. He was a visionary who once said that "with the increasing comfort and speed of transportation, California is fast becoming a winter playground of the leisure class of Americans. I have no doubt that when . . . the place of man's abode will be determined by his will rather than as it is now by his job, Southern California will be the most thickly settled part of the American continent."

The boulevard that bears A. Gaylord Wilshire's name is one of the modern world's great monuments, and I love it. So, like all true Angelenos, I count the acquisition and maintenance of a proper car to be among the duties of citizenship. And that morning in my junior year when I drove my own car into the campus parking lot still ranks as a personal rite of passage that would mystify many people in other parts of the country. It's an L.A. thing.

Los Angeles High's student body was widely regarded as the best dressed in the city, and it was there that I also began to learn more about fashion. In the Cochran family we always were dressed cleanly, neatly, and appropriately for the occasion. While visiting the families of my Hancock Park classmates, I also began to see that clothing could convey not only affluence but also confidence and professionalism. Some of my Jewish friends had fathers who were in the garment business, and sitting next to them in class was like enrolling in a fashion tutorial began to formulate my own notions of how a personal sense of style could be not only a sign of success but also a form of joyful self-expression. I must have hit on something, for today my wardrobe draws nearly as many comments as my cross-examinations.

Throughout my high school years, sports continued to play an important part in my life, though, by then, football had replaced baseball as my main love. At first, my size relegated me to the B team, where I eventually won the starting quarterback's job. By my senior year, I'd even been elevated to the varsity. That year, we went to the city finals and lost to Manual Arts. I never got in the game, but I've also never forgotten the lessons I learned as part of the B team. I particularly recall the sense of responsibility I felt when Coach Siegel would yell to the linemen, "The quarterback is like your mother. Don't let anybody get to him. Don't let them get in there and blindside Cochran." In the classroom, I was learning about competition on an intellectual plane; on the football field, I was learning on an emotional, more elemental level. I began to appreciate the real value of team-work, of when it was time to stick to your game plan and when the circumstances demanded improvisation. I learned how to play when you're behind and how to protect a lead. I learned that a good two-minute drill requires not only steady nerves but also meticulous preparation. Most of all, I began to recognize that stress is a crucible in which everything extraneous is melted away and true character, like some precious ore, is revealed.

Besides being tested on the playing fields, I also had my ROTC training to challenge me. Perhaps a relic of a bygone era today, high school ROTC programs were the norm back in 1955.

Throughout those heady, happy years of high school, I shifted comfortably between two worlds. During the day, I thrived in the affluent, self-confident, preppy environment of L.A. High. Each night, I returned to the familiar warmth of my parents' house on West Twenty-eighth Street, where the food was still usually fried and nearly everyone you knew was black and a Baptist. True, our house began to look a little smaller to me and our immediate neighbors' horizons began to seem a little narrow. But the nightly helping of love my mother served up with her dinners and my father's constant encouragement were things I could not imagine doing without. Together, our parents wove expectation and support into a seamless garment that we believed would protect us against any adversity. They also continued to instruct me in things that were foreign to the lives most of my classmates led.

One of those things was work. We revered work for its character-building qualities. Work meant more than just punching a time clock or collecting a paycheck. For the Cochran family, it represented forward movement in one's life, progressing from point A to point B, and on toward a goal. Work was one factor that determined one's self-worth (or lack of it) and provided others with a means to gauge your value to your family and to your community. In a sense, my family's view of work reflected the old southern adage by Booker T. Washington about taking joy in your task, no matter what it may be, and taking pride in it. I learned to love work at an early age.

In our household it simply was assumed that you would hold a job while you pursued your studies. My first real job, which I took in junior high, was with a local dry cleaner who paid me to sweep up, run errands, and do chores around his shop. Later, I also worked as a paperboy, delivering the morning *Herald-Examiner*. That job required you to rise before dawn and report to the jobber, who paid for the rights to distribute the paper in a certain area. There, you loaded the heavy canvas bags onto your bicycle handlebars and pedaled off to deliver the papers to the subscribers on your route. If you weren't done by the time the sun was up, you didn't keep your job. Each month, you were also expected to go door to door along your route, collecting the monthly payment from each of your subscribers. Your pay was a share of that collection. You soon learned—sometimes painfully—which of your customers were good people who'd had a bit of trouble and couldn't quite come up with that month's subscription price. You carried them for a month because you knew they'd see you right. Others simply were deadbeats, and if you bought their story more than once, it was going to cost you. That was another kind of education.

So, too, was the job I got working for Fawn's, a local caterer, at ninety cents an hour. The owner was a black man with an extensive clientele among Los Angeles' affluent white party givers. On a couple of occasions, I found myself working parties in the houses of my L.A. High classmates. That was amusing, but not half as funny as the time one of the other guys, Charles Young, was hurrying to get the main course on the barbecue grill during a particularly elaborate garden party. As he passed the linen-covered buffet table, tray on high, he tripped, emptying his huge platter of New York steaks right into the punch bowl. That brought everything to a halt—everything, that is, but our boss's legendary temper, which shot past the boiling point and right through the roof. But what I remember most about working as a caterer was the thoughtless condescension with which so many of the guests treated us:

"Boy! Another glass here."

"Son, get these plates cleared away."

"I need that gin and tonic now, not later."

Others simply behaved as if you weren't really there. Even then, it was clear to me that their boorish behavior was as much a matter of social arrogance as it was racial insensitivity. It was instructive to see that money and success did not guarantee courteous or considerate behavior. I also remember thinking, "This job is another reason my father is right about the value of an education." And, to this day, I am careful to show waiters, doormen, and others in the service industries the respect to which they are entitled. I tip generously and will not tolerate discourteous conduct toward serving people by those around me. I'd even try to behave graciously if somebody dropped a steak in my drink.

But the most important thing that occurred during my years at L.A. High happened in the spring of 1954, more than three thousand miles from our tranquil campus. That May in Washington, D.C., the United States Supreme Court handed down its landmark decision in the case of *Brown v. Board of Education of Topeka, Kansas.* Legal segregation with its elaborate mythology of "separate but equal" public institutions for blacks and whites was forever overthrown. I vividly recall how the newspaper accounts of the Court's ruling fascinated me and how carefully I pored over every image in the extensive coverage carried in the next week's photo magazines, *Life* and *Look.* Like so many other African Americans, I was thrilled that the justices' opinion was unanimous, and I will revere Chief Justice Earl

Warren and Justice William O. Douglas until the day I die for the part they played in forging that iron consensus. The day in October of 1968 on which I first was admitted to practice before those two great justices remains one of the most memorable in my life.

But, to me, the most striking images of those exciting days in 1954 were the pictures of the tall, handsome lawyer who had argued *Brown* before the Court. He was Thurgood Marshall of the NAACP Legal Defense Fund. And he was a black man, like me. More important, he had used the law and his storied skill and courage as an advocate to change society for the better. He had made a difference for all of us, black and white. Suddenly, I knew why I wanted to be a lawyer—and another hero had joined my personal pantheon. For the rest of my life, Thurgood Marshall would stand right there next to my father, Joe Louis, and Jackie Robinson.

The effect of the *Brown* decision was magnified for me because it coincided with my own deeper studies in African American history. I had always been a voracious reader, but that year—pushed along, perhaps, by the NAACP's presence at our church, Second Baptist—I had begun to read back to the founding of the Niagara Movement in 1905 by W.E.B. Du Bois and, past him, to the towering figure of the great Frederick Douglass. Like so many before me, I was stunned by the power of his *Narrative of the Life of Frederick Douglass*, an account of his life in slavery, and left to wonder about the brutality that had been visited on my own great-grandparents. I was particularly interested in Douglass's stature as perhaps the greatest of all nineteenth-century American journalists, since my friend Elaine Matthews and I had begun writing "youth columns" for the *Los Angeles Sentinel*. It seemed to me that Marshall's battle against segregated schools put him in a line with Douglass, who first insisted upon the centrality of education to African American progress. I also was drawn to Douglass, as I later was to Dr. Martin Luther King, Jr., by the universality of his values. It is seldom recalled now, but Douglass—despite his own community's pressing needs—was a tireless advocate of all women's rights. The motto of his newspaper, *The North Star*, was "Right is of no sex—Truth is of no color."

Poring over Marshall's photographs and the newspapers' reports of how he skillfully blended cutting-edge scientific evidence and two-hundred-year-old moral arguments to make his case to the Court, I imbued my new hero with the qualities the abolitionist William Lloyd Garrison recognized in his own first encounter with Douglass: "In physical proportion and stature commanding and exact—in intellect richly endowed—in natural eloquence a prodigy. . . . There is in him that union of head and heart, which is indispensable to an enlightenment of the heads and a winning of the hearts of others."

Years later, during the late 1970s, I happened to meet Thurgood Marshall at a reception in Washington, D.C. He was, by then, a former solicitor general and the first African American justice on the U.S. Supreme Court. He also had a reputation as a more than slightly cantankerous old man. I summoned up my courage and introduced myself.

"Nice to meet you, young man," he said simply.

Encouraged by his informal manner, I told him of the impact *Brown v. Board of Education* had had on my life. I told him that he was the legal advocate whose career had most inspired me. "I am pleased beyond words to meet you," I said, "because I became a lawyer to change society the way that you did."

"Thank you," he replied, in what may have been the most precious compliment I ever received. "If you persevere you can do it."

In 1954, that fearless lawyer gave my boyish ambition a man's purpose. More than twenty years later, at a crucial moment in my life, he reminded me never to abandon it. The lesson historian Kelly Miller took from the life of Frederick Douglass applies equally to the career of Thurgood Marshall: "The greatest things of this world are not made with hands, but reside in truth and righteousness and love."

That same fall I noticed my mother was putting on weight. And, whenever I looked up from my plate at the dinner table, she and my father seemed to be smiling at each other. Pretty soon, even a busy, self-absorbed teenage boy could tell why. Early in 1955, the dream she'd had as a young bride came true: She had four children, and I had a brother. My father added an R to our grandfather's name and called his new son RaLonzo. I'd been named for my father, of course, which meant that I didn't have a middle name, just an initial. But this time, Dad decided that our family's hard-won prosperity could support a full-blown middle name for his new son. Ever forward-looking, Dad considered what sort of name might suit a child born into an age of advancing electronic technology. In due course, my brother was christened RaLonzo Phelectron Cochran. Some of our dad's friends weren't quite sure what to make of that. I solved the problem by simply calling my little brother "Flecky."

As my graduation from L.A. High drew nearer, I began to talk to my father about another ambition I had nourished secretly for some time: I wanted to go away to school; I wanted to go to Harvard. Dad listened patiently. More than any of us, he knew the ache of the dream deferred. But the Ivy League, he pointed out, simply was out of the question. We couldn't afford it. I accepted the fact that I couldn't attend Harvard for financial reasons with some disappointment. For me, it would have been a great intellectual challenge, a chance to test my mind against some of the best in the country. As I've gotten older, I've come to understand that there is a part of me that thrives on competition, the opportunity to test my abilities against others who would, hopefully, push me to new heights. But I had two sisters following close behind, top students in their own right. He had promised our mother that there would be an education for "the girls, too." So, I enrolled for the fall semester at the University of California at Los Angeles, the school from which Jackie Robinson had graduated. At the time, my father reminded me that "the Lord has a way of seeing that things work themselves out." And they have, in a funny way. Every fall for the past few years, professors Charles Ogletree and David Wilkins have invited me to come to Cambridge and spend a week or so lecturing and holding seminars for the students of the Harvard Law School. As it turns out, Harvard is all that I imagined it would be.

As it also turned out, UCLA was more than I imagined. From the moment I set foot on the campus, I was in love. The University of California system is one of America's great public treasures, world-class institutions of higher learning open to all, purely on merit. In those years, UCLA—located in the still picturesque village of Westwood, about twenty-five minutes' drive west of our home—was a particular mecca for ambitious young Jews, blacks, and Asian Americans. There were the usual dormitories and off-campus apartments. But, like most of the other African Americans, I was a commuting student, and I never quite got over the fact that while tuition ran forty dollars a semester, parking cost seventy dollars.

The cost of getting out of your car wasn't the only shock. In those days, UCLA and most of the other top public universities had something of an inferiority complex about their standing alongside the elite private colleges. They compensated for it by enforcing rigorous academic standards. I've never forgotten the first day I sat down in History 7A—the United States before the

Civil War—which was a required freshman course and, therefore, taught in a vast, theater-style lecture hall. The professor took the podium, introduced himself, and then instructed us to look at the students to our left and right. "Two of you," he said matter-of-factly, "are not going to graduate."

I don't know who these guys beside me are, I thought, but I'm the one graduating in this trio.

But it was not going to be easy. UCLA made L.A. High seem like a sheltered workshop. It didn't help that I'd elected to major in business administration and minor in political science, two of the most intensely competitive undergraduate departments. I quickly formed a study partnership with two new friends, fellow business administration majors Todd Reinstein and Joe Burton. I was stunned to discover that, while I had worked all summer to put together the financial nest egg that would help carry me through my freshman year, they'd bought *all* the books the previous June and spent the vacation reading them. Before each quiz or examination, Todd, Joe and I would review our notes together. Each time we covered a particular page, we'd put a check mark at the bottom. During one of our sessions, I looked over Todd's shoulder and glimpsed an entire line of check marks marching across the bottom of the page like determined soldiers. I'm in tough now, I thought for about the three hundredth time that month.

Some of our classmates weren't simply hardworking, they were cutthroat. On one occasion, the professor announced that we were to prepare for the next class by reading an article in a scholarly journal that he'd placed on reserve for us in the university library. I had a break before my next class, so I made a bee-line for the stacks. Someone had been there ahead of me. The entire article had been neatly cut from the journal. Nowadays, when I scan *The Wall Street Journal* and come across another story about some corporate CEO who's being lionized for boosting his quarterly profits by laying off another ten thousand workers, I sometimes wonder if he got his start in the stacks at the UCLA library.

In an environment like that, subtle differences count for a lot. Nearly all the African American students, for example, commuted and held down part-time jobs the way I did. So, too, did a substantial number of our Jewish classmates. That was one of the bonds between us. We all were precluded from participating in the best study groups, which were made up of the more affluent students who lived on or immediately off campus. Most helpful of all were the cram sessions run by the white fraternities and sororities. There, you not only were tutored by older members who had already taken your course but you also got a chance to see the actual exam papers from the previous term. It was quite an advantage.

We simply took it as a matter of course that all fraternities were segregated. As a freshman, I pledged Kappa Alpha Psi, the leading black fraternity on campus. By the time I left UCLA, I had become the president of the fraternity, its polemarch. It was a terrific organization, dominated in those days by a cadre of serious-minded young men who had graduated from UCLA and then joined the Los Angeles Police Department, an institution most of them were already using as a springboard into law and politics. Each of the pledges was invited to join the fraternity. I was particularly fortunate. One of my big brothers was a tall, dignified former track star named Tom Bradley, who would go on to become Los Angeles' first African American mayor and the most popular chief executive in the city's history. In that capacity he not only threw open the doors of opportunity for men and women of every color and ethnicity but also took the leading role in reshaping Los Angeles into a modern metropolis. He has remained my mentor and friend to this very day. One of my fellow pledges was a guy named William Baker. Sometime later, he followed Tom Bradley into police work and my sister Pearl to the altar. Bill has been loyal to the force and my sister ever since, though my exasperated father has had to intervene in our lively—though friendly—dinner-table debates more than once over the years. Bill ultimately rose to the rank of Inspector in the L.A. County Sheriff's Department.

Most nights during my years at UCLA, I hopped into my used, two-door 1951 Ford Fairlane and headed home for dinner at West Twenty-eighth Street before hitting the books. Friday nights were the exception. After I turned eighteen, I took the state licensing exam to sell life and disability insurance and went to work for my father at Golden State Mutual. By then, Dad had about forty agents working under his supervision at the district office on 111th and Avalon. Each of them had a specific area in which he was responsible for selling new policies and collecting premiums on the existing ones. That was called "working the debit." Policyholders paid on a monthly basis. Most premiums were a dollar, but some were as high as fifteen dollars. If somebody needed to collect on a policy because of death or disability, you were also responsible for seeing to that, and you carried the check to him or her in person. Golden State Mutual was very proud of its integrity, and even when you were dealing with somebody who'd suffered a tragedy, you felt good that you'd been able to help him or her when the chips were down. People trusted us because we kept faith with them.

My father's knowledge about the debit and the insurance business was legendary. He was a great salesman with an infectious spirit of optimism. Whenever I worked with him, I learned the importance of being an empathetic listener. I learned that people needed and wanted to hear good news, and that if you couldn't provide them with it, the next best thing you could do for them was to let them know that better news was just around the corner. For my father, everything was doable and the word "impossible" did not exist. Life presented you with a series of challenges, and those who took advantage of those opportunities, those who met the challenges head on, led the most fulfilling lives. Working with my dad, I learned to enjoy dealing with people. I began to thrive on "making a way out of no way."

Working the debit was your bread and butter at Golden State. And Dad made sure that I would have to scramble to get mine. He gave me a hundred-family debit in Palm Lane, a tough public housing project at 122nd Street and Wilmington, which since has been cleared away to make room for a county hospital named after Martin Luther King, Jr. These were black folks, many of them from the South, like the Cochrans. But Palm Lane, where people were living month to month and, often, hand to mouth, was a long way from the easygoing gentility of West Twenty-eighth Street. It was further still from UCLA and the hills of Westwood. Still, every Friday after class, I donned coat and tie and hurried down to 111th and Avalon to pick up my debit collection book before continuing on to Palm Lane. I'd quickly learned that the "Friday Night Fights" kept most of my policyholders glued to their television sets. If I moved quickly, I could catch quite a number of customers sitting in their living rooms with some of their weekly paycheck still in their pockets. Part of the trick was to find a variety of ways to graciously decline one of the Pabst Blue Ribbon beers that were an indispensable part of the "Friday Night Fight" ritual and a symbol of hospitality in Palm Lane. That was one of the times being a Baptist from a teetotaling household came in handy.

Before the Second World War, the vast majority of African Americans lived in the rural South. In the years after 1940, the dislocations caused by the war and the introduction of the mechanical cotton picker set more than five million of them on the move. It was the greatest internal migration any nation has ever experienced. For those who were educated, enterprising, and fortunate—like my family—black America's great exodus was indeed a journey of liberation, however incomplete. But for others—less dogged, slightly less resourceful, or simply unlucky—things had not worked out so well. Their long journey seemed to lead nowhere but to places like Palm Lane, to new kinds of deprivation and to a gnawing, increasingly self-destructive frustration.

Yet the longer I worked the Palm Lane debit, the less the differences between these families and my own seemed to matter. Listening to their stories, their hopes and disappointments, I began to discover how deep our connections to one another really were. Faith, family, suffering, fortitude, and our common experience of the majority community's discrimination and indifference bound us to one another as surely as iron chains had once bound together our ancestors in the reeking bellies of the slave ships that bore them out of Africa. With that realization, the voices of Palm Lane took their place in my soul, alongside those of the Little Union Baptist Church. And, as they did, the comfort I had always slipped into between my very different worlds began to fall away. For the first time in my life I felt divided and uneasy.

Busy though I was with work and school, I began to wage a young man's struggle to name my unfamiliar feelings. I thought deeply and read widely and—like so many other young people before me—discovered that I was not alone. Many years before, another young African American, W.E.B. Du Bois—a Harvard man, in fact—had wrestled with similar emotions. He recorded the resolution of his own inner turmoil in what remains the single most powerful description of what it means to be a black American. "One ever feels his two-ness," Du Bois wrote.

An American, a Negro; two souls, two thoughts, two unreconciled strivings; two warring ideals in one dark body, whose dogged strength alone keeps it from being torn asunder.

The history of the American Negro is the history of this strife—this longing to attain self-conscious manhood, to merge his double self into a better and truer self. . . . He simply wishes to make it possible for a man to be both a Negro and an American, without being cursed and spit upon by his fellows, without having the doors of Opportunity closed roughly in his face.

This concept of "two-ness" is one that has eternally intrigued me. It is at the very core of the American racial dilemma. In Du Bois's words, we as Americans and blacks are forever wrestling with this contradiction which has its roots in the anguish that was slavery. We were never viewed as just teachers, doctors, lawyers, scientists, and writers. We were perceived as black teachers, black doctors, black lawyers, black scientists, and black writers. Every decision, every action we made as professionals was and still is defined by this cruel color line.

This new sense of the variety of experience within my own community was a vital part of my education in those years. Part of it occurred after school during my senior year at UCLA, when I took a job as a mail sorter on the night shift at the Terminal Annex Post Office in downtown Los Angeles. Now, that was an experience. Some of what I saw conflicted with the values that I had been raised with. Our group clocked in precisely at 6:06 P.M. and quit at 2:06 A.M. on the kind of schedule only the government could have dreamed up. Most of my coworkers were black, but they weren't quite like anybody I'd met before. There were women, a few of whom clocked in, then left to meet their boyfriends in nearby motels and didn't reappear until just before quitting time. There was a guy who had been to law school and passed the bar, but somehow "things just didn't work out." There were guys with elaborate private theories about UFOs, about conspiracies in the tax code, and conspiracies in the White House.

Terminal Annex was a long, long way from West Twenty-eighth Street. Though the work was never-ending, the paychecks were regular, and I was grateful to earn the money I needed to help me finish UCLA and move on to law school.

One day, during my senior year at UCLA, I joined a group of my Kappa brothers chatting with some girls outside Kerckhoff Hall. I don't recall much of what was said, but I do remember that I couldn't quite take my eyes off an attractive young woman with a bold gold streak in her dark hair. She was older and had an air of sophistication that immediately attracted me. My interest must have been obvious because one of my frat brothers pulled me aside.

"Better stay away from that young lady," he warned. "That's Barbara Berry. She collects engagement rings."

A few weeks later I gave her a ride home. She, too, was from Shreveport by way of the Bay Area, where her father, Youree "Fatso" Berry, had been a popular radio disc jockey. Although both her parents had died within a year of each other, she had managed to get through college on her own. Barbara lived by her wits and had the kind of street smarts that seemed exotic to a young man from a sheltered home like mine. I always had ambition; she always had a plan. We began to see each other regularly, and the two became entwined.

By the time I graduated from UCLA in the summer of 1959, I had made a decision to attend Loyola Law School. Although my alma mater was my first choice, in those days UCLA Law frowned on working students and discouraged them with classes that continued into the evenings and on Saturday morning.

Loyola, which was located downtown, just minutes from my post office job, had a compact, five-day schedule. The choice was made, but it never was a happy match. The Loyola regimen combined the brain-crunching work of a competitive graduate school with the human sensitivity of a Marine boot camp. The school had a thing called the "Two D Rule." Two D's in any one term and you were out, no matter what your overall record or where you were in the three-year program. And just to make sure your anxiety was at a proper pitch, most of the professors told you at least twice a week that even if you managed to avoid flunking out, you would never pass the California State Bar examination.

At Christmastime that first year, I asked Barbara, who was teaching by then, what she wanted as a gift.

"You can't give me what I want," she said.

"Why not?" I asked.

"Because I want a ring," she replied. "I want to be engaged, and I want to get married."

My Kappa brothers had awarded me a $500 fellowship when I entered law school. After buying books, there was $200 left, and I used it to buy Barbara her ring. The following July, despite my mother's reservations, we were married in a big ceremony at Second Baptist Church.

During my first year at Loyola Law School, one of my buddies from L.A. High, Merv Brody, introduced me to a guy named Ron Sunderland, and we all started studying together. Merv took some time off from school, but Ron and I kept on. We ended up best friends for life. His parents, Molly and Sam, lived just off Fairfax—the heart of Jewish Los Angeles—but kept a little mom and pop store down on Century Boulevard in the black community. Ron's wife at that time, Ruth, prepared dinner for us on the evenings we'd meet at his house to study. I remember being struck at the time with how closely the *haimische* atmosphere of their home resembled the warm Southern ambience of our own.

Life settled into a numbing routine of study and work. I saw more of Ron Sunderland, who also was married, than I did of Barbara. Navigating the intellectual complexities of the second-year program in evidence and constitutional law was a full-time job. By the end of the first year of law school, our class had thinned visibly. Of the five African Americans who had enrolled in our freshman class, only two remained.

By my third and final year at Loyola, I already had found work in my chosen profession. That fall I left the post office forever, when I was hired as the first black law clerk in the office of the Los Angeles city attorney. In L.A., the city attorney and his deputies represent the city government and its agencies on all legal matters and prosecute minor crimes, or misdemeanors. Serious offenses, or felonies, are prosecuted by the district attorney, an elected official of the county government. I loved the city attorney's office from the moment I walked in. My supervisors quickly spotted my fascination with trial work and assigned me to represent the city in small claims court. In California, lawyers aren't allowed to practice in small claims, which in those years handled cases with no more than $200 at issue. From the first day, I won more than I lost.

The next year brought both joy and anxiety. Early in 1962, our oldest daughter, Melodie, was born; in June, I graduated from law school. Any elation I felt was fleeting. The following month, I was scheduled to take the bar, and Ron and I planned to study full-time in the interim. Barbara was home in our Dalton Street apartment with the new baby, unable to resume teaching until the fall.

"I can't afford to take this thing more than once," I told Ron. "In fact, I'm not sure how I'm going to afford taking it this time."

We had a new family's bills and nothing coming in when fate intervened. One day after a long study session with Ron, I was driving down Avalon Boulevard, when some guy rear-ended my yellow and black Ford Fairlane convertible. I loved that car, but I could have kissed him. I settled the case myself shortly thereafter and came home with $2,000. It was enough to get us through the summer with a little left over. As a gesture of faith in the future, I took the surplus from my auto settlement and put it down on a white Chevrolet Impala with red upholstery.

"Now," I told Barbara, "I'm going to pass the bar exam because I have to." I knew that $2,000 wouldn't last forever.

Because of that Ford Fairlane, I nearly didn't last long enough to take the bar exam. Its exhaust system had somehow become damaged, but money was tight, so I couldn't get it fixed. Even with the windows rolled down, the carbon monoxide fumes from the exhaust worked their way up through the floorboards. I was on my way to UCLA to take the bar exam, and I was so tired from all of my studying that it took some time for me to realize that the poisonous fumes were making me nauseous. Not some run-of-the-mill light-headed nauseous, but floor-spinning, forehead-sweating, stomach-churning way-beyond-queasy nauseous. Somehow I got through that exam and said, "This is preposterous, this old car." I said, "I will not put myself through this again. I will never own another junker."

After I took the bar, I returned to my clerkship with the city attorney, sweating out the months until the results were announced on Monday, December 17. Some of my classmates had had the presence of mind to get post office boxes. A particular day's mail is slipped into a P.O. Box immediately after it's sorted between midnight and 2 A.M. That meant the guys who had rented boxes got their results hours before the rest of us. One of them woke me at 2:30 A.M.

"I've paaaaaassed," he screamed into the phone.

I never got back to sleep that night. At 4 A.M. I was turned away from my own local post office by a sleepy clerk. I went home, dressed, and headed for the office to join the other nervous clerks. At precisely 8:50—the earliest possible moment—one of my colleagues, George Logan, telephoned the clerk of the state supreme court. You were allowed to ask for your own results and those of two others. George had passed. He asked about me.

"Cochran, Johnnie L.," he said into the phone. The pause that followed seemed endless.

"Yes, 4233 South Dalton. Yes, that's right. . . . He passed?"

"Yes, yes, yes," I screamed, nearly drowning out George's inquiry about Ron Sunderland's results.

A few minutes later, I telephoned the William Morris Agency in Beverly Hills, where Ron was working as a clerk.

"Ahem," I began portentously. "Good morning, Attorney Sunderland, Esquire."

"You're lying," he said suspiciously.

"I am not," I laughed.

"If you're lying to me, I'll kill you," he warned.

"You heard me, Attorney Ronald B. Sunderland. I, Attorney Johnnie L. Cochran, Jr.—also Esquire—am saying under oath that you passed the California State Bar exam. Congratulations."

Given the volume of the shrieks that followed, we could have dispensed with the telephone.

The joy and pride my parents felt when I told them that I attained my dream filled me with an indescribable happiness. My father said he never doubted that I would achieve my goal. My mother choked back tears as she said she was so proud of what I had accomplished. Within an hour, the news of my passage of the California bar exam was already a part of family legend.

A few weeks later, I knotted a fresh new tie, hopped into my gleaming Impala, and drove downtown to report for work, not as a clerk but as a freshly minted deputy city attorney, fully qualified to take up the practice of my new profession.

It was January 10, 1963, and the dream that had first been spoken at my parents' table on West Twenty-eighth Street, that had found its wings in Thurgood Marshall's epic victory for justice, that had kept itself alive through three dreary years of law school drudgery—that dream was real at last.

I was a lawyer.

4

A Soul Divided

LIKE THE COMMUNITY IT SERVED, THE LOS ANGELES city attorney's office in the early 1960s was dominated by the conservative values of the white establishment that still ran the town. During my tenure there, I was one of only three African Americans on the staff. One, a gifted young woman named Consuelo Marshall, went on to become a federal judge. The other, my close friend Charles E. Lloyd, became a trial lawyer, like me. The city attorney's office offered three things every young lawyer needs: supportive colleagues, a steady paycheck, and loads of hands-on experience.

My initial assignment was in traffic court, and the very first day on the job I tried twenty-eight traffic tickets. I won them all and went on winning them day after day.

"Officer," I would inquire, "did you see Mr. Smith run that red light?"

"Yes, sir, I did," the officer would reply—no matter what the alleged offense's time of day, no matter what his distance from the intersection, no matter what his angle of vision, no matter what obstacle lay in between.

The unfortunate Smith would, of course, deny his infraction. The judge would, of course, accept the officer's word:

"Twenty-five-dollar fine. Pay the clerk, Mr. Smith. Next case."

In short order, I graduated to trying drunk-driving cases. Sometimes the defendant would elect to have the judge decide his case. That's called a "court trial." Other defendants would insist on their right to have the matter heard by a jury. But whatever the format, I never took the presentation of the case for granted.

I participated in over 125 jury trials in my first two years, and I'd like to say that I enjoyed every minute of handling the drunk-driving and misdemeanor battery cases. And, working what was essentially a legal assembly line, I had plenty of opportunities to experiment. For example, while examining the defendant in one court trial, I left the podium, walked to the witness stand, and bent over the partition.

"Mr. Cochran," the bemused judge asked, "exactly what are you doing?"

"Your Honor," I replied, "every time I ask one of these defendants how much they'd been drinking, they tell me 'just two beers.' I simply wanted to see if maybe there was a cue card down here that they're reading from."

As the judge rolled his eyes in weary agreement, I knew my point was made.

On another occasion, during a jury trial, I was cross-examining the defendant, a bartender charged with serving liquor to an obviously intoxicated patron.

"Mr. Jones," I said, "you testified that you drove this man home on the night in question. Is that correct?"

"Yes, sir," Jones replied.

"And was he a good friend of yours?"

"No, but he was one of my regulars."

"So, you often drove him home?" I asked.

"Oh, no, Mr. Cochran, but it was raining that night."

"Well," I said, "that was very, very thoughtful. Was his car broken down?"

"No, no, it was okay."

"So, even though his own car was running, you went out of your way to drive him home through that awful storm, even though you'd put in a full night's work behind that busy bar. That really was kind of you," I said.

"Well, thank you, sir." The defendant beamed.

"Are you a churchgoing man?" I wondered, larding my voice with all the admiration I could muster.

"Not really, Mr. Cochran," the smiling defendant said. "But I really felt like it was the right thing to do since I'd never seen him that drunk before."

"Thank you very kindly, no more questions," I said, a smile spreading across my own face. The jury twittered, the red-faced judge looked into his lap, and Jones and his attorney shared a look of silent, open-mouthed horror.

But while I was comfortable with both trial formats, it was clear to me from the start that the one thing both judge and jury had in common was an almost unshakable predisposition to believe the police. And, as case after case rolled through my busy schedule, it also was clear to me that the stories those police officers told were remarkably—some might even say incredibly—alike. Every suspected drunk driver they stopped had provided them with an absolutely classic case of probable cause. Once stopped, every one of those defendants behaved in precisely that way and displayed precisely the symptoms required to obtain their conviction for driving under the influence of alcohol. The officers' written reports were invariably flawless, recounting in perfect detail how they had conformed to every nuance of the drunk-driving statute. Like any trial lawyer, I was happy to win. But, as victory followed victory, the nagging feeling grew that I was the beneficiary not of good police work but of an elaborate choreography. God help the defense lawyer or defendant who tried to point that out, however. In Los Angeles in those days, you could be held in contempt for calling a police officer a liar. Cops, attorneys, courts, defendants—we all were dancing to the same music. And that tune was being orchestrated down at police headquarters.

To understand why, it's necessary to step back from my own story for a moment and consider that of the Los Angeles Police Department, an institution unique in the history of modern urban America. Nowhere else in our country have the development of a law enforcement agency and that of the community it polices been so intricately intertwined. Los Angeles' two preeminent social historians, for example, are men of very opposite sensibilities. One of them, Kevin Starr, is a patrician San Franciscan, as at home in the corridors of government as he is in the halls of academe. The other, Mike Davis, grew up in the shadow of Fontana's steel mills and honed his politics in the rough-and-tumble of the intellectual New Left. There is one thing on which they completely agree: "Basically, what you have in Los Angeles is a police culture addicted to heavy-handed exercises of power," Davis says. "Nowhere else in this country is that history as continuous as it is here." To Starr, the story of Los Angeles' unquiet relationship with its police is a window on the essential nature of the city itself. "Once you begin to talk about L.A.'s police," he says, "you *have* to talk about the community itself. For better or worse, our cops are the deepest taproot of our community."

That root extends back to the bitter conflict that dominated Los Angeles during this century's first decade—the fight between trade unionists and the city's businessmen and industrialists over the open shop. These oligarchs, who had built their fortunes on plentiful cheap land and lots of cheap labor, were determined to keep unions out of "their" city. In the streets, that determination was backed up by the police with their truncheons and mass arrests. The department's active role in the street violence that erupted sporadically throughout the open-shop period was decisive in creating its culture.

Decades of labor turmoil reached their climax in the municipal election of 1910, when the *Los Angeles Times*, then the oligarchs' ideological mouthpiece, was bombed. Twenty of the paper's employees were killed. Three labor activists—James B. and John J. McNamara and Ortie McManigal—fled to the Midwest and were later returned to Los Angeles to stand trial for the bombing. Labor and the Socialist Party, whose mayoral candidate, Job Harriman, stood a strong chance of election, alleged a frame-up and retained Clarence Darrow, then America's leading defense attorney, to represent the accused. Their trial reached a sensational and, for labor, crushing conclusion. Darrow had become convinced his clients inevitably would be convicted of a terrorist act, which they had, in fact, committed. He pled them guilty as part of a deal that allowed them to escape the death penalty. But before Darrow could get out of town, the police arrested him on a trumped-up jury-tampering charge. With the help of a legendary local defense lawyer named Earl Rogers, Darrow ultimately won acquittal, but he never quite recovered from the wounds inflicted on him. American working people had lost their greatest legal champion through the machinations of the Los Angeles Police Department.

Meanwhile, Harriman lost the election, and L.A.—with the assistance of the police department's new "Red squad" and the state's draconian "antisyndicalism" statute—was made safe for the open shop for another thirty years. At times, however, police misconduct became so blatant that it embarrassed even the department's wealthy backers. In 1923, for example, the famed muckraking author Upton Sinclair and some friends staged a candlelight vigil in support of striking dockworkers at the Port of Los Angeles. As Sinclair read aloud from the First Amendment of the Bill of Rights, he was arrested by Police Chief Louis Oaks, who ordered the writer to "cut out that Constitution stuff." Over the next eighteen hours, Sinclair and his friends, including a socially prominent Santa Barbara millionaire, were held incommunicado and hustled secretly from one jail to another, ostensibly on suspicion of criminal syndicalism. Brutally rousting a bunch of longshoremen was one thing; the legal kidnapping of a millionaire and Sinclair, whose book *The Jungle* had almost single-handedly secured passage of the nation's 1906 Food and Drug Act, was another. Scandal ensued, and the humiliated oligarchs agreed to free Sinclair and his friends, drop all charges, and deal with the problem of Chief Oaks. A short time later, the chief was arrested while parked on a local lovers' lane. Both he and his companion, a naked young woman, apparently had partaken freely of the half-empty bottle of whiskey found inside the car. A few days later, Oaks resigned.

During that period, the Los Angeles Police Department also earned a reputation as one of the country's most corrupt. Acting in concert with city hall officials, the police took a lucrative share of L.A.'s burgeoning bootlegging, gambling, and prostitution rackets. Public outrage mounted, culminating in a reform movement that, in 1938, forced the recall of the notorious mayor Frank A. Shaw, whose downfall was attended by two particularly lurid and closely followed trials. In one of them, Shaw's brother and bagman, Joe, was convicted on sixty-six counts of bribery and selling city jobs, including positions in the police department. In the other, Police Lieutenant Earl Kynett, the Red squad's leader, was convicted of a car bombing that nearly killed a private detective who was working for the reformers.

The reformers swept into power by Shaw's fall had two attributes characteristic of the progressive movement in which their politics were formed—a visceral antipathy toward nonwhites and a nearly religious faith in the virtues of managerial government. When it came time to deal with police reform, those two attitudes had consequences that have shaped events right down to the trial of O. J. Simpson. As Starr sees it, "Uniquely in urban America, the Los Angeles Police Department became an independent agency and, somehow, more than that. I don't think it overstates things to say that there accrued to the department part of the sovereignty of Los Angeles itself." At least one exercise of that sovereignty soon became clear. If the police became more neutral toward labor in the post-Shaw era, the change simply allowed them to shift their attention to enforcing racial segregation, which they did with relish.

In essence, the police reforms amounted to a kind of Faustian bargain. The people of Los Angeles said to their police, "Look, if you guys will stop stealing, we'll give you a free hand." Most people also welcomed the increasing militarization of the force, particularly its growing reliance on widely scattered automobile patrol units that further isolated officers from the communities they policed. Militarization was good, as far as the white majority was concerned, because it kept the police out of sight until you called them, and then they came pretty quickly. More important, it allowed Los Angeles to police its vast area with very few officers, which meant very cheaply. Latinos and African Americans took a different view of this process since they were treated differently by the reformed police department from the start.

Initially, this disparity fell most harshly on the Mexican Americans and recent Latino immigrants who, since the 1940s, have comprised the city's largest minority group. In August of 1942, the body of a young Mexican American was found near a flooded East Side gravel pit subsequently dubbed "Sleepy Lagoon" by an overexcited newspaper reporter. Within days, the police had arrested twenty-four alleged members of a Chicano "gang." During the course of the investigation, the suspects were held incommunicado; two of them were badly beaten by their police interrogators. Seventeen of the young men were convicted and sent to prison in what was then the largest mass trial for murder in American history.

As the late journalist and historian Carey McWilliams wrote not long afterward, "For years, Mexicans had been pushed around by the Los Angeles police and given a very rough time in the courts, but the Sleepy Lagoon prosecution was a climax. . . . From the beginning the proceedings savored more of a ceremonial lynching than a trial in a court of justice." In fact, an appeals court overturned all seventeen convictions just two years after the trial.

The postwar era, which brought my family and so many other African Americans to Los Angeles, accelerated the overall pace of social change. Racial antagonism was no longer the only point of friction between the police and their community. That was particularly true after the department came under the sway of a rigid former military officer named William Parker, who believed that the best way to ensure an honest police force was to people its ranks with former soldiers and marines with no personal ties to the community. He purposefully recruited new officers from among discharged young servicemen in the South and Midwest, and they brought with them not only the racial prejudices common to their regions at that time but also deeply rooted Bible Belt notions of public rectitude. The department's vice and Red squads became public inquisitors, joined by their colleagues in the County Sheriff's Department, who didn't want to be seen as "soft" on immorality.

In 1957, Wallace Berman—subsequently to be recognized as one of the most important and original artists Los Angeles ever produced—was arrested when police, acting on an "anonymous citizen's complaint," raided an exhibit of his work at the city's most important contemporary art gallery, the Ferus. A small nude drawing was seized, and Berman, who had begun his career drawing album covers for African American jazz artists, was convicted of displaying lewd material. He was spared fifteen days in jail when a friend, actor Dean Stockwell, paid his $150 fine. The conviction cast a deep chill across Los Angeles' emerging contemporary art scene and left both the police and sheriff's vice squads with a taste for more of the same.

It was inevitable that, sooner or later, their attention would fall on Lenny Bruce, who, by the time I became a deputy city attorney, was performing his iconoclastic, profanity-studded comedy routines at the Troubadour, a West Hollywood club not far from the Ferus Gallery. Those wonderfully convenient "anonymous citizen's complaints" apparently came pouring in, and the Sheriff's Department dispatched a young vice deputy named Sherman Block to sit through one of Bruce's performances with a tape recorder under his shirt. On the basis of that visit, criminal obscenity charges were filed against the comedian, and the case ended up on my desk. By then, I was the up-and-coming young trial lawyer in our office with a growing reputation for courtroom flair. But fate and the First Amendment were against me this time.

Bruce, a rumpled, sad-eyed man with an alcoholic's pallor under a five o'clock shadow, didn't impress me much. He appeared somehow defiant and doomed at the same time. His attorney was something else entirely. Three minutes with him

and I knew I was in tough again. His name was Sydney Milton
Irmas—Syd to his friends, who seemed to be spilling out of
every nook and cranny of the courthouse. He was tall, tanned,
handsome, impeccably groomed, and immaculately turned out
in a dark suit accented with a white pocket square. The shine
on his shoes was blinding. I knew him by reputation, a millionaire businessman and philanthropist and a trial lawyer
whose every gesture bespoke good-humored confidence and
competence. He had an aura of honesty and integrity written
all over him, and—I must admit—it was an inspiring sight to a
young attorney who was doing well and hoping to do better. I
just sat there in my regulation city attorney's dark suit, white
shirt, and dark tie, my nose stuck in my notes. It may have
been the only time in my career when I simply faded into the
background.

Things didn't get any better when we moved on to the law. As
it turned out, most of the jokes on which the complaint turned
were inaudible on Block's tape. The spit-and-polish young deputy
had worn a shirt so stiffly starched that the crackling of the fabric
was all you could hear through most of the tape. We could make
out only two of Bruce's routines, both of which, liberally laced
with vulgarities, involved political personalities. I took particular
exception to one that satirized a visit to then-President Lyndon B.
Johnson by a group of black businessmen. As they left the Oval
Office, Bruce had the group discussing the necessity of teaching
the chief executive "to speak jive." I was ready to spin out an
argument on that one. But it was clear that the judge—a fervent,
lifelong Democrat—was more concerned with Bruce's interpretation of a photo that had appeared in *Time* magazine shortly after
the assassination of John F. Kennedy. As its caption said, the picture in question showed the First Lady "reaching out over the
rear of the car to help a Secret Service agent aboard." On Deputy

Block's tape you could hear Bruce saying that it looked to him "like she was hauling ass to save ass."

The judge began to sputter, and his faced turned a shade of crimson so virulent that I wondered if he could stave off a stroke long enough to give me a conviction. I relaxed the way prosecutors, accustomed to getting their own way, so often do. Irmas, however, knew his man. He engaged the judge in a spirited discussion that led straight to the First Amendment and then back through the applicable case law to our situation. They batted the facts back and forth, then Irmas concluded by saying, "Your Honor, the very fact that we are arguing in this fashion means there is, in some sense, social relevance to what this man is saying."

As it turned out, the judge was an even stronger civil libertarian than he was a Democrat. Case dismissed. But my first celebrity trial wasn't a total loss. Syd Irmas and I became very good friends and later went on to try cases together. Sherman Block, the young deputy with the impenetrably starched shirt, later was elected sheriff of Los Angeles County three times. Sometimes, clothes do make the man.

Nor was our judge the only one who had begun to take a dim view of Los Angeles' war on "obscenity." A year before I tried the Bruce case, Los Angeles Police Department vice officers had arrested a Hollywood bookstore owner named Bradley R. Smith for selling them a copy of Henry Miller's *Tropic of Cancer*. Smith was convicted of violating the city's obscenity law and lost his store to bankruptcy. Fortunately for all of us, the American Civil Liberties Union took up his cause. Not long after Lenny Bruce was acquitted, the California Supreme Court struck down the ban on Miller's novel. Justice Mathew O. Tobriner wrote the court's unanimous opinion, whose eloquence exerted a powerful influence on other state courts then considering similar statutes:

"Man's drive for self-expression, which over the centuries has built monuments, does not stay within set bounds. The creations which yesterday were the detested and the obscene become the classics of today."

The *Tropic of Cancer* decision erased Los Angeles' local obscenity statute and, for all intents and purposes, took the LAPD out of the business of policing culture. To Deputy City Attorney Johnnie L. Cochran, Jr., that came as a relief.

Losing the Bruce case did nothing to diminish my standing within the office. But neither my colleagues' regard nor my superiors' encouragement could resolve the crisis of conscience into which I seemed to slip more deeply with each passing day.

By March 1965, I had become one of the city attorney's top trial lawyers. But, increasingly, the cases that came my way were what we called "148s." That is, they involved defendants charged with violating Section 148 of the California Penal Code, which prohibits resisting arrest or interfering with an officer in the course of his duties. Every Monday, I would arrive for work and confront a courtroom filled with men who were there to answer one or both of those charges. The defendants invariably displayed visible injuries ranging from cuts and bruises to fractured limbs. The officers with whom they allegedly had struggled never had so much as a visible scratch. Ninety percent or more of the defendants had something else in common: They were African American men.

Everyone in the courtroom knew precisely what was going on. LAPD officers privately referred to penal code section 148 as "the attitude test." If they believed a black man had "flunked the attitude test," they would administer what they called "curbside justice," or "a little wall-to-wall interrogation." In other words, they beat the hell out of him. The severity of that beating, like the decision to administer it, depended entirely on the whims of the officers involved. It quickly became apparent to me that the policeman on the street is the single most powerful person in the entire American system of criminal justice. Most of the people with whom that officer comes into contact are relatively powerless, sometimes unpopular, often friendless. At that moment, the policeman literally has the power of life and death. Even if he chooses not to take your life, he may beat or maim you. He may lie about your conduct and—in a system that accepts his word as gospel—thereby change your life forever. In Los Angeles, the police had become accustomed to exercising all that power virtually unchecked by any authority higher than their own headquarters.

From day one, it was equally clear to me why we deputy city attorneys were being asked to prosecute such bogus cases. Pursuing criminal charges against these poor battered men made it virtually impossible for them to file civil suits against the city to obtain compensation for their injuries. In other words, our office had elected to become a silent co-conspirator with the police as a way to save the city money. At first, I thought that I could sort the wheat from the chaff, that I could find a way to prosecute the legitimate 148s—of which there obviously were some—and dispose of the others. But in a very short time, I became painfully aware of just how badly I was deluding myself.

I vividly recall the day I was sitting at the prosecution table, listening to a 148 defendant tell his story from the witness stand. This man—a black man from South Central, of course—had run afoul of officers working out of LAPD's 77th Division, a station infamous for its implacable racism. The defendant was a small, soft-spoken man, who had been badly beaten by a pair of beefy cops during a routine traffic stop. Both his eardrums had been ruptured, the orbit of one of his eyes had been fractured, and his body was covered with bruises. He seemed so small and powerless and was so obviously truthful, so obviously terrified and bewildered by what had happened to him, that tears began to well up in eyes throughout the courtroom. When he finished his testimony, there was a painful silence.

"You may cross-examine, Mr. Cochran," the judge said.

"No questions, Your Honor," I quietly replied.

The judge and defense attorney shot me puzzled looks. I didn't bother to look at the cops. The defendant was acquitted, and I knew precisely what I had to do. I went to see my superiors that very day and told them I no longer would prosecute 148s.

"I have drawn the line," I said. "I'm not doing this anymore."

To their credit, my supervisors understood my objections. Moreover, I was perhaps their top trial attorney, and they wanted to keep me on board. They assured me that other, equally challenging assignments would be found for me. They were sincere; I was loyal. We were all professionals, men and women of the world. We had reasoned our way to an accommodation. But over the next few nights, my conscience gave me no peace. My own hands were now clean, but I was still drawing a paycheck from an institution that was—in the prosecution of most 148s—betraying its public trust. Worse, the consequences of that betrayal were falling most heavily on my own community, on the people among whom I grew up, among whom my mother and father still lived and worked, among whom my wife and I planned to raise our own family. Once again, I was face to face with my "two-ness." There was no inherent conflict between my role as a prosecutor sworn to uphold the law and my identity as an African American. But there was an irreparable contradiction between my silent acquiescence to injustice and my sense of duty to my community.

Like an unquiet spirit, an old memory began to torment me. In 1963, not long after I had joined the city attorney's office, I had taken Barbara and little Melodie on a much-deserved and long-deferred vacation to Yosemite National Park. At first, our time in that breathtaking place was like a blessing. But our holiday happened to coincide with Dr. Martin Luther King, Jr.'s storied March on Washington. To this day, I recall the morning I passed a news rack outside the lodge in Yosemite Valley and found myself transfixed by the headlines and the accompanying photographs of the march. There were all these people—white and black—standing shoulder to shoulder for justice, and I was not among them.

God, I should be there, I thought, guilt's hot spray rising through my gut like a geyser. Suddenly, my hard-earned family holiday felt like a self-indulgent evasion. Like the hungry Esau, I had traded my birthright for a mess of pottage.

If you grew up black in the 1960s and you didn't march with Dr. King, if you didn't go on the Freedom Rides, if you didn't help lay the foundations for the War on Poverty, then you didn't do enough. I didn't. I had my reasons, but they weren't good enough. While I wasn't quite sure how to resolve my dilemma over the city attorney's office, I was certain I didn't want another memory like that.

Sleepless, I tossed and turned through anxious nights. Gradually, I began to listen to the voices that always have been there for me. I remembered the Gospel admonition I first heard echoing off the clapboards of the Little Union Baptist Church: "A man cannot serve two masters." I thought of my mother on the night I first told her I wanted to be a lawyer: "John, just promise me this. Be the best that you can be." I pictured the fearless Thurgood Marshall on the steps of the U.S. Supreme Court, his great work of righteousness like an invisible crown upon his brow. I realized Du Bois's description of how Frederick Douglass had resolved his own inner struggle because he "bravely stood for the ideals of his early manhood—ultimate assimilation *through* self-assertion, and on no other terms."

I knew what I had to do.

At the dinner table that night, I told Barbara of my decision to leave the city attorney's office and enter private practice. "No, you aren't going to do that," she said, frowning and shaking her head. "Why would you even think about leaving a good job like that? What's wrong with you, Johnnie? You can retire from a job like that."

I sat watching little Melodie methodically turning her dish of peas into puree with her fingers and tried to put myself in Barbara's place. The $608 I made each month and the life we were building together represented the first real security she had known since her parents' deaths. I tried to explain what staying in the city attorney's office would mean. I told her how confident I was that I could make a go of private practice. Barbara would have none of it.

"Don't leave," she said with an air of steely-eyed finality. "This is a mistake."

But we both knew I was going to leave. It was the first visible breach between us, and, over the years, it would widen into a chasm. I left the office in March 1965. My colleagues, many of whom have remained my friends to this day, gave me a lavish going-away party. I didn't go far though, just out to West Washington Boulevard, where I joined another black attorney, a former deputy district attorney named Gerald D. Lenoir. From the start, I relished the sense of accomplishment private practice provides. But I also began to get a sense of what the issues that had propelled me out of the city attorney's office looked like from the other side of the courtroom aisle.

Gerald D. Lenoir was a small man, five feet five inches tall, weighing in at maybe 130 pounds, but he had a lot of fire. A real passion for the law. He was from New Orleans, so I felt an immediate connection with him. Plus, he really believed in the importance of criminal defense. I learned a lot from him in a short period of time. Gerald also had a great sense of humor. A lawyer needs that. If he had a client who had messed up while testifying, he would come back to the office later and tell me how he'd taken the person aside during a recess. "Johnnie," he'd tell me, "I looked him in the eye and said, 'You just lost yourself a lawsuit.' " Of course, he hadn't really said that, but I know he was thinking it.

On Mondays, when Lenoir and I returned from court, our waiting room usually contained a number of prospective clients with black eyes, limbs in splints, heads swathed in bandages.

"Don't tell me," I'd say, as they sat down in the chair opposite my desk, "you're charged with resisting and interfering with an officer in the performance of his duty. Or, you're charged with battery on a police officer."

"How can you tell?" the client would ask.

"Oh, something about the way you look," I would say.

But beneath the gallows humor, my sense of frustration was mounting. Given the propensity of judges and jurors to take the word of virtually any police officer against any black defendant, there was little I could do for most of these injured men but use my contacts with my former city attorney colleagues to negotiate a deal, usually a plea of "no contest" to the lesser charge of disturbing the peace. The city was protected from any legal liability, and my client was spared a harsher penalty. It was what lawyers call a "result," but it was nobody's idea of justice. Worse, each of these cases—and hundreds more like them—were fanning the embers of social anger that, even then, were burning just beneath the community's surface. What Chief William Parker's Los Angeles Police Department called "keeping the lid on" amounted to a low-level police riot proceeding night after night in the streets of the city's black neighborhoods. What Lenoir and I were seeing in our West Washington Boulevard office was a fraction of the problem. By the mid-1960s, the problem of unchecked police misconduct was *the* defining issue among black Angelenos of every social class.

But along with its frustrations, private practice had its rewards. Not long after I joined Lenoir, Barbara and I purchased our first home, a Spanish-style house with white stucco walls, red-tile roof, a beautiful little courtyard, and yellow-trimmed windows. It was in a middle-class, predominantly black neighborhood called Leimert Park, where many of my Kappa brothers also owned homes. The day we moved in is indelibly etched on my memory: August 13, 1965. That also was the night that black Los Angeles' smoldering anger flared into full-scale rage in what has come to be called the "Watts Riot."

The Watts Riot was an act of communal self-destruction, an unconscious, though purposeful, expression of hopelessness born of legitimate anger and frustration. What other reason could a people have for destroying their own community? Most of the burned-out stores and businesses were never rebuilt. The vast majority of the people injured or killed were African American. Their deaths were treated as little more than statistics.

The Watts Riot was a catharsis for me and a lot of other people in the black community. I understood more fully the rage, frustration, and despair of the people on the streets. It reconnected me in a very real way to the anguish of the disenfranchised. Once a person becomes successful, it's very easy to say, "That doesn't apply to me." The truth is, however, that there but for the grace of God goes any one of us.

As I watched all this unfold, I was overcome with a sense of tragedy. It wasn't just middle-class revulsion against the lawless turbulence of the poor. In my heart, I had bridged the distance between West Twenty-eighth Street and Palm Lane many years before. But everything I had learned and lived—from Little Union to the L.A. County Court House—had taught me that, throughout our history, wherever moral and legal lawlessness held sway, black people suffered. Our struggle had never been with America's Constitution and its laws; rather, ours was a struggle to convince white Americans that we, too, were entitled to the Constitution's protections and that they, too, were subject to its restraints. The burning of Watts, no matter how great the provocation—and it was great—could not advance that struggle.

The Watts Riot started, predictably enough, when two young black men in their early twenties, Marquette and Ronald Frye, were stopped by a pair of highway patrolmen two days earlier for reckless driving. What should have been a routine stop got nightmarishly out of hand. When the men's mother arrived at the scene, an argument broke out between the Fryes and the two white officers. A crowd gathered, shouting at the policemen as they arrested Marquette and his mother. Some eyewitnesses claimed that the police used excessive force in making the arrests. The crowd got angrier—raising an increasingly vocal defense of Mrs. Frye. The policemen called in reinforcements. Tempers ignited and some youths threw rocks at the officers, who retreated to their cars. The crowd, at an emotional fever pitch, scattered when a sizable police presence arrived. Though no longer concentrated in one area, the crowd and its collective outrage was still strong. They went on a rampage through the neighborhood, and within a short time, street fighting, sporadic gunfire, looting, and arson spread to many other black neighborhoods.

In Watts, the protests escalated from rock throwing and looting to widespread arson and sniper fire, which claimed several lives. Police Chief Parker stressed crowd control. He wanted the ringleaders arrested, so vast numbers of residents were lined up against cars and walls, searched, and hauled away. Parker wanted to gain and maintain the respect of the populace, both black and white. His tactics may have gained him what he wanted with whites, but they further angered blacks. Those people must know we mean business, he said to the press. Parker bluntly stated that necessary force would be used to restore order, to effect arrests, and to protect officers from bodily harm. Apparently, the irony of the situation escaped Chief Parker. What the LAPD deemed "necessary" and what African Americans who took the brunt of that force believed was "necessary" had sparked the riots in the first place.

Large groups of African Americans were taken into custody on a number of charges ranging from possession of stolen weapons and breaking and entering to felonious assault, theft, arson, and inciting to riot. About one-fourth of the juveniles arrested were later released and their cases dismissed. Most were put on probation.

The riot lasted six days. Thirty-five people were killed and another 1,032 were injured. In a 150-block area, over 600 buildings were damaged by looting and arson, with more than 200 of those destroyed by fire. The property loss totaled more than $200 million, and 3,938 adults and 514 juveniles were arrested.

During the riots, there was something surreal about being forbidden to travel the streets of the city I loved so much. In "downtown Watts," where our Cousin Cloteal once primly ordered us to "be on your best behavior," the air was filled with the acrid stench of fires and the keening wail of police sirens. Suddenly there were armed troops in the streets. South Los Angeles was an armed community.

Watching the televised news reports on the disturbances, I remember thinking back to something I had heard during a Passover Seder to which one of my Jewish classmates had invited me. That great Jewish holiday commemorates the night on which God sent the angel of death to the homes of the Egyptians, thereby forcing the evil Pharaoh to free the children of Israel from slavery. One of the many bonds between the black and Jewish communities is the central place the figure of Moses, the Israelites' liberator and lawgiver, occupies in the spirituality of both communities. The story of how our faith in a just God led us out of bondage is a sacred memory in both black and Jewish households. In observant Jewish homes, part of the Passover ritual involves discussion of what the Talmudic sages and other scholars have taught concerning the exodus out of Egypt. The exchange I recalled as I watched Watts burn concerned God's instruction to Moses that his people should mark their doorposts with the blood of a lamb so that the avenging angel might recognize them and pass them by.

Why, one of the sages wondered, was such a mark required? Why would an all-knowing God need a sign to recognize his enslaved children?

Because, another wise man replied, once the angel of death and disorder is unleashed in a community, no one is safe.

Watts and so much more that has transpired in urban America since then have proven just how right those ancient sages were.

I've returned to these thoughts many times over the years. But at the time, I was too busy to entertain them more than briefly. When the violence began that hot August night, my law colleague, Lenoir, was out of town, driving his two daughters back to the University of Wisconsin, where they were enrolled. Within hours, circumstances and my partner's absence had brought me face to face with one of the paradoxes of a criminal law practice: Our community and city never had been convulsed by a more far-reaching tragedy; the law office of Lenoir and Cochran never had enjoyed a more lucrative month. African Americans were being arrested in droves. Our phones were constantly ringing. Our offices were flooded with clients, all of whom seemed to have cash. So many cases were pending that the arraignment courts virtually ran around the clock. Flushed with exhilaration, I represented one client after another. Night after night, I made my exhausted way home, slumped into a chair, and emptied my bulging pockets onto the kitchen table. Often, when I smoothed the crumpled bills, the day's receipts would amount to as much as $5,000, at the time astonishing money for a small practice like ours.

But as I sat there in the kitchen of our new home listening to the news reports of Chief Parker's comments about the disorders, I was forcefully reminded that there was a lot more than cash flow at stake. "We're on the top, and they're back on the bottom," Parker said of his officers' reassertion of authority over the streets of South Los Angeles. "We've got them dancing," he said, "like monkeys in a cage." He was describing my clients, my community, my people, my family. These were not the ravings of some garden-variety bigot but the public pronouncements of the widely admired architect of America's most highly praised "modern" urban police force. As I angrily turned them over in my mind, I reached two conclusions about the practice of law to which I have clung ever since:

Once engaged, defense attorneys must give themselves without reservation to protecting the constitutional rights of each and every one of their clients. For it is the zealous defense of the individual—however unpopular, however revolting the alleged crime—that guarantees the right of the peace-loving, law-abiding majority to live secure in its freedom. It is this unyielding commitment to equal and indivisible justice for all— no matter what the personal cost—that makes a defense attorney more than just a profiteer of pain.

I also knew that if I were to be a worthy heir to the tradition of Thurgood Marshall, I would have to assume the responsibility of using my legal skills to change things for the better. He had looked at the South's segregated schools and known what he had to do. As I listened to Chief William Parker and thought of the carnage and bitterness his department's arrogant, deceitful bigotry had wrought upon Angelenos of every color and faith, I knew I had to do what I could to root it out. Still, it was a daunting prospect. As a former prosecutor, I had an insider's firsthand knowledge of just how tightly the thread of police misconduct was woven into the fabric of our civic life. I knew how many powerful people and institutions had a stake in the conspiracy of silence that allowed this evil to perpetuate itself year after year. I knew how ruthlessly the department's hierarchy would fight to defend its lawlessness.

I had the vision. The question was: Did I—a young man, not yet thirty—really have the strength? But as I was Thurgood Marshall's disciple, so I was my father's son. I knew I was not alone and there, on that August night so long ago, I sought the Lord in prayer, and he led me to these words from the First Book of Samuel:

> And Saul said to David, Thou art not able to go against this Philistine to fight with him: for thou art but a youth, and he a man of war from his youth. And David said unto Saul, Thy servant kept his father's sheep, and there came a lion, and a bear, and took a lamb out of the flock: And I went out after him, and smote him, and delivered it out of his mouth: and when he arose against me, I caught him by his beard, and smote him, and slew him.

I did not know it at the time, but I would fight my Philistine for many years to come. And, whenever I have wearied of the battle, I have reminded myself of the need to keep faith with the decision to which I believe God guided me on that hot August night in 1965, while all around our quiet house my people bled and my city burned.

5

A Wanderer in the Wilderness

IN THE AFTERMATH OF THE WATTS RIOT A CHORD WAS struck deep within me and renewed my sense of purpose. I will never advocate lawlessness, and, in all honesty, what transpired over the course of those six days in August 1965 vacillated wildly between legitimate political protest and senseless criminal acts and touched nearly every gradation in between. I could not condone those criminal acts, but I certainly better understood their source. I will always believe that there are other recourses, other means by which individuals can seek redress for their grievances—the criminal and civil justice systems.

The Watts Riot renewed my commitment to effect change in the criminal and civil justice systems, to make the courts, the police, and other agencies more responsive to the community I served, the community in which I lived, and the community for which I have boundless respect and affection. Like Dr. King, I believed that the solution lay in working within the system, not dismantling it entirely. From the ashes of Watts, my optimism rose phoenixlike.

Buoyed by these feelings, I decided to set a new course for myself. My decision to set off in a new direction had nothing to do with Gerald Lenoir, it simply was time to strike out on my own.

Like nearly all the black attorneys of my generation, I'd come to professional maturity admiring Leo Branton, Jr., for many years Los Angeles' preeminent black lawyer. Branton came from a distinguished family. His brother, Wiley, was for many years a beloved professor at Howard University Law School and, ultimately, its dean. Leo Branton was professionally accomplished, financially successful, and strikingly stylish. His clients included a number of leading black celebrities, but he probably was best known as the great Nat King Cole's personal attorney. That fact—unremarkable today, but stunning at the time—said a great deal about both men. In those days, the lucrative field of entertainment law was an all-white boys' club; even today, it remains perhaps the most segregated of all legal specialties. As a shrewd businessman and skilled negotiator who enjoyed his clients' complete confidence, Leo Branton dealt with the entertainment industry's hard-nosed executives on his own terms. At one point, he even helped Cole realize a longtime ambition to purchase a mansion in Hancock Park. As the first African American to crack the neighborhood's restrictive real estate covenant, which forbade sales to blacks or Jews, Cole was welcomed by a large group of neighbors—most of them listed in the local *Blue Book* or *Social Register*—who staged a protest rally in front of his family's new home.

Branton's record of success for his clients was a remarkable achievement in an era when the relationship between black artists and their white agents and attorneys could be described most charitably as paternalistic. Branton also enjoyed the visible symbols of his achievements. He had a mansion of his own in Lafayette Square, then the neighborhood of choice for affluent African Americans, drove a Rolls-Royce, and had an office on Wilshire Boulevard, one of the marks of a successful law practice.

The stylish home and the Rolls still were well beyond my reach, but after carefully reviewing our financial situation, I calculated that I could afford a Wilshire Boulevard office—just barely. Finding one, however, was another matter. I located a likely space in the Union Bank Building at Wilshire and Western, which was then in the center of one of the city's better business districts. There were no other black tenants in the building, and, after meeting the leasing agents, I began to suspect why. A certified deposit check wasn't enough; they also insisted on poring over my accounts receivable. The negotiations dragged on endlessly. Finally, as I left one of our meetings, one of the agents' employees, an attractive young woman with blue eyes and blond hair, tugged at my elbow.

"Can we talk privately?" she asked.

Her name, she told me, was Patty Sikora.

"What can I do for you, Miss Sikora?" I asked, somewhat puzzled.

"Please, just Patty," she said. "What's happening here just isn't right. You should know that when you leave, my bosses say things like, 'Oh well, talk is one thing, but we don't want that nigger in this building.' It isn't right, and I wanted you to know how I felt," Patty said.

I was touched by her honesty and her willingness to put herself at risk for a stranger. I thanked her and pressed on with the negotiations. Ultimately, the building's agents leased me a twelfth-floor office, but not before demanding that my father cosign the agreement.

The new "Law Office of Johnnie L. Cochran, Jr." was hardly palatial. It consisted of a small office—mine—furnished with a desk and two chairs—one of them mine—and a small anteroom for my "staff," Albertine Mitchell. Her equipment consisted of a rented IBM typewriter and a telephone, both of which perched precariously on a folding TV tray one of us had brought from home. What we didn't lack were clients. Criminal defense continued to be my mainstay, but I began to handle an increasing volume of civil actions, many of them involving people referred by my father or one of his agents. People came into my office, sometimes desperate, sometimes frightened, always in search of someone to guide them through what appeared to be an impenetrable web of procedures and paperwork. For most people, hiring an attorney is an unsettling experience. More than anything else, I had to show them that the institution itself, the courts, wasn't as inflexible and inhuman as they thought.

I was their advocate. I understood how vulnerable, how awestruck, and, in some cases, how helpless they felt. Although the case might involve a son or a daughter or a father or a wife facing a court fight, representation often meant that I became involved with the whole family on some level. During a trial, looking out into the gallery of spectators would be the equivalent of thumbing through a family photo album. Every one of the clan would be rooting for a victory, for me to secure justice for their loved one. That's a heavy load, but a responsibility I bore willingly.

It always was particularly gratifying to have a prospective client sit down in the chair opposite my desk and say, "Mr. Cochran, I don't know if you remember me. But you used to sell me insurance when I lived on Palm Lane."

We were so busy that, within a few months, I was joined by a partner, Nelson L. Atkins, another former deputy city attorney.

Nelson had occasionally worked in the evenings at my law office. Though Nelson had joined the city attorney's office after I left, I had known him since high school. We shared a common background, and I had a real affinity for him and his family. Not only was he a sharp lawyer, he was also like a younger brother whom I could count on.

But while we went from one professional success to another, it was impossible to ignore the fact that our business was being conducted in a city whose racial tensions were still tuned to an almost unbearable pitch. Even so, in May 1966, they were pushed up what must have been a full octave when Los Angeles police officers shot to death a young African American man named Leonard Deadwyler.

I seriously doubt that there is a single black Angeleno over forty who cannot recite in detail the facts of the Deadwyler case. On that night in May, Leonard Deadwyler and a friend had made a stop while taking his pregnant wife to buy baby clothes. During the stop, Leonard's wife, Barbara, who was in her eighth month of pregnancy, suddenly began to experience what she believed were labor pains. Mrs. Deadwyler had already delivered three children, and all had been born after very short labors. So Leonard, Barbara, and their friend quickly got in the family car and sped up Avalon Boulevard toward the L.A. County Medical Center, which in those days was known to people in the community as "Big General." At that time, there was no freeway connection between the Deadwylers' neighborhood and the hospital; they had no choice but to take local streets. The family had only recently come to Los Angeles from rural Georgia, where a motorist in distress or on an emergency mission would announce his situation by tying a white handkerchief to his car's radio antenna. When they spotted that signal, other drivers would give way and police officers would offer assistance. Before setting off, a frantic Leonard Deadwyler had tied a flag-sized piece of white fabric to his antenna.

Los Angeles, however, was another world in more ways than one. Within a short time, the Deadwylers' speeding vehicle attracted the attention of LAPD patrol cars, which set off in pursuit. But Deadwyler, who, based on experience, believed his wife was set to deliver at any moment, pushed on. Though the only law Leonard had broken was the speed limit, one patrol car finally pulled alongside the Deadwylers' car. Using a technique officially reserved for apprehending motorists suspected of a felony, Officer Robert Taylor leaned out of the cruiser's window and pointed his drawn gun at the Deadwylers, ordering them to stop. Leonard quickly pulled to the curb. Another officer, Jerold Bova, leaped from his patrol car and, drawn revolver in hand, approached the terrified Deadwylers. For reasons he never was able to explain clearly, Bova—gun at the ready—leaned into the open driver's side window and attempted to remove the ignition key. At that moment, the officer would subsequently claim, the Deadwylers' car lurched forward. Bova later said that forward motion caused him to close his grip reflexively on his revolver, which inadvertently fired into Leonard's chest.

Deadwyler toppled over into the lap of his wife, who screamed in horror and disbelief as her husband's blood soaked her dress. As his life hemorrhaged onto the floor of his own car, a bewildered Leonard Deadwyler looked up at the man who had shot him and said, "But she's having a baby."

Those were the last words he ever spoke.

The killing of Leonard Deadwyler pushed Los Angeles once again to the brink of civil strife. The black community was awash in angry rumors. The anxious city authorities knew that this police shooting could not be handled in their habitual business-as-usual style. It was at that moment that I received a telephone call from my former UCLA classmate Dr. Herbert Avery. After his graduation, Herb had gone on to Howard University Medical School and then returned to Los Angeles to practice. He was on staff at Big General.

"Johnnie," he said, his voice brittle with urgency. "I'm out here at County General with a patient of mine. She's the widow of the fellow who was shot by the police. This is a terrible situation."

"It's worse than terrible," I agreed. "Is there something I can do, Herb?" I asked.

"You've got to come right out here," he replied. "She's here now. I've told her about you, and she really wants to see you."

Thirty minutes later, Herb Avery ushered me into an examination room, where I first met Barbara Deadwyler. She was a small, shy, painfully pregnant woman who wept almost constantly. She was almost too frightened to talk. But, between sobs, she managed to tell me the story of her husband's killing.

As she stammered out her husband's last words, she looked up at me and said simply: "I can't understand how this could happen."

"I'm sorry to say it, Mrs. Deadwyler," I replied, "but I'm afraid I do understand this. I think you need a lawyer." Briefly, I described for her some of the legal remedies she could, if she chose, pursue. To this day, I clearly remember being struck by the fact that she never asked about monetary compensation. Instead, she fought back her tears, cleared her throat, and asked: "You mean, people will know what really happened?"

"I think they should," I said.

"Please," Barbara Deadwyler said, "you've got to help me."

"Well, I'll try," I replied, squeezing her hand.

Barely eight months after I had taken my private decision in that silent Leimert Park kitchen, my own Philistine loomed before me like David's Goliath.

Within a day or so, our office arranged for the coroner's office to release Leonard's body and helped Mrs. Deadwyler with the funeral arrangements. The autopsy results were troubling in at least one major respect: They put Leonard's blood alcohol level at 3.5. The police later would claim that he had failed to comply with their orders because he was drunk. But a person with that much booze in his bloodstream isn't intoxicated—he's unconscious. Moreover, both his wife and his friend were certain that Leonard had not drunk enough to be inebriated. Even then, the Los Angeles county coroner's office seemed inordinately prone to error.

There was nothing ordinary, however, about the attention being paid to the Deadwyler case. Partly, that was attributable to the fallout from Watts; partly, it was because the spectacle of the police shooting to death a man rushing his pregnant young wife to the hospital had touched a chord in the conscience of a white majority previously unwilling to believe that police misconduct occurred. The *Los Angeles Times*, which recently had won a Pulitzer Prize for its coverage of the Watts Riot, covered every phase of the Deadwyler case in detail. So, too, did the city's other daily, the *Herald-Examiner*. Up to that point, both papers had behaved as if the city's black community was all but invisible. The seven local television stations, each of which had its own news operation, devoted unprecedented airtime to the Deadwyler affair, as did many of the dozens of radio stations in the L.A. area.

Given the level of community outrage and media scrutiny, it soon became clear to the civic establishment that the Deadwyler case would have to be handled in an extraordinary manner. The first official to confront that fact was Los Angeles County

District Attorney Evelle J. Younger, a smart prosecutor and shrewd politician who was extremely popular among his deputies because he had used his skills to improve their salaries and working conditions. Politically, he represented a species now unfortunately missing from our system, the moderate Republican. It was Younger who had to decide whether to prosecute Officer Bova for shooting Leonard Deadwyler to death. From the outset, he recognized that whatever his decision, it was critical that it be reached in such a way that a majority of the community would accept it as fair. To accomplish that, Younger elected to request a coroner's inquest to "establish" the cause of Deadwyler's death. He hoped that such a public proceeding would put "the facts" on which his eventual decision would be made squarely before the public. To that end, he began to discuss with his aides the unprecedented possibility of televising the inquest. Almost simultaneously, KTLA, a local TV station, approached Younger with just such a proposal. It was accepted, and the Deadwyler inquest became the first legal proceeding in California history to be carried live on television.

Coroner's inquests, which rarely are convened today, have a distinctive protocol. They are presided over by a "hearing officer"—in this case, Charles Langhauser—and there is a seven-person jury. Our panel was unusually diverse for the time, consisting of four whites—three men and a woman—one African American man, one Latino, and one Asian American man. In those days, all questions were asked by a single deputy district attorney, who also called the witnesses. In this instance, however, the D.A.'s office also called the witnesses we wished to question and allowed me, as the Deadwyler family lawyer, to take a place at the counsel table.

The deputy district attorney, a serious, highly principled prosecutor named John Provenzano, also agreed to put all my questions to the witness since I was not allowed to speak. This

cumbersome formality quickly was transformed into what ultimately became the inquest's coda, as the methodical Provenzano
prefaced each of my numerous questions with the phrase "Mr.
Cochran wants to know . . ."

The inquest was convened in the largest hearing room in
downtown Los Angeles, but the place was still packed to overflowing. Some 400 people tried to get into a room at the Hall of
Records that held only 150 seats. So the inquest was moved
to larger quarters. The headline in that afternoon's *Herald-
Examiner* read: INQUEST PANDEMONIUM. But for all that, the
proceedings went forward over the next six days in an orderly,
thorough fashion. Television turned it not only into a civics
lesson for millions but also into a badly needed and successful
confidence-building exercise in the justice system itself. KTLA's
daytime rating rose to historic heights. My experience in that
inquest has made me an advocate of cameras in the courtroom
ever since.

The dogged seriousness of the KTLA journalists and the
extreme sensitivity of the times even conspired to create some
unintentionally amusing moments. One involved my name.
KTLA's broadcasts were anchored by George Putnam, at the
time one of Southern California's most popular television
newsmen. He also happened to be the son of the aviatrix Amelia
Earhart. Over and over, Putnam felt compelled to remind his
viewers that my given name, in fact, was *Johnnie* Cochran and
that "no disrespect or condescension" was implied by his use "of
the diminutive form of address."

The hearing room buzzed with anticipation when the widow,
Barbara Deadwyler, appeared to give her testimony. It may seem
commonplace now in this era of high-tech high security, but for
the first time deputies searched some of the people attending the
proceedings. They frisked men and examined briefcases, purses,
and camera cases. Mrs. Deadwyler answered John Provenzano's

questions in a soft, controlled voice. She described how her husband arrived at her sister-in-law's house after running an errand and agreed to take her to the store to buy baby clothes for the child she was expecting. While making a stop on the way, Barbara Deadwyler explained, she started experiencing pains in her stomach and back and remembered that her obstetrician had warned her that the baby might be early.

"There was a person in front of the store where we were parked, and I told him to go in there and tell my husband to come out." She measured her words carefully, aware of everyone in the courtroom listening intently. "Tell him it's time. He better take me to General Hospital."

"Did you smell any alcohol on your husband's breath after he left the store?" the prosecutor asked.

The widow calmly answered no.

She continued by telling how her husband asked several people in front of the store for the best route to the hospital and was told to take Avalon Boulevard to the freeway.

"Did you notice any speed limit signs or street markers?" Provenzano stood just to her left, careful not to block the jury's view of her.

"I was hurting too much to notice," she replied. Barbara Deadwyler did not avert her gaze or flinch at all. But when asked about her husband's death, the expectant widow swallowed hard, tipped her head back, and drew a deep breath before continuing. "I asked the officer why he shot him." Her voice picked up in intensity as she proceeded. "He didn't say anything, he just put his gun back in his holster and turned around and walked to the back of the car."

When asked to do so, Mrs. Deadwyler told how her husband "fell into my lap and I tried to brace him up." She told how the officers helped her husband out of the car and how he "suddenly went limp" as they eased him to the ground.

"I got out," she recalled. "I went around to my husband. I looked at him. He was just . . . Well, I looked at him. I gently shook him, but he didn't say anything and he didn't move."

Mrs. Deadwyler endured two hours on the stand and remained nearly rock solid throughout. She held up but was near collapse afterward. We escorted her to a first-aid station where she was treated for exhaustion. I don't know how she managed. She was a woman of great courage.

During the hearing, tension reached a dangerous level when a large number of black nationalists, attempting to stage a sit-in protest in an adjacent room, faced off with baton-carrying sheriff's deputies. All spectators were cleared from the courtroom and proceedings adjourned until the following day.

Through my indirect questioning of the police witnesses, I was able to establish that the pursuing officers, as well as the shooter—Bova—repeatedly had violated their department's own published procedures. Clearly, their reckless negligence had led to Deadwyler's death. But following a relatively brief deliberation, the seven-member jury handed down a split verdict, which such panels are allowed to do. The majority found that while Leonard Deadwyler died "at the hands of another," Officer Bova's discharge of his revolver had been "accidental."

Younger, who later would be elected attorney general of California, was in court for the verdict. After it was read, he delivered an extraordinary on-camera talk, ostensibly addressed to the jurors but actually aimed at the community at large. He thanked the panel for its service and then said: "I want you to know, for whatever it's worth, that we have closely followed the evidence, as you have. And we have reached exactly the same conclusion as a majority of jurors have reached. We feel that criminal prosecution is not justified in this case. And, as far as our office is concerned, in the absence of further evidence or new witnesses, the case is considered closed."

And so it remained. Jerold Bova, who in a split second deprived Barbara Deadwyler of her husband, and the children of their loving father, ultimately finished his police career by retiring as a captain of the department's Pacific Division, one of the LAPD's most desirable posts.

Younger also praised me for my role in the inquest, thanking me for bringing additional witnesses forward and expressing his gratitude for the measured way in which I had conducted myself.

His sentiments, welcome though they were, did little to lift the sense of bitter disappointment I felt. Following dismissal of the jury, both Provenzano and I went before the cameras, too. John, who died early in 1996, was a prosecutor of the old school, a capable and civilized advocate, dedicated to the steady pursuit of justice as he understood it. We remained friends to the day of his death. Today, when I confront one of the self-righteous, win-at-any-cost, ideological young zealots who try far too many of the L.A. County D.A.'s cases, I recall one of Provenzano's post-inquest comments with particular respect.

"I felt we tried to bring out everything we could that was pertinent to the issue at hand," Provenzano said, scowling through a truly formidable pair of black horn-rimmed glasses. "Sometimes we may have been repetitious. If so, that was at the expense of nothing but time. Certainly, we didn't expend truth in order to avoid repetition."

While I had my own thoughts on the verdict, my first obligation was to my clients, the Deadwyler family. So, when my turn came at last to speak to the cameras, I took the opportunity to give the entire city what I felt was a vital message from Barbara.

"Prior to coming back for the verdict in this inquest," I said, "I spoke on the phone to Mrs. Deadwyler and she asked me to relay a message to you. She's a very good person, as I'm sure you were able to tell. And her husband was also a good person. She is naturally very sorry that his life was lost. But she is hopeful that despite the verdict, despite what different individuals may feel, we may now from this point go forward and there will be no more bloodshed, no more killing or no more disorder, if you will. This is her sincere desire and I am relaying it to you for her."

During a lull in the whirlwind surrounding the shooting and the inquest, I thought of Leonard Deadwyler's funeral, the hundreds of people who turned out to support his widow, the solemn words of faith and comfort from the Reverend Joseph B. Hardwick that were carried out to those who waited outside of the Praises of Zion Missionary Baptist Church in the South L.A. neighborhood. The Reverend Hardwick told us that day: "We don't want this man's death to be in vain, we will not hide this in a corner, we want it to be brought out into the light." The image of the young widow, mother of three children with another on the way, crying during the service while being fanned by a nurse, still haunts me.

Los Angeles had never seen anything quite like the Deadwyler inquest and neither had twenty-eight-year-old attorney Johnnie L. Cochran, Jr. I had learned lessons that would prove critical in the years ahead. One was that a high-profile trial imposes almost unimaginable stress and pressure. I discovered by accident that there is only one way to survive them unscathed: Never forget that you are there to represent your client's interests and for no other reason.

I also learned that "two-ness" had an external, as well as an internal implication. Because of my professional conduct during the inquest and, particularly, because of my public recitation of Barbara Deadwyler's sentiments, Los Angeles' white legal establishment suddenly came to regard me as a "reasonable Negro" and as a "responsible spokesman for my community." They nodded knowingly about the "beneficial" impact my experience as a prosecutor had had on my development.

Within the African American community, people saw something quite different. For the first time, they had *seen* one of their own standing up and, on his own terms, demanding that the authorities confront the ongoing injustice inflicted on black Angelenos on a daily basis. When I stood up for Barbara Deadwyler, I was in a sense standing up for all the black mothers who had sent their husbands, sons, and brothers out never to see them again. I was feeling the pressure speaking for the whole community. I knew that with the Watts Riot only a year behind us, the situation was volatile. I had to balance the needs of the community with the needs of the client. At the Second Baptist Church, I was no longer just Johnnie Cochran's smart young son but a presence in my own right. Suddenly, I was recognized nearly everywhere I went.

"Hey," people would say, "aren't you the lawyer on TV?"

To this day, I meet older African Americans who look closely at my face, then say, "Weren't you the young lawyer in the Deadwyler case?" "You know, we're real proud of you."

Perhaps most important, my new visibility gave me the opportunity to carry back into the community a message in which I believe as deeply today as I did then. Leonard Deadwyler was a man whose wife was entitled to some measure of justice. She did not receive it. But it was important to fight for redress of that wrong within the courts and not in the streets.

My resolve to continue that fight was undiminished. I replayed the inquest over and over in my head. I had seen once again how skilled the LAPD officers were in testifying, how well schooled they were in concocting innocent explanations for the harm they did, even when they clearly were wrong or negligent. More important, I had seen firsthand that they never, ever would admit they were wrong. That refusal was the foundation of the stone wall their siege mentality had led them to construct between their department and the entire community—white as well as black. In their minds, it was "us versus them" every moment of the day and night. Somewhere in that blind, unbending fanaticism, I was convinced I ultimately would find a fatal weakness.

I remember telling my partner, Nelson Atkins, that uncovering that flaw would be our firm's special mission. "We've got to learn everything we can," I told him. "We're going to lose some cases, but ultimately we're going to win them."

Unfortunately, one of those we lost was Barbara Deadwyler's civil suit against the Los Angeles Police Department for the wrongful death of her husband. We never charged her a nickel for our work on the inquest and—as civil lawyers usually do— we assumed all the costs of preparing her suit. It took us four years and tens of thousands of dollars to bring it to trial in 1970, a substantial sum for the time. But, by then, I was unavoidably engaged in a lengthy murder trial. Nelson actually tried the suit and, through no fault of his, lost. It was almost unbearably painful for Barbara, but in those days you lost those cases. Nobody was surprised.

We lost the Deadwyler case because the majority of the jurors could not accept the fact that police officers do not always tell the truth, that they make mistakes and sometimes are grossly negligent. This was a difficult loss, compounding the already tragic loss Mrs. Deadwyler suffered. By all that is right, Leonard Deadwyler should still be alive.

Barbara Deadwyler and I have remained in frequent touch ever since. She never remarried, but despite her grief, disappointments, and hardships as the single mother of four fatherless children, she has never surrendered to bitterness. Her son Michael was born healthy, one month after his father's death. In that sense, the Deadwyler case continues to educate me to this day. For every time I speak with Barbara Deadwyler, I am reminded that there is a cardinal Christian virtue called fortitude. And, in his grace, a merciful God has conferred that virtue abundantly on generation after generation of black women so that they might stand as inspirations to their men and others all around them.

In late 1966, Nelson and I brought in another attorney to form the firm of Cochran, Atkins & Evans. Our new partner, Irwin Evans, was a smart, fun-loving man, a former all-city football player at Manual Arts High School, and a college wrestler. We all called him "Big Red" because of his size and reddish hair. My most enjoyable years in practicing law were with Cochran, Atkins & Evans. We had all gone through the lean years, and now that we saw that the community really needed us, it made the struggle worthwhile. It wasn't all seriousness, though. Nelson called my new visibility "the Cochran halo effect," and there was a lot of good-natured kidding about the impositions it made on them. Once, for example, my involvement in a protracted civil trial prevented me from appearing on behalf of a client charged with a criminal offense. I telephoned Nelson the night before the court date and asked if he could appear for me to request a continuance or postponement until the civil matter was resolved.

"No problem," he said.

It should have been a routine process. Unfortunately, Nelson ran into a particularly bad-tempered judge that day.

"There aren't going to be any continuances, Mr. Atkins," the judge snapped. "We have a jury panel assembled. You're Mr. Cochran's partner. You're here, and we are going forward. You will try this case—today."

Nelson gulped, asked for thirty minutes to read the file, then went to work picking a jury and trying the case. The next day, that jury went out, deliberated for a few hours, then came back with an acquittal.

As the clerk read the words "not guilty," the client wheeled around and began to pump Nelson's hand enthusiastically.

"This is terrific," he almost shouted. "Tell Johnnie Cochran he did a great job on my case."

Nelson just began stuffing papers into his briefcase and muttering something about "that halo effect."

Those were heady years for an ambitious young attorney. Unfortunately, though, my personal life was virtually a mirror image of my orderly, successful career. In gradual stages, almost unnoticed at first, Barbara and I allowed our relationship to move from cool to cold to contentious. Looking back, I now can see that the fault line that ultimately tore us apart was there from the beginning. In fact, we were drawn together for precisely the wrong reasons. I wanted to become more as I believed Barbara was when I first met her—in control of her own destiny because of her willingness to take risks and to rely on her wits. She wanted to become more as she believed I was—quiet, steady, predictable, and sheltered in the reliable bosom of middle-class security. We both got where we wanted to go, and, as the years went on, that journey drew us unrelentingly in opposite directions.

Those sorts of misplaced expectations are common in youthful marriages. In another era, it might even have been possible to work through them. But this was the late 1960s, when social and personal experimentation seemed virtually mandatory and the confusion between self-fulfillment and self-gratification afflicted far too many of us. In August 1969, we had a second daughter, Tiffany. But despite our mutual delight in our new child, our marriage moved still further in the wrong direction, from contention to turmoil. Our arguments became more frequent and heated, but they never once escalated past the point of angry words. As bad as our relationship became, physical violence never played a part in it. I never at any time physically struck Barbara Cochran, as I have never struck any woman in my life. We separated and reconciled repeatedly.

On a number of occasions, I moved back into my parents' house on West Twenty-eighth Street. Their reaction to all this ran true to their personalities. My mother, whose reservations about Barbara had never quite abated, hid her unhappiness with my problems by asking me what I wanted for dinner and by urging me to "do the best that you can, John." My father, by contrast, always had been fond of Barbara. Moreover, his religious principles also led him to put a high value on the sanctity of matrimony. He came from a time and place in which you married for life. When difficulties arose, you coped with them, and what you couldn't cope with, you endured. Dad couldn't hide his displeasure with my failure to abide by those standards. He worried a great deal about the impact all this would have on the children. So did I.

Like my father, I am both by inclination and by conviction a conciliator. From him I learned that unnecessary confrontation is not only wasteful and frequently ineffective but also embittering for everyone involved. Reason and compromise, on the other hand, solve problems and create the sort of relationships and goodwill on which future progress can be built. Our dad taught us those lessons implicitly in the way he dealt with his wife and children. Later, he conveyed them to me explicitly when he showed me how the delicate business of running an insurance agent's debit had to be conducted.

He saw no reason why these same notions—which had, after all, worked so well within his own family—couldn't be applied to the problems Barbara and I were having. Repeatedly, Dad urged me to try to see Barbara's side of things more sympathetically. One of the continuing points of friction between us, for example, had to do with Barbara's spending. For reasons that I suspect had to do with being orphaned as a teenager, Barbara assuaged any upset or insecurity with shopping, particularly for clothes. In fact, from the moment we were married she insisted on having a monthly clothing budget of $75. That wasn't a negligible sum when my gross weekly salary was $152 per week. As the years passed, her clothing budget skyrocketed.

"Enough is enough," I would tell my dad.

"Look, son," he would urge me gently, "you have to see her side of things. It's important to her. It's a small thing. Let her have her way."

And so I did. But though we made repeated efforts over the years, things between Barbara and me were never right again. It remains one of the few situations in which I feel I failed to live up to the example my father and mother set for me.

And the human heart, no less than nature, abhors a vacuum. As my remaining affection for Barbara poured itself out, another flowed in to take its place. One evening, in my office at Wilshire and Western, Patty Sikora—the leasing agents' secretary with a heart—came to seek my help with her divorce. At that moment, my estrangement from Barbara and my anxiety about our children had never been deeper. Patty also had two daughters and was fighting to free herself from a rocky marriage that had left her emotionally battered and filled with self-doubt. We talked family law. Then, we told each other our troubles. We quickly discovered we felt more than sympathy for each other. We found comfort in one another and—after a time—came to care about each other deeply.

My separations from Barbara became longer and more frequent. Patty's divorce became final during one of them, and, since she was no longer my client, we began to date. In 1973, Patty and I had a baby boy we named Jonathan. Though his mother and I never married, Jonathan was a doted-upon child of the extended Cochran family from the start. His proud grandparents displayed his bronzed baby shoes on their mantel, and Barbara sometimes acted as baby-sitter so that his adoring sisters could spend more time with him. I bought my son and his mother a house and arranged for their support and his education. After Jonathan's birth we made the decision not to marry. For her own reasons, Patty decided she wanted to make Cochran her legal last name, which she did. We have never lived together as husband and wife. Patty and I drifted apart. However, I've always maintained a close relationship with my son, and I have supported all three of my children financially throughout their lives and I continued to assist their mothers for years after we had ended our relationships. Best of all, my three children maintain a close and affectionate connection with one another, the extended Cochran family, and—happily—not only with me but also with the genuine partner in life I ultimately was fortunate enough to find, my wife, Dr. Dale Mason Cochran.

One of the many graces of beneficent Providence is that it allows our weakness, willfulness, mistakes, and even follies to bring forth unexpectedly gifts of incalculable value. Certainly, Providence favored me in that way. Melodie, Tiffany, and Jonathan are my constant hope and my greatest treasure. I would not trade that for this world or any other.

Just as the turmoil of the late 1960s and early 1970s had made itself felt in my personal life, my professional career was also buffeted by the currents of social change. Because America is, in fact, a nation of laws, our courts are always at the cutting edge of social change. And, for that reason, to be an active American trial lawyer is to be intimately engaged with the spirit and issues of your time. It probably was predictable, therefore, that my own practice would plunge me into the whirlpool of militant political radicalism that welled up in so many African American communities in the late 1960s.

In Los Angeles, as in so many cities, the Black Panther Party was the most visible and controversial symbol of that confrontational—sometimes violent—new tendency.

Huey Newton and Bobby Seale, who founded the party in 1966, took their doctrine of community determination and armed self-defense from the writings of separatist Robert Williams, who had once been the head of the NAACP chapter in Monroe, North Carolina. Williams, writing in his book *Negroes with Guns*, spoke of the need to meet racism and oppression with armed struggle, to meet force with force. The Black Panthers, carrying firearms, patrolled their communities and met resistance from local police. In May 1967, the group made national headlines when they entered the state capitol building in Sacramento with rifles and shotguns to lobby for their right to bear arms. By the end of that year, both Newton and Seale were arrested and jailed on weapons charges. Reviled in some quarters, revered in others, the Black Panthers gained support among some segments of the community with their free schools, clinics, and food banks.

Nationally, the party quickly became the target not only of surveillance by the Federal Bureau of Investigation but also of infiltration, disruption, and even assassination by law enforcement at all levels. In Los Angeles, the FBI found eager allies in the LAPD's Criminal Conspiracy Division. That unit, one of the successors of the department's notorious Red squad, was Chief William Parker's organizational darling. He continued to fill its ranks with carefully selected ex-servicemen—most of them Southerners—and watched over their paramilitary training. Throughout 1968 and 1969, tensions between the LAPD and the Panthers spiraled upward, a process that was exacerbated by a network of informants and agents provocateurs placed inside the party by both federal and local authorities.

During the late summer of 1968, two police officers on West Adams Boulevard stopped a car carrying four black men, some of whom were Panthers. No one is quite clear on what happened next, but a shoot-out erupted. Three of the car's occupants were killed. Both officers were wounded. The fourth passenger escaped and became the object of a highly publicized citywide manhunt that further escalated racial tensions. A few days later, the fugitive, who feared giving himself up to the LAPD, surrendered directly to a judge and was placed in the custody of the County Sheriff's Department, which operates Los Angeles' county jail. The fugitive was charged with assault and intent to commit murder. After a two-week trial, a superior court jury deliberated just two hours before acquitting him.

A few months later, in January 1969, two of the Panthers' leaders at UCLA—Alprentice "Bunchy" Carter and John Huggins—were shot to death under circumstances that remain unclear.

By then, the mutual animosity and fear between the Panthers and police virtually guaranteed further bloodshed. A little more than a year after the West Adams shoot-out, in the predawn hours of December 8, 1969, elements of the LAPD's Criminal Conspiracy Division, along with a sprinkling of FBI agents, quietly surrounded the Panthers' Central Avenue headquarters. The authorities later testified that they went there to serve a misdemeanor warrant, though nobody ever explained why federal law enforcement officials would have risen before the sun to serve papers for a minor state crime. Nor did anyone ever convincingly explain why all the LAPD officers went there that early morning dressed in black and carrying assault weapons.

Unknown to the Panthers, more than a dozen of whom were sleeping in the fortified headquarters, one of their number—Melvin Smith—was an FBI informant and agent provocateur. Not so coincidentally, he also happened to be the one who first spotted the cops.

"The pigs are coming in," Smith shouted and opened fire from one of the building's sandbagged windows. The police naturally returned fire. Over the next five hours, Central Avenue—where the air once had been filled with the sounds of music, laughter, and commerce—rang with the din of what the *Los Angeles Times* subsequently called "a miniwar." The Panthers fired from the headquarters' fortified upper windows; the police shot back. Both sides had automatic weapons. The police fired tear gas into the building; the Panthers tossed Molotov cocktails back. Investigators later would count more than a thousand empty cartridges on the building's floor. Finally, the besieged party members surrendered, hanging a white flag above a doorway over which there was a sign reading: FEED HUNGRY CHILDREN— FREE BREAKFAST.

Miraculously, no one was killed. Three of the officers and six of the Panthers were wounded. Thirteen party members were arrested and charged with more than seventy criminal offenses, the most serious of which was conspiracy to murder police officers.

None of the defendants could afford to retain his own attorney, which is how I became involved in the case. We were appointed by an old friend, Superior Court Judge George Dell, to represent the indigent defendants because the L.A. County public defender's office, which was known for providing first-rate legal representation for poor clients, had a conflict of interest. They had represented the informant in this case, Melvin Cotton Smith.

Until 1994, Los Angeles judges were free to appoint any lawyer they chose. The system was rife with cronyism. Many criminal defense lawyers, particularly those just starting out, built their practices around such appointments. But, until quite recently, black attorneys got relatively few appointments and women almost none. Many judges demanded a certain kind of deference and courtroom deportment from the lawyers they appointed. Lawyers too aggressive or zealous on their client's behalf often weren't invited back. At Cochran, Atkins & Evans, we took few appointments, principally because a three-lawyer firm with an increasing volume of civil cases couldn't really afford to work for the $100 per hour the county paid. We continued, however, to take some interesting appointments as a form of public service.

Judge Dell appointed me to represent a Panther named Willie Stafford, and, like the other twelve defense lawyers assigned to the case, I immediately was plunged into a murky new morass of radical politics, governmental espionage, officially instigated dirty tricks, and plain old-fashioned criminality. Two years later, after an eight-month trial that was then the longest in California history, all thirteen attorneys would emerge as changed men.

Some of the Black Panthers were serious social activists driven to extremism by the reckless atmosphere of the times; some of them were just thugs who'd latched on to a sexy new gang m.o. If the Panthers hadn't been around, the thugs would have been just as happy—and just as destructive—as other street gangs. By the time I started dealing with party members, the FBI, working through its network of informants and agents provocateurs, had used the thugs' violent, treacherous propensities to turn the whole organization inside out. At that point, the Panthers were split into two factions, one of them led by David Hilliard and Huey Newton, who was in and out of jail, and the other by Eldridge Cleaver, who, along with his wife, Kathleen, was living in self-imposed exile in Algeria. Our clients included members of both factions.

Left to his own devices, my client, Stafford, was one of the thugs. But, once inside the Panthers, Willie had the good fortune to attach himself to the leader of the L.A. office, a Cleaver supporter named Elmer "Geronimo" Pratt. Geronimo and his wife,

This is me at six months old in April 1938. I was the epitome of wide-eyed wonder, optimism, and innocence. Some of that naiveté has worn off, but the wonder and optimism keep pumping through my veins.

"The Chief," as we affectionately call him. Johnnie L. Cochran, Sr., in 1942. He is only twenty-five years old and has just been named district manager of the Louisiana Industrial Life Insurance Company in Shreveport.

My beloved Mother, Hattie Bass Cochran, at age twenty-four, circa 1941. By this time she had a husband and three children. She was always a beautiful lady.

All photos, unless otherwise indicated, are from the Cochran family archives.

This photo was taken in 1945 just after we'd moved to California from Shreveport. From left to right, that's my sister Pearl, my sister Martha Jean, and me.

The 1945 class photo of Webster Elementary School in Alameda, California. I'm in the back row, looking like a good country lawyer in my suspenders. Apparently, I'm working on mastering the stern look that would come in handy later with reluctant witnesses.

By July 1955, the family had moved to Los Angeles. My brother RaLonzo was born that year. Standing, from left to right, that's my father, Jean, and me. Seated are my mother, RaLonzo, and Pearl. I had acquired my taste for fancy ties even then.

The big night. Prom. May 1955, Los Angeles High School. That's my first girlfriend and date, Sandra Jackson. The Eiffel Tower stands in the background. Even then I dreamed of traveling to faraway places.

C. R. Roberts and I were the Polemarches of the local undergraduate chapter of the Kappa Alpha Psi fraternity. We are surrounded by the Kappa sweethearts.

Graduation day from Loyola's School of Law in June 1962. The fulfillment of a dream and a lot of hard work. More obstacles await me—a malfunctioning car and the California Bar exam.

Here I am with attorney Gerald D. Lenoir following one of our early victories in a criminal case.

William C. Collins was found not guilty of murder and robbery charges in March 1966. This was my first murder case. I went on to win the next nine cases without a loss.

This is the home office of Golden State Mutual Life Insurance Company. My father worked there for thirty-five years, and I worked for them during my college years.

I've had a career full of heart-wrenching moments, but watching the pregnant, grieving Barbara Deadwyler testify about how her husband was shot and killed by an LAPD officer was one of the most difficult. She is accompanied here by a sherrif's deputy and her twenty-eight-year-old lawyer.

Over one thousand people tried to crowd into Courtroom 12 on May 20, 1966, to hear testimony at the inquest into Leonard Deadwyler's death. Racial tensions were still high following the Watts Riot, and eventually spectators had to be cleared from the courtroom. The inquest was televised live in Los Angeles.

Several defendants leaving the courtroom in the 1971 Black Panther trial.
At that time, it was the longest-running
trial in California history. It also
marked the beginning of a new phase
in my politicization.

Kathleen Cleaver addresses the
media in 1972 after testifying on
behalf of the Black Panthers.

Our first step on the long journey to change the way the LAPD treated all its citizens.
Mr. and Mrs. Jeff Leonard receive the $25,000 settlement the city awarded in the
police shooting of their son William. We are flanked by my partners, Irwin Evans
and Nelson Atkins.

The Cochran family gathers in 1976. Top row (left to right): Jean Cochran Sherrard, RaLonzo Cochran, Johnnie L. Cochran, Jr., Bill Baker, Sr., Fred Sherrard, Billy Baker, Jr., and Pearl Cochran Baker. Middle row (left to right): my three-year-old son, Jonathan Cochran, Barbara Cochran, The Chief (Johnnie Sr.), Hattie Cochran holding her granddaughter LaToi Cochran, Robin Anderson, and Arlyce Baker. Bottom row (left to right): my daughters, Tiffany and Melodie, and my niece Cherene Sherrard.

In 1977, I received the Lawyer of the Year Award from the Criminal Courts Bar Association. That's me, the Honorable E. Talbot Callister, presiding judge of the Criminal Courts, and Robert L. Roberson, first vice president of the Criminal Courts Bar Association.

On January 2, 1978, I was sworn in as assistant district attorney by Judge Paul G. Breckenridge. I was the third-ranking prosecutor in the county of Los Angeles and the first African American to serve in that position. I'm particularly proud of the fact that I continued to try cases and initiate several reforms, including the Rollout Unit, the Domestic Violence Council, and the Sexual Assault Program.

John Van de Kamp is the man who lured me from private practice to the district attorney's office. I gained valuable insight into how the criminal justice system works. I put that knowledge to good use many times.

Gil Garcetti and I at a reception in 1980. Though Gil and I have often opposed each other, we still maintain a fairly cordial relationship.

I'm proud of a lot of things I've done, but I'm most proud of my beautiful children. Today, Jonathan is at UCLA, Tiffany works as a TV anchor, and Melodie is an electrical engineer and computer expert.

Out in front of my home in 1980. I'm with nine-year-old Tiffany and five-year-old Jonathan.

As an assistant district attorney, I met often with the press. I believe that, with a few notable exceptions, I've always maintained a positive relationship with the media. As the following press clips indicate, there was a lot of attention focused on the D.A 's office and the LAPD during my tenure.

Through the efforts of many on both sides, the LAPD's misconduct was well documented and reforms were enacted.

"He was our pride and joy." With those simple words describing their slain son, Ron, Donell and Helen Settles touched a community and set into motion events which eventually exposed a pattern of official misconduct and abuse of power that helped to topple Signal Hill's city government. That booking photo held by Deputy D.A. Gil Garcetti clearly shows evidence of the beating he sustained prior to his death by choke hold. In the middle photo, witness Gloria Zabala demonstrates at the inquest how officers held their guns to Settles' head during his arrest. I have seen many senseless deaths, but none more than that of Ron Settles, whose life and promising football career were cut short by brutal, sadistic police officers.

After leaving the D.A.'s office in 1982, I set up a private law practice, once again on Wilshire Boulevard.

I was appointed to the airport commission in 1982. Here, in 1984, Cliff Moore, executive director of LAX, Commissioner Liz Armstrong, former mayor Tom Bradley, and I attend the opening of the Bradley International Terminal at Los Angeles International Airport.

One of the added bonuses of being on the Los Angeles County Airport Commission, besides the $25-per-meeting stipend, is the opportunity to work with some wonderful Angelenos. Here, Liz Armstrong, Sam Greenberg, and I attend a groundbreaking ceremony in 1982.

While serving on the airport commission, I've traveled around the world and made many new friends. Pictured here with Dale and me are our friends Lieschen and Stuart Hill.

Newspapers from the early 1980s tell the story of our continuing battle to ensure justice for all.

My lovely bride and I on our wedding day, March 1, 1985. We were married in Bel Air, California, surrounded by family and friends. The smiles say it all.

In 1987, the family gathered for my parents' fiftieth wedding anniversary. I've never seen a more loving and devoted couple. Gathered around them is the fruit their labors bore. Remarkable. That's the only word that I can think of to describe the two people who gave me my life and so much more.

Dale and I attending a gala fund-raiser in 1988.

My mother and father and I in 1989. They were always my biggest supporters, attending many of the trials I was involved in. Though my mother has passed, I still feel her support and encouragement every day.

My father looks on as I present a check from Dale and me to Syd Irmas of the L.A. Family Housing Corp. Cochran Villa provides subsidized, low-income housing for formerly homeless families. As my parents always taught me: Those to whom much is given, much is required. Cochran Villa opened in 1991.

In January 1991, I received the Los Angeles Civil Trial Lawyer of the Year Award for 1990. Justice Allen Broussard does the honors, making me the only lawyer to win both the Criminal Trial Lawyer of the Year and the Civil Trial Lawyer of the Year awards.

Sandra—whom everyone called "Red"—also were among the defendants.

We didn't know it at the time, but Geronimo Pratt had been singled out by the FBI as the Los Angeles Panther it most wanted off the street. Looking back, it's not hard to see why. Pratt was a highly decorated army veteran who had served two combat tours in Vietnam. He earned one of his three Purple Hearts when he scooped up and tossed away an enemy grenade that had been thrown into his platoon. The grenade went off, leaving Pratt with a permanently injured hand. Even amid the callous indignities of police custody, Pratt stood out. He was intensely serious, but not forbidding. A deep and commanding quiet seemed to surround him.

I saw it waver only once—and then only in a flicker. Some of the defendants, including Pratt's pregnant wife, Red, had been released on bail. One morning, the police found her lifeless body stuffed into a sleeping bag dumped alongside a quiet dirt road. She had been shot through the stomach. Pratt's attorney, Marvin Zinman, and I were with him when a police detective came to inform him that his wife and unborn child had been murdered. To the day I die, I will retain two memories of that awful moment—Geronimo's nearly imperceptible but successful struggle to retain his composure and the smirk that played across the detective's face.

Red's killing set in motion what was perhaps the single most tumultuous courtroom scene I have ever witnessed. The twelve remaining defendants were seated at three counsel tables. Most of the Newton loyalists, who were out on bail, sat together at the first two tables. The Cleaver supporters, including my client and Pratt, sat at the third. By the time we next appeared in court, Pratt and his people had determined to their satisfaction that Red had been assassinated at the behest of the Newton faction.

As the judge took the bench and the courtroom settled down, waiting for the jury to be brought in, someone gave a pre-arranged signal. The Cleaver people jumped up, grabbed chairs, their lawyers' briefcases, and anything else that came to hand and began attacking the Newton followers. They fought back. A general brawl broke out.

It was like nothing any of us had ever seen before. As we defense lawyers scrambled to get clear of the melee, one of the trial's annoying mysteries was solved. To enter our high-security courtroom, you had to pass through a metal detector. The judge, of course, was exempt from that screening, but so, too, were the district attorneys. We always were perplexed by that. As Judge Dell and the prosecutors backed, shoulder to shoulder, toward his chambers, we saw why they were exempt: All of them had been concealing guns beneath their coats. As they withdrew, somebody triggered an alarm. Suddenly, a phalanx of shotgun-bearing deputy sheriffs swarmed through the swinging doors and into the courtroom. They began beating our clients, and, within seconds, the courtroom floor literally was awash in blood.

Gradually, order was restored. But as we began to sort things out—and to agonize over what impact news of the melee might have when it inevitably reached our unsequestered jury—things got even more complicated. Just before the lunch break I received a personal call. Barbara and I were then in the midst of one of our several legal separations. My lawyer was across the street in what's euphemistically referred to as "family law" court, where he was scheduled to appear to answer Barbara's demand for a modification to our support arrangement. Unfortunately, he said over the phone, I would have to come to court, though only briefly. Like everything else that day, things went wrong. By the time I arrived back at the Hall of Justice, our scheduled lunch break was long over.

As you might imagine, Judge Dell was in no mood to be indulgent. He held me in contempt. That night, when I got back to the office, all I could do was sit and replay the day's events. It was hard to believe everything that had happened: My client had helped foment a riot in the courtroom; I had discovered the lawyers on the other side were secretly armed; my estranged wife had gone after my bank account; and a judge had held me in contempt. All in all, it was a trial lawyer's notion of a day in hell.

As bad as that day was, I knew how important it was to shake it off. An extended criminal trial is, in a strange sense, a kind of parallel universe. It demands that your "other" life accommodate itself to its particular rules and is unforgiving of those who fail to comply. You deal with your personal problems outside the courtroom and maintain your focus within. It was during the Panther trial that I learned just how hard that can be.

A little more than two months after our opening statements, my mother once again fell ill. In the intensive care unit of the old Good Samaritan Hospital on Wilshire, doctors diagnosed an intestinal blockage. Over time, Dad, Pearl, Jean, and RaLonzo had come to rely on me in such situations. I inquired about specialists, but my mother's surgeon—whose office was on Washington near my old office—insisted that he could handle the problem. Over the next two months, he performed two operations on her, both of them unsuccessful. She developed a raging infection and a 106-degree fever. I looked into her eyes and knew she was dying.

At my request, an old friend, Dr. George Jackson, Jr., a cardiovascular surgeon, came in to see her. We had gone to Mount Vernon, L.A. High, and UCLA together before taking our separate paths to law and medical school. He knew my family well. George came out of my mother's room, put his arm around my shoulders, and led me down the hall, away from the nearby nurses' station.

"I don't want to say anything bad about anybody, Johnnie," George said quietly, "but if you want to save your mother's life, you will get her off Washington Boulevard. You will get her to another doctor."

"Who's the best man in town for this?" I asked.

"There's a young white doctor, Carl Schwab, down in Orange County," George said without hesitation. "He's got nimble fingers."

No surgeon likes to come in behind a colleague and clean up his mess, particularly with a patient on the verge of death, as our mother was. But Schwab agreed. He examined Mother and ordered the staff to get her ready for surgery.

"Your mother," he told me, "has about a twenty-percent chance of making it." It was not the kind of thing I could tell Dad or my sisters, so I kept it to myself as we sat in the waiting room and prayed our way through the next eight hours. I will never forget the sight of an exhausted Carl Schwab walking alongside my mother's gurney as they wheeled her out of the recovery room. We were all there to meet them.

"She's going to make it," Schwab said with a smile that spread from ear to ear.

I'm seldom at a loss for something to say, but I didn't have the words then—and I don't have them now—to express our gratitude to that man whose willingness to use his skills and risk his reputation saved our mother's life.

Altogether, Mother spent three months in the hospital. Each evening I would leave the Hall of Justice, where the Panthers were on trial, and go to the hospital to be with Mother; Dad; RaLonzo; Jean and her husband, Fred, an accountant; and Pearl and her husband, Bill, a deputy sheriff. When Mother would drift off to sleep, I'd go back to the office or home to prepare for the next day in court. It was a grueling schedule, but that's part of a trial lawyer's life.

But even that grinding routine had its own moments of high excitement, the most memorable of which was provided by my brother-in-law, Bill. One night, while he was on duty, the rest of us—gathered as usual in Mother's hospital room—decided to watch a little television for diversion. When we flipped on the set, we discovered the station was broadcasting live from Marina Del Rey, where a bunch of armed robbers had taken hostages and barricaded themselves inside a jewelry store.

Suddenly, one of the law enforcement officers surrounding the place walked forward, laid down his sidearm, and went inside in an attempt to talk the robbers into surrendering.

"This is just like the movies," the breathless television reporter whispered into his microphone.

"That's Bill," the assembled Cochrans shouted at the television screen with one voice.

"Is he crazy?" poor Pearl cried to no one in particular.

Moments later, my fearless brother-in-law emerged unscathed from the store, the hostages freed, the robbers in custody, and not a shot fired. He later was decorated for valor by the Sheriff's Department. I remember driving home that night thinking that after a quiet evening at home with the Cochran family, a simple conspiracy-to-commit-murder trial could seem downright restful.

Finally, they let Mother come home. You're never too old to take a childlike joy in the security that comes with your parents' well-being. Jean, Pearl, and I expressed ours by making a banner we strung across the front of the house our mother loved so much. It read: WELCOME HOME, HATTIE COCHRAN: A TRULY REMARKABLE WOMAN. Pain would be Mother's intermittent companion for the rest of her life, and she was forced to pay constant and tedious attention to her diet and medication. But she would shower us all with love and unflinching loyalty for another twenty years, and in all that time not a syllable of self-pity or complaint ever fell from her lips.

Mother's homecoming was welcome on more than one level because the intensity of the Panthers' trial was unremitting. After the brawl, the sheriffs refused to unchain our clients, even in the courtroom lockup. What's more, they attempted to discourage us from conferring with our clients in that room, the only private venue we had within the Hall of Justice. When we persisted, the presiding judge and the Sheriff's Department had a sign put in each courtroom's lockup, advising the defense attorneys that "the bailiffs' first responsibility is courtroom security." In other words, if you guys get kidnapped or held hostage, you're on your own. We all knew who that was aimed at.

As we moved toward final argument, something else was nagging at me. Again and again, it seemed to me that the prosecutors were almost unnaturally prepared for our every move and witness. Sometimes, it seemed that they could read our minds. Maybe, I thought, they're that good; maybe they're just lucky. As it turned out, they were neither. They were the skulking beneficiaries of lawless treachery. Years later, as the result of a Freedom of Information Act request in connection with another case, I would discover that one of my co-counsels in the Panther trial was an FBI informant. His name was Arthur Alexander, and, according to the government's documents, he regularly provided the bureau with confidential information on our clients and their lawyers. When he was confronted with his misconduct, Alexander said he informed because he feared the Panthers were plotting to escape. His excuse was as contemptible as his conduct. Sadly, he would not be the last of his loathsome species I would encounter.

After months of controversy and testimony, the Panther case came down to this:

The prosecutors contended that the defendants had conspired to murder police officers. To that end, they alleged, the party's L.A. chapter had stockpiled weapons inside its fortified Central

Avenue headquarters, then lured officers there in order to ambush them. The crux of their allegations was contained in the testimony of the informant Melvin Smith, who they insisted was a former Panther who'd turned state's evidence.

We, on the other hand, had presented testimony that the police had subjected the Panthers to a purposeful campaign of harassment, disruption, and terror in the hope of provoking a violent incident. We did not deny that the party had stockpiled weapons and fortified its headquarters. But we presented evidence that they had done so in anticipation of precisely the sort of military-style raid the LAPD, in fact, had staged.

From the start, I had resolved that when it came time to argue this case, it wasn't going to be another 148, in which legal deceit passed itself off as courtroom gentility. Times had changed, and so had juries and the defense bar, even if the bench and prosecution had not. Demographically, for example, our jury more closely reflected the new Los Angeles than those I had watched rubber-stamp injustice in my city attorney days. Our panel was composed of six African Americans, three Chicanos, two whites, and an Asian American. I knew that, given the opportunity, they would weigh our evidence against a reservoir of life experience that was bound to contain a clear-eyed skepticism about both the LAPD's motives and Melvin Smith's credibility.

On Thursday, December 9, 1971, I rose to make my closing argument in defense of Willie Stafford and the other Panthers on trial with him. Both my mother and father came to hear me. From the start, I went after Smith with every rhetorical weapon I could muster. It was crucial that the jurors see him for what he was, and, with that foremost in my mind, I described his conduct in the resonant language of the time. Melvin Smith, I told them, was "lower than a snake," an "Uncle Tom" who had fomented trouble for others to ingratiate himself with the police. When that wasn't enough, I told them, he turned himself into a "flunky" for the prosecution. And, I said, the lead prosecutor, Ronald M. Carroll, was only too glad to accept Smith's help in his "callous disregard for the rights" of the defendants.

"Mr. Carroll is somewhat happy with the status quo and doesn't want a change," I told the jurors in reference to the prosecutor's denigration of the Panthers' various social programs in the community. "I can understand some of these things that Mr. Carroll can't, and I ask you to consider your own experience in weighing the credibility of all the testimony."

That was too much for Judge Dell, who interrupted my argument to warn me against "borderline tactics," which he described as "unworthy of you, Mr. Cochran."

I plunged ahead. So did another of the defense attorneys, James Gordon, whose argument was equally frank. The police officers involved in this incident, he argued, were "racists, who went to the Panther headquarters under false pretenses and then lied in court. . . ."

"If you find the defendants guilty," he said, "you are exonerating the police action and setting a precedent . . . that the doorways of the people in the ghetto can be kicked down at will."

After the jury was sent out to deliberate, Dell, whose displeasure with our conduct seemed to grow with each passing day, called the defense attorneys before the bench. He had appointed us to this case, and he thought that gave him the right to dress us down. "You gentlemen have been entrusted by the court with this appointment, and you have failed in that trust," he lectured us. "I'll never appoint any of you lawyers again."

At that point, of course, none of us cared. Far more important to me were the reactions my parents expressed. "I'm very, very proud of you, son," said my father, the conciliatory businessman and deacon of the church. "You said what needed to be said," added my mother, who never had asked me to do anything more than to "be the best that you can be."

Eleven days later, the jury returned its verdict. Seventy-two counts had been alleged against our clients, and I never had heard so many "not guiltys" in my life. The Panthers were acquitted on all the serious charges, including conspiracy to murder police officers and assaulting police with deadly weapons. Nine, including Stafford and Pratt, were found guilty of the minor charge of conspiracy to possess contraband weapons.

Though he had censured us for the way we obtained those verdicts, Dell praised the jury for its decisions. "I have never seen a jury that worked harder or more conscientiously than in this case," he said. "The final verdict you reached was not very much different than the one that I would have reached." Dell also complimented them for not being influenced by "the fireworks that occurred during the trial. . . . A jury under these circumstances might easily have been stampeded and found everyone guilty."

Nowadays, when juries that acquit routinely are vilified, I sometimes remember crusty old George Dell's remarks and reflect that while things always change, it isn't always for the better.

6

My Brother's Keeper

HONEST CRIMINAL DEFENSE LAWYERS WILL TELL YOU that they live in terror of innocent clients, if only because the overwhelming majority of criminal cases end in a conviction of one sort or another.

The defense attorney's constitutional duty is to make sure that the state proves his or her client's guilt according to the procedural rules and beyond a reasonable doubt. By fulfilling that obligation, the defense lawyer becomes the guardian of due process, which is what really holds the ever-nascent tyranny of even the most democratic state at bay and prevents the rule of law from degenerating into mob rule.

But when your client is innocent, that constitutional obligation is joined by a profound moral and human duty. Defense of the innocent is an obligation more intimate and individual than even a physician bears. Unchecked disease, after all, destroys only the body; injustice unimpeded can maim its victim's very soul.

In the months following the Panthers' trial, I would have that axiom burned so deeply into me that, even today, I feel as if it is inscribed directly on my heart.

The Panther verdict came down just two days before Christmas 1971. The season's glad tidings were all the more welcome that year.

At the time, another lawyer, Frank A. Evans, Jr., and I owned a supper club in South Los Angeles called "There." With its mahogany-paneled walls, warm lighting, topflight chef, and congenial bar, the club soon became a popular hangout for local sports celebrities. Muhammad Ali was a frequent visitor, though as a devout Muslim, he did not drink. The opportunity to rub elbows with sports stars, along with courteous, professional service, which I'd learned to recognize in my catering days, quickly made There a favorite spot among the city's growing black middle class. It would be years before diet and discipline became synonymous in the American mind, and our kitchen was very much a creature of its time. A typical Sunday brunch at There, for example, would, in the words of our menu, "start with our King Crab Cocktail Supreme, move on to a tureen of soup du jour, followed by prime rib of beef au jus, roasted according to an old English recipe in our specially designed ovens, and finish with cheese cake in a hot Cherries Jubilee Sauce. To accompany your meal, we suggest a bottle of cabernet sauvignon." My cholesterol level notwithstanding, that still sounds pretty good.

I always gave a Christmas party for my friends and professional associates at the club, and that year we also invited the jurors who had decided the Panther case. It was a memorable and emotional evening for all of us, our pleasure in each other's company deepened by the spirit of that blessed season with its promise of "peace on earth to men of goodwill." More than any of the reams of favorable publicity I received after the verdict, I still treasure the note those twelve jurors sent me:

"Dear Mr. Cochran," it read. "We would like to thank you for the lovely party you gave in our honor. Everyone had a wonderful time and it was just great to meet all the attorneys personally after our months together in court. We thank you and wish you our best in future cases." It was signed, "Jurors of Dept. 101."

So, as 1972 began, I felt an almost intoxicating sense of confidence and optimism. My colleagues and I had emerged victorious from the longest conspiracy trial in California history, and I personally had won the last ten murder cases that had come my way. I was hot. So I wasn't really surprised when I received a call from Geronimo Pratt, who had remained in custody after the verdict because he was also facing murder, robbery, and assault with a deadly weapon charges as the result of another incident.

Pratt and I had become close during the Panther trial. We were two very different men with two very different backgrounds from which we had derived two very different ideas about how to change America for the better. But we shared two other things that were more important—an abiding belief that America had to change and a deep, almost affectionate respect for each other. Pratt already had a lawyer, a fine Pasadena attorney named Charles Hollopeter. I pointed that out to Geronimo when he called my office from the jail one afternoon early in 1972.

"I like Hollopeter," he said. "But I want you to be my lawyer, too. I want you to be on my case. I saw the way you were with Willie Stafford. I saw you argue for him. I want you to argue for me like that. I love the way you argue, Cochran."

He was flattering; I was intrigued. Hollopeter and I conferred, and it was clear that we'd have no trouble working together on the case. A few days later, the judge—Kathleen Parker—appointed me. I didn't know it at the time, but I had just crossed over into a twilight zone of deceit, dishonesty, betrayal, and official corruption whose darkest corners have yet to be illuminated.

The crimes with which Pratt was charged were chilling, brutal, and simple-minded. On December 18, 1968, the police alleged, Geronimo and another black man had gone to a public tennis court in Santa Monica's Lincoln Park. There, they allegedly accosted a young white couple, Caroline Olsen, a twenty-seven-year-old schoolteacher, and her thirty-five-year-old husband, Kenneth. The robbers, who were armed, ordered the victims to lie facedown on the court. They then shot Mrs. Olsen once in the back and her husband five times. All of the wounds were inflicted by the same .45 caliber semiautomatic pistol. The robbers took eighteen dollars from Caroline Olsen's purse before fleeing the scene. Eleven days later, Mrs. Olsen died. Her husband, through some miracle, recovered.

In a lineup staged two years after the shooting, Olsen identified Pratt as one of his assailants. Later, during one of the most damning moments of Pratt's trial, Kenneth Olsen would point to my client from the witness stand and say: "That's the man who murdered my wife!"

Pratt, the authorities charged, was linked to these crimes by one critical piece of evidence and a witness whose testimony would corroborate the surviving victim's testimony. The evidence was a .45 caliber handgun that had been seized from a house frequented by the Panthers following the 1969 killings of Carter and Huggins. According to tests performed on the weapon, its chamber mechanism produced distinctive markings similar to those found on empty cartridges recovered at the tennis court. However, the far more definitive rifling left on bullets fired through the recovered .45's barrel did not match the marks on slugs extracted from the victims' bodies. That was crucial, since every rifle or pistol barrel leaves a unique signature on the bullets that pass through it. The police claimed, though, that their key witness could explain that discrepancy, as well as much more.

That witness was himself a former Black Panther, a middle-aged hairdresser and former Los Angeles county sheriff's deputy named Julius Butler. In the wake of the Carter and Huggins murders, both Butler and Pratt had sought the leadership of the party's L.A. chapter. When Pratt won, he expelled Butler because, as he later told me, "I never did trust that guy." Despite their bitter differences, which made it highly unlikely that Pratt ever would have confided in Butler, Julius testified that Pratt had confessed the tennis court shootings to him. He also said Pratt told him he had removed and destroyed the barrel of the gun used in the crimes.

Those were the facts on which the prosecution's case against Geronimo Pratt turned. They would have made any defense attorney's job difficult. What Hollopeter and I didn't know was that there were other, illegally hidden facts that made Pratt's conviction inevitable.

Unbeknownst to us, during the late 1960s, FBI director J. Edgar Hoover had ordered the bureau to undertake a covert "Counter Intelligence Program" (COINTELPRO, for short) to spy on, infiltrate, and disrupt dissident political groups. Hoover launched COINTELPRO on August 8, 1967. Hoover, a staunch foe of the civil rights movement, earlier had targeted Dr. King, Roy Wilkins, Whitney Young, Stokely Carmichael, H. Rap Brown, Elijah Muhammad, and other established leaders. The program's other goals were to "prevent the coalition of militant black nationalist groups" and to "prevent the rise of a black messiah who could unify, and electrify, the movement."

Publicly, Hoover had kept his lifelong racism as deep a secret as his homosexuality. But, as we now know from documents obtained under the Freedom of Information Act, he was obsessed with the Black Panthers and ordered his lieutenants to take whatever measures were necessary to "neutralize" the party and its leaders. Pratt, with his military experience and decorations for bravery under fire, was one of COINTELPRO's particular targets.

Agents spied on him almost constantly. Though we did not know it at the time, the FBI had wiretap records that showed Pratt making phone calls from Oakland just three hours before the tennis court shootings hundreds of miles south in Santa Monica.

We did not know that Julius Butler was a confidential informant not only for the FBI but also for the Los Angeles County district attorney's office, a fact that was hidden from us by the prosecutor, Deputy D.A. Richard Kalustian, with whom I had attended Loyola Law School.

We could have impeached Butler's testimony if we had known he was a government informant. The number of government witnesses who perjured themselves in this case was unprecedented. Of course, we did not know they were doing this at the time. There was much more that we would eventually learn.

We knew nothing about the COINTELPRO's Ghetto Informant Program, which was started in October 1967 as a community surveillance measure. A network of informants was recruited from black areas to inform on real and suspected militants, community organizers, even "owners and clientele of African American bookstores." The government wanted to gauge "changes in the attitude of the Negro community toward the white community." We learned much later that FBI field agents were required to have a specified number of black informants. Hoover terminated the informant program along with the COINTELPRO initiative in 1971 following a break-in at an FBI field office, in which an antiwar group seized documents that revealed the intent and scope of the clandestine plan. The materials were later leaked to the press and to Congress.

We also did not know that, during the trial, the FBI tapped my office phone and that, according to an appellate court which later reviewed the case, the bureau maintained "an informant within the defense environs." To this day, that particular quisling's name is unknown to us.

We did not know that, shortly after the crimes, Kenneth Olsen had been shown a photographic lineup and had unhesitatingly identified a man named Ronald Perkins as the killer. Perkins, however, was in police custody at the time of the crimes. Mr. Olsen also had told police that his wife's murderer was less than six feet tall and wore a safari-style jacket. Two years later, when the police created the new fifteen-man photo lineup out of which Kenneth Olsen finally identified Pratt, my client's picture was the only one to depict a man under six feet and wearing a safari jacket. All this was known to Kalustian. The original photo lineup, by the way, has disappeared, the only time in my experience such evidence has been lost in a murder investigation.

With all that hidden from us, I began the trial with my habitual optimism. If anything, my spirits were higher than usual. Barely two months before, my hero and mentor Leo Branton had come out of retirement to win another controversial black activist, Angela Davis, an acquittal on murder, kidnapping, and criminal conspiracy charges growing out of a 1970 jailbreak. I had carefully studied Leo's masterful tactics in that case, particularly his use of new scientific data demonstrating that stress and racial differences dramatically reduce the reliability of eyewitness identifications. I thought such research might show our own jury how Kenneth Olsen, through no fault of his own, was mistaken when he pointed to Pratt as his wife's killer.

In a criminal trial, the prosecution puts its case on first, followed by the defense, and then the prosecution's rebuttal witnesses. The surviving victim's testimony was the centerpiece of the state's case against Pratt, and I still recall talking to my client in the county jail's attorney room the night after Mr. Olsen identified him as the murderer in front of our jury.

"I didn't kill this woman, Cochran," he said to me for what must have been the one hundredth time. "I wouldn't do that. It's not my style. This whole case is about something else."

"Oh, man," I wearily sighed for what must have been the two hundredth time. "What is this about except this crime? You are innocent, but you're really being paranoid."

"You'll see," Pratt replied flatly. "They're after me, and they're going to do whatever it takes to get me, Cochran. Even paranoid people have real enemies, you know."

I didn't even bother to grimace over that old joke. I just packed up my things and headed home to prepare for the next day's testimony. As much as I liked and respected Geronimo Pratt, I refused to follow him into his never-never land of official plots and governmental conspiracies. Time to get back to work, I thought as I walked back to my car. Time to rejoin the real world. I had faith in the rule of law as applied by our criminal justice system under the norms ordained by the Constitution. I did not believe that an agency of the United States government would conduct its business with all the foul underhandedness of the Borgia court. I trusted in the integrity of my old classmate, Richard Kalustian. He was a stand-up guy; we wore the same school tie.

Geronimo Pratt and I were about to learn which of us was living in a dream world.

In the midst of the prosecution's case, we won one important skirmish. Five days after being ousted from the Panthers, Julius Butler had written a letter recounting Pratt's alleged confession. He sealed it in an envelope and gave it to a Los Angeles police officer named Dwayne Rice. Butler asked Rice—whose snitch he sometimes was—to hold the letter as "insurance," to be opened only if something untoward happened to him. The letter, which ultimately led to Pratt's arrest, had come to light during an investigation into an internal police matter. What did not emerge until years later was that as Rice concluded that initial meeting with Butler on a public street, he was confronted by waiting FBI agents, who demanded a copy of the letter. How they knew what was in the sealed envelope remains a matter of speculation.

I fought hard to keep the letter out of evidence, and Judge Parker agreed it was inadmissible. I wanted Butler on the witness stand, where the jury could judge his credibility for themselves. On Monday, June 19, 1972, Julius Butler, then thirty-nine, was sworn in as a witness. He told the court that the night of Caroline Olsen's murder, Pratt had come to his West Adams beauty shop and told him, "I'm going on a mission." Butler testified that Pratt wanted him to tell the other Panthers if he didn't return. Geronimo came back later that same night, Butler testified, looking "very nervous." "He said he had shot some people in Santa Monica, but didn't know whether he had killed them," Butler alleged.

The day after the shooting, according to Butler, Pratt returned to the shop with a newspaper containing a story about the attack on the Olsens. Butler swore that Pratt pointed to the article and said, "That's what I was talking about." Under prodding from Kalustian, Butler also claimed to recall that Pratt told him "that he had done the shooting because the other guy couldn't shoot" at the helpless couple. It was at that time, Butler alleged, that Pratt told him he had destroyed the barrel of the handgun used in the crime.

On cross-examination, I showed Butler all the consideration he deserved. He bobbed; he weaved. He twisted, turned, evaded, whined, wheedled, and temporized. The only direct, unequivocal response he gave was one we now know to be a lie.

"Are you now or have you ever been an informant for the Federal Bureau of Investigation or any other law enforcement agency?" I demanded.

"No," Butler said emphatically. "Never."

I looked over at our jury—nine whites and three African Americans. Some of them gazed at Butler with perplexity, some with outright loathing. None of them looked very happy. I looked over at my old classmate Dick Kalustian, who knew Butler was lying through his teeth. He looked straight ahead and never flinched. What he knew then—and what we know now—was that Butler had informed thirty-three times to the FBI and had been listed as a confidential informant by Kalustian's own office on January 27, 1972, nearly six months before Pratt's trial began.

We opened our defense by going straight to the heart of the prosecution's case—poor Mr. Olsen's moving testimony. To demonstrate its unreliability, we called as a witness a pioneering psychologist, Dr. Robert Buckhout, whose laboratory research had convincingly demonstrated that eyewitness accounts, particularly those of stressful events, almost always were inaccurate. That was particularly true, his research showed, when the accounts involved identification of people of another race.

There was something, after all, I told the jurors, to the "traditional American myth that white men can't tell one black man from another"—not if he's a black man the white man sees for a handful of seconds during a brutal crime that occurred four years before. Buckhout, in fact, testified that in his "scientific opinion," Mr. Olsen would have been incapable of accurately recalling individual facial features glimpsed that long ago under such traumatic circumstances.

At our request, Kathleen Cleaver returned from her self-imposed exile in Algeria. She testified that she had seen Pratt frequently during the two weeks before Christmas 1968 while both were in the San Francisco Bay Area at Black Panther Party meetings. She could not swear, however, that she saw him at the precise time of the murder since so much time had passed. Other party members, who might have corroborated her testimony, refused to testify for Pratt because they were members of the Huey Newton faction. We, of course, did not know that the FBI's wiretap records would have supported her account. We also now know that the bureau's operatives followed Pratt almost constantly from early in 1968 through December 18, 1968, the day of the crimes. The logs of that surveillance, like so many other state and federal documents related to his case, are mysteriously missing.

Pratt was an effective witness on his own behalf. He looked directly at the jurors when he flatly denied murdering Caroline Olsen and callously shooting her husband. From across the courtroom, you could sense his soldier's contempt for the cowards who had. He gave a credible account of his own whereabouts when the crimes were committed, and he denied ever confessing to Julius Butler. In fact, he chuckled slightly when he said he always "had been a little suspicious of Julius" and never would have confided in him on a serious matter.

Any defense attorney will tell you that there is nothing more nerve-racking than having your client on the witness stand. Kalustian used a textbook cross-examination technique. First he'd walk toward the witness, then move back toward the jury. He'd stand facing them, letting them read his facial reactions to Pratt's responses while under attack. This created a type of split-screen effect. On one screen, the jury saw the prosecutor's face, on the other the defendant's. Each told a different story. The jury got to see both the point and the counterpoint of the hardline questioning. Nonverbal signals said a lot. For a defense attorney, this is the moment when you can measure the jury's degree of sympathy toward your client. But Pratt testified so credibly and weathered Kalustian's cross-examination so well that our confidence surged. But "pride goeth before a fall," and we made a mistake.

Kenneth Olsen initially had described his assailant as a "clean-shaven black man." Geronimo Pratt has always worn a neatly trimmed mustache and goatee. Late in the trial, Pratt's brother Chuck, who had gone to UCLA with me, produced a Polaroid snapshot he said he had taken the same month as the murder. It showed Chuck's young son sitting in the lap of his bearded Uncle Geronimo.

"Are you sure it was taken in December?" I asked.

He was sure. I took his word and checked no further. I should have. The photograph was admitted in evidence, and Kalustian had his opportunity. The final rebuttal witness he called was an employee of the Polaroid film company, who examined the numerical code on the back of the snapshot and testified that it proved conclusively that the film was manufactured in May of 1969. Kalustian was able to wrap up his case by leaving the jury with the impression that we had tried to put something over on them. I learned an invaluable lesson—at Geronimo Pratt's expense.

After deliberating six days, the jury informed Judge Parker that they were "hopelessly deadlocked." I asked for a mistrial, but Parker insisted the panel continue its deliberations. We did not know it at the time, but they were split ten-two for conviction. Neither of the holdouts was an African American. Two days later, a single juror was still holding out. Finally, on Friday, July 29, on the tenth day of deliberation, the jury sent out a note that they had reached a verdict.

We all stood to receive their decision. While Alice Nishikawa, the court clerk, read the first verdict—"guilty" of first-degree murder—Pratt swore under his breath, shrugged off my cautionary hand, and blurted out: "You're wrong. I didn't kill that woman. You racist dogs. I'm not going to sit here and listen to the rest of this." Judge Parker ordered Pratt removed from the courtroom. After a brief interval, he returned to waive his right to be present while the rest of the verdicts—all guilty—were read.

"I told you, Cochran," he said to me as we parted that day. "They're going to do whatever it takes to get me."

I went home that night as dejected as I have ever been. In my mind, I replayed the philosophical debates Geronimo Pratt and I had waged virtually from the time we met. In a way, our differing points of view mirrored the split that divided black families and friends across America in those days. I was very much a man of Dr. Martin Luther King's school. I believed then, as I still do, in the moral imperative of nonviolence. I believed then, as I still do, that courageous people, working within the system, can arouse the popular conscience against injustice. Geronimo Pratt held to the school of Malcolm X and the other militant theorists of his generation. He believed that the gates of justice never would yield to anything but a battering ram propelled by forceful hands. I believed then, as I still do, in the essential goodness of my fellow human beings. Geronimo Pratt, who had seen war in the villages on a foreign shore and in the city streets of his native land, could not tear his eyes from his fellow man's capacity to do evil. Somehow that night, I felt I had let our side of this great argument—my side and Dr. King's—down.

There is an insult in the African American community that dates back to Du Bois's day: "You're not black enough." That night, as I measured myself against Geronimo Pratt, I wondered about myself. "Two-ness," again. It was a bleak moment. Like many of its kind, it marked the end of one phase of my education. I never again would unhesitatingly trust my client's fate to the system's basic fairness. I had learned that prosecutors and law enforcement officials, convinced of their own righteousness, would do anything to make the system yield the "right result." I had learned that during that journey to justice on which I had embarked all those years ago in the kitchen on West Twenty-eighth Street, I would encounter not only the courage of saints but also the treachery of Judas. I had learned that if I was going to be the lawyer I had always wanted to be, I would have to be tougher, more skeptical, and, most of all, braver in the pursuit of truth.

Never again would I accept anything as it appeared at first glance without delving deeper beneath the surface and then deeper still. Never again would I accept the "official version" of anything. That's what the loss of the Geronimo Pratt case taught me: a healthier kind of paranoia.

Geronimo Pratt paid the tuition for all those lessons of mine. That is, in part, why I have labored through all these long years to win his freedom. That is why I have never forgotten him. But through the years, our conversations have deepened along with our friendship. We are brothers, in fact; we have both moved a long way and no longer are so far apart.

Today, I owe Geronimo Pratt not only a debt of justice but one of love. Together, we both have learned just how wise Dr. King was when he taught us: "If you don't stand for something, you'll fall for anything."

7

Jonah and the Whale

THOUGH I DID MY BEST NOT TO SHOW IT, ANGER WAS
my constant companion in the days following Geronimo Pratt's
conviction. I knew I was keeping dangerous company. Uncon-
trolled and unchanneled, anger will burn through your soul like
a lava flow. It will incinerate discretion, judgment, discernment,
wisdom, proportion, and, most of all, charity—all the virtues
essential to a decent life. In the end, when every other impulse
has been consumed, unchecked anger melts your inner life into a
reeking, stagnant pool of bitterness.

And yet, I was angry.

There are times, like the Pratt trial, when you empathize so
deeply with a client and identify so closely with the issues
involved that the ethical and moral issues are difficult to separate
from your personal feelings. As much as you try to separate
them out, it's not always possible. Lawyers are human, and it

sometimes feels as if you are on trial along with your client. Maybe this was why I was so angry. I was angry that I had been naive enough to believe that the government would play according to the rules, angry that I had been gullible enough to believe that this case would be tried on the facts alone.

This defeat humbled me in many ways. I also learned many valuable lessons. As the philosopher Jeremy Taylor wrote in his seventeenth-century commentary "Sermons": "Humility is the most excellent natural cure for anger in the world."

It was the Cochran way to carry on, no matter what the setback—to "keep on stepping," as my father often said. I did my best to do that. I worked on my cases, visited my parents, played with my children, continued halfheartedly trying to patch things up with my unhappy wife. Inside, however, I waged a struggle as difficult as any case I've ever tried. Day followed weary day. Long after everyone else was in bed, I sat alone with anger and listened as it chanted its mesmerizing litany of injustices.

It was the "dark night" of my soul. But in its depths, grace—unasked for and undeserved—bestowed one of its merciful lessons upon me. Dimly, I began to understand that faith never is more vital than when God seems silent and withdrawn.

Humbly, I opened myself to the wisdom my father, the Reverend C. A. W. Clark, and all my other pastors had set before me. I recalled that when Christ—unjustly accused and condemned—allowed himself to endure the humiliation of death on the cross, he achieved more than victory over sin. He sanctified for all time not only our human suffering and failures but also that sense of "brokenness" which every honest man and woman ultimately must recognize deep within themselves. Humbly, I began once more to listen not just to my anger but to the wisdom that might subdue it to a decent and constructive purpose.

I had a use for my anger after all and, finally, an answer to the troubling questions my debates with Geronimo Pratt had left in my mind. It wasn't enough to *hate* injustice; you had to *love* justice for its own sake. And justice, like truth, is indivisible. It must apply as equally to the cop, the prosecutor, and the judge as it does to the prisoner in the dock and the advocate defending him. The change I sought in our system was not its overthrow but the realization of its ideals through the application of its laws and principles equally and to all.

My Philistine still stood before me, and, within a matter of weeks, we once again were locked in battle.

One night in late August of 1972, shortly before my first trip north to visit Geronimo at San Quentin, a twenty-three-year-old black factory worker named Philip Eric Johns was asleep in his apartment in Inglewood, a community surrounded by and indistinguishable from southwest Los Angeles. Acting on a tip from "an informant," James P. Hurley and Daniel R. Tregarthen, two LAPD detectives working out of the department's notoriously racist 77th Division, went to Johns's apartment to arrest a man suspected of committing a series of holdups in nearby neighborhoods. Either their "informant" was lying or Hurley and Tregarthen simply stumbled into the wrong apartment. Johns had no criminal record and worked long, hard shifts beside his father in the Goodyear Tire & Rubber plant not far away. It was tough, dirty labor and, when the two detectives—supported by Inglewood police officers—broke into Johns's bedroom in the middle of the night, they found a tired young man, deeply asleep with one arm tucked beneath his pillow.

Hurley and Tregarthen, who were in plainclothes, would later claim they thought Johns was "feigning sleep" and "concealing a weapon" under the pillow. They testified that as they stood over his bed with drawn guns, he suddenly roused from his slumber and lunged at them, grabbing at one of their gun barrels. The detective at whose weapon he allegedly clutched shot Johns three times; the detective standing at the foot of the bed shot him twice. Philip Eric Johns was dead in seconds. At least two of the bullets—one of them the fatal round that pierced Philip's heart—were high-speed .357 magnum loads banned by LAPD policy.

The written report filed by an Inglewood officer, who stood in the door of Johns's bedroom and watched the whole tragedy unfold, did not corroborate the detectives' account. Despite that fact, the LAPD's internal affairs investigation found—in the words of Police Chief Ed Davis—"absolutely no evidence to justify disciplinary proceedings or criminal prosecution" of Hurley and Tregarthen.

That was too much even for the normally docile Los Angeles County grand jury. It opened its own investigation, calling more than forty witnesses, including the actual suspect in the robberies, a man named Carl Spotsville, who had surrendered directly to a judge because he feared the LAPD would kill him. He testified that he had never met Philip Eric Johns and had never been in his apartment. On October 5, 1972, the grand jury handed down a two-count indictment of both detectives, charging them with manslaughter and "assault by an officer under color of authority." Stung by this unfamiliar intrusion, the department and its allies quickly circled their wagons.

Chief Davis was a worthy heir to the imperious William Parker. Today, he's probably best remembered for his proposal that the department be given a portable gallows so that it could summarily hang airline hijackers at the airport. On another occasion, he suggested that the city council buy his narcotics officers a submarine so they could intercept drug smugglers before they came ashore. His response to the indictments in the Johns case was to pile additional boulders atop the LAPD's traditional stone wall. Within hours, he issued a statement blasting the grand jury and expressing "complete confidence that these men will be exonerated when the charges are reviewed by trained judges."

Trained by whom? I wondered at the time.

Los Angeles' mayor, Sam Yorty, also made a public statement predicting the officers would be acquitted. "Regret for what happened," he said, "should not obscure the fact that the officers acted in the line of duty and under circumstances which suddenly developed at the scene."

I followed all this with more than normal interest because, while the grand jury was meeting, Johns's mother, Mrs. Johnie Choyce, had come to my office to ask that I represent her family. She lived in a small, rural town called Wasco, near Bakersfield at the south end of California's Central Valley. It had been a long, hot drive down to my office, but I still recall her quiet composure as she explained why she felt it was important to obtain some redress from the police.

"I don't want my son's death to be in vain, Mr. Cochran," she said. "I hope, somehow, some good will come out of this, that it will have some meaning."

She told me that when her sister, Mrs. Herberteen King, who lived near Philip, called and told her of his death, "I just left the house and started to walk. It was dark outside, but I just wanted to walk. I couldn't think of anything else to do then, but now I have."

Most of all, I remember the moment when Johnie Choyce reached across the desk and handed me the deeply creased sheet of paper the coroner had found folded inside her dead son's wallet. On it was a handwritten poem entitled "I'll Be Listening." It began:

> All I want is one chance to prove
> that I can do all the things I need to do
> to make the world a better groove for me and you.

It ended:

> Let it be said when your life is done
> that your life was spent for something
> worth more than worldly fun.
> That the battle against evil for sure you've won
> but mostly to hear the Lord say job well done
> I'll be listening.

Something about Mrs. Choyce reminded me of my mother and grandmother—of all proud and strong black women, the beating heart of their families. Mrs. Choyce's determination and character were etched in her face and reaffirmed in the words she spoke. I would carry those ironic stanzas from her son's poem in my head throughout the trial. I knew what I must do.

Within days, I filed a $5 million suit against the Los Angeles Police Department on Johnie Choyce's behalf. But by that time, the department's defenses were in high gear. The police commission, acting on a demand by Chief Davis, unanimously recommended that the city council authorize the city attorney not only to defend the indicted detectives but also to retain private counsel at public expense to assist them.

In the meantime, Philip Eric Johns's body had been exhumed from the graveyard near Wasco's True Light Baptist Church and returned to Los Angeles for a second autopsy, this time in the presence of a pathologist I had hired. That examination confirmed that Philip had been shot twice in the chest and three times in the back. It also revealed extensive powder burns on his chest and gunshot residue on a single middle finger of one of his hands. One expert later would testify that the residue probably was the result of a reflexive defensive gesture. The second autopsy also disclosed that Philip Eric Johns had suffered a broken jaw that— like the powder burns—had gone undetected during the initial investigation. It was business as usual at the coroner's office.

It also was business as usual at City Hall, where the council took up the question of who would pay to defend the indicted detectives. When the council president opened the question for public comment, a virtual parade of white and black civil rights leaders and civil libertarians spoke in opposition to any use of public funds. But, in the end, the council's conservative majority sided with the city's Republican mayor and police chief and their hand-picked police commissioners. Among the members opposed was a black city councilman, my Kappa brother, Tom Bradley, soon to be elected mayor.

At a press conference after the vote, I called the decision "a callous act on the part of the city council and the majority community. It shows an utter disregard for the conflict you have when, on one hand, you have the district attorney prosecuting the case and, on the other hand, you have a city attorney or a lawyer employed by the city defending the case. That's hardly an adversarial proceeding.

"Tolerance of such an obvious conflict of interest," I continued, "shows the complete insensitivity of the majority community to the shooting of a black man."

That kind of sweeping rhetoric was a hallmark of the times. In fairness, it deserves to be recalled that three of the council members who voted against defending Hurley and Tregarthen were white—two Jewish men, Marvin Braude and Ed Edelman, and Pat Russell, then the panel's only woman. Their vote was courageous, and we have a duty to remember such things.

Both detectives ultimately were tried and acquitted.

Due to a logjam of cases in the system, it took four years to bring Johnie Choyce's civil suit to trial. When we finally got a courtroom, it was in Torrance, a virtually lily-white suburb fifteen miles southwest of Los Angeles, which then had a reputation for conservative juries. Syd Irmas and I tried the case together. The witnesses, the facts, and the law all were on our side. But we had an all-white jury, some of whose members openly referred to the African American court reporter as "burr head."

We lost.

I was back sitting alone in the dark.

In the years since Geronimo Pratt's conviction and Philip Eric Johns's killing, my reputation had grown along with my victories. I had forced the city of Los Angeles to make its first-ever cash settlement in a wrongful death suit growing out of a police shooting. In that case, I had represented Mr. and Mrs. Jeff Leonard, whose unarmed son, William, had been shot in the back and killed by a police officer who had gone to the wrong house while answering a domestic dispute call. The settlement was a mere $25,000, but the precedent was enormously significant. Still, I thought to myself, the cop who did the shooting was exonerated of any misconduct by the department and probably was on the street that very night. In another case, I had set what veteran court watchers claimed was an unofficial record, when the jury in a robbery case I tried returned an acquittal in slightly less than twenty minutes.

But I also had taken and lost the cases of two young African American men who had been choked to death when LAPD officers, attempting to take them into custody on minor charges, applied the department's latest "suspect control" technique, the bar-arm choke hold.

Now there was this: no justice for Philip Eric Johns, no justice for his grieving mother, Johnie Choyce. She had trusted me with her most precious possession—her son's memory. And all she had asked was that I take it and make sure that her son's final moments of terror and pain should not have been in vain. After four years, the only thing I could do was hand her back the memory and tell her that's all there ever would be.

I didn't drink. I didn't weep. I didn't stir. I didn't even pray. I don't think I've ever spent a bleaker night. After ten long years of battle, the Philistine still loomed before me and the field seemed his for the taking. I had not won, but I was not beaten.

I did the only thing I could: I made a place for Johnie Choyce in my heart, alongside Barbara Deadwyler and Geronimo Pratt. Then I threw myself deeply into the practice of law. A year later, I won the Los Angeles Criminal Courts Bar Association's coveted Jerry Giesler Award. That honor is the highest award a Los Angeles criminal lawyer can receive. Given the size and skill of our local defense bar, it's an honor every recipient cherishes. I am no exception.

Business was booming, when—out of the blue—I received a call from the then Los Angeles County district attorney, John Van de Kamp. He had a confidential matter to discuss with me, he said, and wondered whether we could meet privately. I, of course, agreed, and a date was set.

John Van de Kamp came from an old Los Angeles family whose name was familiar to any Southern Californian who had ever purchased one of their cakes, pies, cookies, or prepared foods. Theirs was old money—the sort of stuff that bought mansions, beach houses, ranches, and thoroughbred racehorses. After law school, however, John had chosen to pursue public service. A liberal Democrat with an active social conscience, he had managed to make a name for himself as a tough, highly effective career prosecutor while maintaining his personal opposition to capital punishment.

At his suggestion, we had agreed to meet at the Los Angeles Athletic Club in the downtown financial district. The Athletic Club is one of several private dining and social clubs in the central city. We found a private corner beside one of the tall, heavily draped windows in the club's gracious main reception room. John quickly came to the point. The time had come to make some changes in the Los Angeles County district attorney's operation, which by then was the largest law office in the United States. He had followed my career from the time of the Deadwyler case. He said he was impressed.

"I'm offering you the position of assistant district attorney," John said. I would be the number three man in the office, he explained, with general administrative responsibility for all six hundred prosecutors and specific responsibility for the eighty-five deputy D.A.'s assigned to the Juvenile Division, the Consumer and Environmental Protection divisions, the Sexual Crimes Unit, and the Special Investigations Division, or SID.

For the moment, at least, I was speechless. SID investigates all allegations of governmental corruption, including police shootings. I stammered out a series of reservations—I was a defense attorney; I had a living to make; I never would be accepted. Van de Kamp shrugged them all off.

"Look," he said, "this will give you a chance to do more than talk about these problems. I'm asking you to come inside and do something about them. If things need cleaning up, help us do it. You've done all the talking there is to do. If you'll come in with me, we can make a difference. It's time, Cochran," he said, "to put your money where your mouth is."

He didn't know it, of course, but he was also offering me the chance, at long last, to put my efforts where my heart was. And yet, my sense of alienation from the legal establishment, my skepticism of law enforcement and its motives, never had been deeper. I felt a profound ambivalence. It wasn't just that I was reluctant to abandon a lucrative law practice I'd worked so hard to build. I didn't want to be a token presence, a bit of black bunting in the window of a shop that would go on selling the same shoddy goods. I asked for a few days to think it over, and John graciously agreed.

Many in the African American community believed that the system rarely produced favorable results for its residents. Blacks, with good reason, believed that a large number of innocent defendants with dark skins were convicted solely because of racism. They believed the system's corruption was evident not only in its results but in its administration, from the judges to the arresting officer on the street. I believed that this appointment would be my opportunity to initiate change from inside the system.

I quickly discovered that none of the people I consulted shared my anxieties. My father saw it in perhaps the starkest terms: It was an "opportunity to help others," and it had to be taken. My old classmate, friend, and confidante Elaine Matthews was unequivocally enthusiastic. Syd Irmas and Tom Bradley, the latter by then mayor of Los Angeles, strongly urged me to accept, though for different reasons.

This, the ever-practical Syd told me, is "an investment in your future. As good as you are, you're going to be a much more versatile lawyer when you leave that office. What you sacrifice now, you'll more than make up for later," he said. "I want you to take that job."

Bradley, who was fighting to open L.A.'s corridors of power to people of all colors and faiths, saw a chance for me to do a little of the same. "John Van de Kamp is a good man," he said, "and he wants you *because* you've demonstrated you won't take any crap from anybody.

"You've been an advocate for the poor and those denied justice, and that's why John asked you," Bradley said, his voice picking up force as he spoke. "He wants to stop routine police abuse, too. He's a visionary elected official, and he deserves your help. And he's told me personally that he is willing to give you the power and support you'll need to make real changes in the D.A.'s office.

"There's no decision here," said Bradley, suddenly very much the mayor. "Take the damn job, and enjoy it."

I phoned John Van de Kamp and accepted. I thanked him sincerely for the opportunity and for the confidence he had shown in me. "I will give you my absolute best," I promised.

"I know that," he said. "That's why I asked you. Now, let's go make a difference—together."

There had been only one voice raised in opposition to my decision, and that, unsurprisingly, belonged to Barbara. At the time, I was making about $300,000 per year in my law practice. The job Van de Kamp was offering paid $49,000. Barbara looked at those numbers and shook her head in disbelief.

"Are you out of your mind?" she asked. "You're making real money, lots of it. Only a crazy man would give that up. You have responsibilities, you know."

"I know I have responsibilities," I replied, fighting to keep an even tone to my voice. "That's why taking this job is the right thing to do. And I'm going to do it."

"Johnnie," she said coldly and for the last time, "don't do this. It's a mistake."

A short time later, I was sworn in as Los Angeles County's first African American assistant district attorney. I had agreed to serve for a three-year term. My appointment was regarded as a milestone in many sections of the community, and the swearing-in turned into something of a gala. Not only did John Van de Kamp speak but also Mayor Tom Bradley, my pastor, and a number of legal colleagues, including Howard Weitzman. My family, friends, and professional associates crowded the overflowing courtroom where I took the oath.

Cards, letters, and telegrams of congratulations poured in. One of the warmest was a note from California's Republican attorney general, my old adversary Evelle J. Younger. "It is gratifying to see someone with your background, experience, and ability serve in this important position," he wrote. "I am sure you will bring constructive and dedicated leadership to that office. You are bound to do an outstanding job as Assistant District Attorney, just as you have always done in every endeavor you have undertaken."

One message, however, stood out from the others, in part because it was the only one I received from a former client. It was a greeting card inscribed with a congratulatory verse:

> The news of your promotion
> Is a happy thing to hear
> Sure hope it brings you
> more success
> With every coming year.

Enclosed with the card was a recent snapshot of the sender. On the back it was signed simply "G." It was from Geronimo Pratt.

I took up my new duties in January of 1978. Just prior to that, Barbara had taken Melodie and Tiffany and moved out of the hillside home we shared without even bothering to tell me. While in the office that afternoon, I got a call from a neighbor inquiring, "Why is the moving van parked in front of your house?"

I hurried home as soon as my appointments permitted and found the doors open and every stick of furniture and every appliance gone, including the refrigerator. As I later discovered, she'd also cleaned out our joint bank accounts. There wasn't even a note. I was shocked, but not really surprised, by Barbara's unexpected departure. We had separated many times in the past twelve years. Perhaps my decision to accept the position in the district attorney's office was the final straw. Any real upset I felt was dulled by a sense that this crisis was finally nearing a resolution. Within the year, we were divorced.

That night, though, I called Elaine Matthews, who was going through her own divorce. She came over, surveyed all that emptiness, and said, "Well, Johnnie, you're better off. Think of it as a fresh start—though it's probably a little fresher than you planned."

Elaine wasn't just funny, she was right. Being single once again allowed me to throw myself completely into my new job, and, from the start, it was clear this new role would require all I had to give. One of the reasons public prosecutors—and particularly those in the L.A. County district attorney's office—so often lose their big cases is that they have a civil service mentality. Most of the time, most of them work nine to five, five days a week. Once they make the right grade on the office pay scale, they do little or nothing to hone their trial skills. They take as few risks as possible and trust that they can make up the difference by drawing on the overwhelming resources of law enforcement and the huge reservoir of public support they enjoy. Thus, when they run into the kind of topflight opposition they often face in a big case, they are utterly outclassed and ill prepared for the rigors and hours seasoned private trial attorneys accept as a matter of course.

In the late 1970s, John Van de Kamp set out to change that and a great deal more about the way his office conducted the public's business. I brought my own skills to the job, and so did John's number two man, an extraordinary lawyer named Steve Trott, undoubtedly the best prosecutor I've ever seen in a courtroom. He was principled, intelligent, articulate, highly skilled, and meticulously prepared. Before attending law school, he'd had a successful career as a professional folk singer and, briefly, as a magician. That background as a performer, coupled with his obvious sincerity, gave him a real rapport with juries. In multicultural Los Angeles, it also didn't hurt that he spoke a number of foreign languages fluently, including Spanish. Though he lacked any of the appetite for self-promotion common among the more ambitious deputy D.A.'s, like the erratic Vince Bugliosi, Trott was the opponent L.A.'s defense lawyers feared most. He went on to serve in the Reagan administration's Justice Department before accepting an appointment to the federal appeals court. His personal politics were conservative and Republican; Van de Kamp and I were liberal Democrats. But we nonetheless were a team committed to changing our agency's notions of business as usual.

We were in the office seven days a week, and I don't think I actually saw a sunset for the first two years. But I loved the work. And, to my surprise, I found I felt its successes and frustrations as intensely as I had my similar experiences as a defense lawyer. From the start, Van de Kamp knew I would need a particularly able deputy to head SID. He chose a rising young prosecutor named Gil Garcetti for the job. Though he had little trial experience and few courtroom skills, Garcetti was a good administrator with keen political instincts. We quickly formed a close partnership that weathered more than its share of stormy weather.

In fact, Gil and I hadn't been together long when we suffered one of our worst disappointments. Early in 1978, a couple of Southern California Gas Company employees went to a house in South-Central Los Angeles. The gas bill hadn't been paid, and they were supposed to shut off the service. The homeowner, an African American woman named Eula Love, had no intention of doing without the fuel she used to cook and to heat her house. She ran the gas men off with a shovel. Two LAPD officers were called to the scene. An altercation ensued, and they shot Eula Love to death. Garcetti and I investigated, and I recommended that manslaughter charges be filed against both policemen, one of whom had a long history of treating African Americans brutally. Van de Kamp and Trott disagreed. They were in charge. There would be no prosecution of Mrs. Love's killers. My former law partners, Nelson Atkins and Irwin Evans, filed suit on behalf of her family and ultimately compelled the city to settle for just under $1 million.

It was clear to me that cases against police officers would have to meet a higher-than-usual standard of proof if they ever were going to be filed in court. With that in mind, Garcetti and I founded the so-called Rollout Unit within SID. It put a deputy D.A. and a district attorney's investigator on the scene of every police shooting within our jurisdiction. After that, we no longer had to rely completely on law enforcement agencies to probe their own potential misconduct. It didn't take long for the new unit to make itself felt. I particularly remember one story that made its way back to our office. A sheriff's deputy had a guy he was pursuing turn and pull a knife. The deputies' usual practice in such instances was to shoot—and sort things out later. This deputy just drew his gun and held the suspect at a safe distance until other officers arrived. When he got back to the station, the other deputies demanded to know why he hadn't "dropped the scumbag."

"Because I don't want to be investigated by Cochran and Garcetti," he reportedly snapped.

We knew then we were having an impact.

I also pushed hard for other reforms. In the Sexual Crimes Unit, we recruited more women prosecutors and instituted a system we called "vertical prosecution" of accused rapists. Under that arrangement, a single deputy D.A. handled a case from start to finish, thereby sparing victims the trauma of recounting the story of their abuse over and over. At Van de Kamp's request, I became the founding chairman of Los Angeles County's Domestic Violence Council. At our urging, LAPD fundamentally changed the way it handled reports of domestic violence. Up to that time, officers responding to such a call would look around and, if they didn't see a body or too much blood, simply would shrug the matter off as a "family dispute." Under guidelines our council promulgated, the department began to inform battered women that they were entitled to protection and assistance and to provide them, on the spot, with a list of nearby shelters and helping agencies.

In fact, during O. J. Simpson's trial, one of the prosecutors—Scott Gordon, the office's domestic violence specialist—approached me with the brochure the D.A. now provides all battered women.

"Johnnie," Gordon said, "look what you started." That meant a great deal coming from Scott, who as an ex-cop had answered more than his share of those tragic calls.

One of the things I also discovered about my new office was that it sometimes required me to speak uncomfortable—even controversial—truths to people among whom I might otherwise have been inclined to tread softly. In 1979, for example, a young black LAPD officer named Bernard Parks—later the department's deputy chief—invited me to address the National Organization of Black Law Enforcement. The topic was unspecified, but I had something on my mind. Shortly before, *Ebony* magazine had published its courageous report on the devastating impact so-called black-on-black crime was having among urban African Americans. My own preoccupation with the issue had been growing, and I wanted to speak out.

But when I raised the possibility with my friends, most of them advised against it. Such a speech, they said, inevitably would be seized upon and misused by white racists, particularly in law enforcement. I would risk being called an "Uncle Tom," they warned. As usual, my father took a far more independent view.

"I don't see it that way at all, Johnnie," he said. "You're like Nixon going to China. You can do what needs to be done because nobody expects it of you. Besides, it's the right thing to do." And that sentiment is what always finishes things in my dad's mind.

The message I carried to those black law enforcement officers was measured but blunt. The problem of black-on-black crime, I argued, was approaching crisis proportions. It could not be tolerated. While we could not waver in our struggle to eradicate crime's root causes, we could not allow the persistence of those causes to serve as an excuse. As African Americans active in the criminal justice system, I said, we had a special responsibility to act in this matter since our community was suffering the most.

To my immense pleasure—and relief—the response among African Americans at that meeting and elsewhere was overwhelmingly positive. In Los Angeles, we launched a new dialogue between black law enforcement officers and black prosecutors in the offices of the D.A. and city attorney. By pooling information, we quickly became aware of just how serious the plague of gang violence had become. Out of that discussion came the district attorney's new Hardcore Gang Unit.

One of the first prosecutors I assigned to the unit was an unusually bright, hardworking young lawyer named Lance Ito. About that same time, I hired a tall, serious attorney as one of our new prosecutors. His name was Bill Hodgman. Years later, fate would reunite us under circumstances no one could have foreseen.

Because of our vigorous pursuit of police misconduct cases, Gil Garcetti and I became the target of a great deal of sniping and bad feeling on the part of the office's more conservative prosecutors. In 1980, the feeling against me escalated when Geronimo Pratt returned to Judge Kathleen Parker's court for what proved to be his last hearing for many years to come. On my personal stationery, I wrote the Department of Corrections a letter once again asserting Pratt's innocence.

A furor erupted. Van de Kamp called me on the carpet. The

office's position, he said, was that Geronimo Pratt was guilty and that his trial had been fair and untainted. As assistant district attorney, I was creating a problem by taking a contrary stance in public.

"I don't agree," I said. "You can take this job and shove it. I know this man is innocent."

"Well," Van de Kamp said coolly, "you're entitled to your opinion."

"You're darned right I am," I snapped. "It's what I said before I took this job, it's what I'm saying now, and it's what I'll be saying long after I'm gone."

To his credit, John let the matter drop. But some of my colleagues were not similarly inclined. I've always had a taste for exotic pets. In those days, I had an aquarium in my office. Its star resident was a beautiful red fire eel, rare and expensive. One morning, I came to work and found it dead on the office carpet. The aquarium had a top to prevent such accidents. The top was still firmly in place. There was a lot of snickering around the office about "Cochran's dead eel." I never saw the joke, but I got the point.

I think I felt the impact of that incident with particular force because of something that had occurred a short time before. John Van de Kamp, who was running for reelection, held a Sunday-afternoon fund-raiser at Hollywood's Magic Castle, a club that, as the name implies, specializes in all sorts of theatrical magic. It was a wonderful event, and I took ten-year-old Tiffany and seven-year-old Jonathan, both of whom thoroughly enjoyed themselves.

The sunny afternoon seemed just as magical as the show, and, after it was over, I had promised the children we would go shopping for some toys they wanted. We were in my brown Rolls, driving down Sunset Boulevard at about thirty-five miles per hour, when I heard the siren and saw the lights of an advancing police car closing in behind us.

Suddenly, I heard the blare of a loudspeaker: "Pull over."

I slowed and pulled over to the curb. As we rolled to a halt, three other police cruisers screeched to a stop around us. The officers inside leaped out and, with guns drawn, took up crouching positions behind the open doors of their cars. I sensed my children's silent terror. I thought of Leonard Deadwyler and of how his wife, Barbara, wept in fear. This is how it must have felt, I thought.

"Get out of the car," one of the officers barked. "Put your hands over your head, and move to the curb."

I knew too much about what could happen to act on the anger and humiliation I felt. At that moment, those cops were the most powerful men in Los Angeles, more powerful than the assistant district attorney, more powerful than any judge or jury. They could end my life and those of my children in a second and go on to explain the whole thing away—just another tragic accident.

I went to the curb, hands above my head, still dressed in the silk shirt, suit, and tie I had worn to the district attorney's fund-raiser.

One of the officers, an older man with graying hair, approached our car, his gun aimed directly at the backseat where Jonathan, my seven-year-old son, sat shaking.

"Don't point that gun at my son," I said.

Both children were crying by then. "Daddy, please make them stop," one of them sobbed.

"Daddy's in trouble now," one of the other cops laughed.

I had left the bag with my identification sitting on the driver's seat. The gray-haired cop snorted loudly as he reached inside and scooped it up. He opened it, fumbled around, and then pulled out my gold district attorney's badge with the numeral "three" emblazoned on it.

He dropped badge and bag, staring at me in disbelief.

"Get your sergeant out here now," I hissed.

Over the next few minutes, he stammered out a confused and contradictory story about my car matching the description of a stolen vehicle.

It was my turn to snort. "You thought this car was stolen? Do you see those license plates—'JCJR'? I've had those personalized plates on every car I've owned for the last fifteen years. You stopped me because I'm a black man driving an expensive car and for no other reason. That's unconscionable. Now get your supervisor out here. I want a report made on this."

Putting those bigots in their place was the easy part. Explaining what had happened to my traumatized children seemed suddenly impossible. It was their first brush with racism. They were fearful and confused, and I was deeply, deeply ashamed that I had not been able to shield them, as my parents had protected me from so very much.

Poor little Jonathan just sat beside me and quietly cried. Tiffany, the future journalist, was full of questions.

"Daddy," she said, "I thought you and the police were on the same side."

"I'm on the same side as the good police," I replied.

"Aren't all the police good?" she asked.

"No, sweetheart, I'm afraid not," I said.

"Why did they stop our car?" she asked.

"I'm not sure, sweetheart," I lied.

"I think it's because we're black," she said and turned to look out at the sun-drenched streets of Hollywood that somehow had lost their luster. I knew what she was feeling, though she didn't yet have a name for it. It was "two-ness," and there was nothing left to do but sit silently together and share what could not be denied.

Gentlemanly John Van de Kamp was enraged when he heard of the incident. So, too, was my friend Bernie Parks. I even received an apology from Daryl Gates, L.A.'s chief of police. But my perspective was changing. Things I might otherwise have put aside began to loom larger in my mind.

One day, for example, John, a couple of other prosecutors, and I were meeting in his office when somebody came in asking for approval to obtain a warrant to search the office of a well-known black lawyer in South Los Angeles. A brief discussion ensued, then suddenly died. I caught a couple of sidelong glances.

"What do you guys think I'm going to do?" I demanded. "Run out of here and warn 'the brother' you're coming? Last time I checked, we were all on the same side."

"Two-ness," again.

Syd Irmas had been right. As the end of my three-year term approached, I began to get offers from a variety of major law firms. It was time for a change—and not only for that reason. For now, I had done what I could on the "inside." Reform forced from there would be painfully slow and incremental and inevitably would entail compromises I was increasingly loath to make.

Like Thurgood Marshall, I had decided that my purpose as a lawyer was to change things for the better. But to do that, I had learned, sometimes you really do have to stand alone outside and pound on the door with both fists.

Time to go. Time to get stepping.

8

"He Was Our Pride and Joy"

MANY ATTORNEYS BELIEVE THAT CRIMINAL LAW IN-
evitably surrounds its practitioners with an aura that is at best
raffish and, sometimes, downright disreputable. I've never shared
that sentiment. To me, the criminal defense lawyer—usually
underpaid and always underappreciated—is the single most vigi-
lant sentinel on the rampart of American liberty. But many of the
friends who encouraged me to join the district attorney's office
believed that a stint at the prosecution's table would "clean up"
my résumé, opening the way to judicial appointment or even
public office.

None of my own aspirations inclined in that direction. But
apparently, my friends were right. As my term in the D.A.'s
office wound down, I began to receive feelers from some of Los

Angeles' largest established law firms. It was a time of discreet but opulent lunches with well-groomed, well-mannered men in gracious restaurants, of chummy early-evening cocktails in soothing, clubby settings. It was fascinating. It was flattering. It wasn't me.

I had no intention of giving up criminal defense work, but I was firmly resolved not to be limited to it, as so many of my black colleagues traditionally had been. What I envisioned was my own sort of full-service law firm, one that somehow would embody the tireless idealism of Thurgood Marshall and the stylish savvy of Leo Branton. It would do criminal, personal injury, entertainment, and sports law. It might even involve itself in municipal finance, which was then a lucrative, though virtually segregated, legal specialty. It nonetheless interested me because equal access to the credit markets clearly was one of the keys to solving urban America's mounting problems. I wanted a firm that would include men and women of all races and ethnicities but one that would always be particularly attentive to the needs of the African American and other disadvantaged communities.

But no matter what I envisioned, I also had to face facts. The previous three years had been rewarding but hardly lucrative. I had made $149,000, out of which I met my own expenses and mortgage, while supporting my three children. I was not, as they say, in a "capital formation" mode.

Once again, I turned to Syd Irmas for advice. And, this time, he responded not only with good counsel but also with a proposition. He invited me to join him in the Century City offices of Trope and Trope, one of Los Angeles' leading domestic relations firms. Syd, who always has believed that low overhead is the key to a successful law practice, had worked out a terrific arrangement: Trope and Trope would give us office and secretarial space, and, in return, we would refer to it any divorces that came our way. In the meantime, Syd and I could work on our own cases, cooperating whenever we had a client who required more than one attorney.

So, on January 2, 1981, I drove not into downtown but toward the sea—to my new offices in Century City, a shimmering enclave of gleaming office towers, luxury hotels, expensive shops, trendy restaurants, and theaters just south and west of Beverly Hills. Century City, which is far enough west to catch the ocean breezes, is home to many of the city's leading entertainment companies, as well as to the law firms and financial service companies that depend on them. At the time, my new environment felt like a bracing hybrid of Wall Street and Hollywood, a long way from mid-Wilshire and just the place for a bright young former prosecutor eager to make his fresh start.

Our new arrangement worked just as Syd predicted, and having the opportunity to practice law side by side after so many years of friendship was a priceless experience. But, as the months wore on, I began to feel a haunting sense of disconnection. The cases were good; our prospects were better. But this place was not *my* place. These clients were not *my* clients. Most important, the firm's purpose was *not* my own.

"Two-ness," again. And, by then, I had learned through hard experience that the dilemma it posed never could be resolved from behind the desk of a chic and comfortable Century City law office, where manners were polished, voices were modulated, and everyone knew how to play the game. Frederick Douglass had a similar sentiment in mind when—with his usual prophetic clarity—he wrote:

> If there is no struggle, there is no progress. Those who profess to favor freedom, and yet deprecate agitation, are men who want crops without plowing up the ground. They want rain without thunder and lightning. . . . The struggle may be a moral one; or it may be a physical one; or it may be both moral and physical; but

it must be a struggle. Power concedes nothing without a demand.
It never did and it never will.

That, I began to realize, was the real lesson of my years in the
district attorney's office, as productive and satisfying as they
may have been. Douglass was right about the nature of power,
its natural inertia and reflexive self-protection. My three years as
a "powerful insider" simply had confirmed what I always had
suspected peering in from the outside. Looking back, it is hard
not to see the hand of Providence at work. For just as these
sobering thoughts began to afflict me, the means to act on them
presented itself.

It was a hot day in June of 1981, and the sleek, fashionable
people strolling in the sunlight beneath my office windows were
in shirtsleeves and summer dresses. My business lunch had taken
longer than expected, and, as I hurried back through the door of
Trope and Trope, my secretary, Jackie Simms, told me that the
couple who were my next appointment were already seated in
my office.

I went in and made my apologies to Helen and Donell Settles,
a middle-aged African American couple whose obvious pain and
immense dignity seemed somehow a somber reproach to the
heedless, sun-washed scene outside. Like my father, Donell Settles had sold insurance for Golden State Mutual, and I already
knew why he and Helen had come. The exploits of their twenty-
one-year-old son and only child, Ron, were familiar to anybody
in Los Angeles who read the sports pages. As an all-city running
back at Wilmington's Banning High School, a perennial football
powerhouse, Ron had broken a string of records. He went on to
do the same at California State University, Long Beach, and—
with his senior season still before him—was listed as a prospect
by the Dallas Cowboys.

The pro football scouts, however, never would see Ron play another game. Neither would anybody else.

Just days before his parents took their seats in my office, Ron Settles was found dead—allegedly by his own hand—in the Signal Hill jail, where he'd been taken following a routine traffic stop.

A decayed relic of Southern California's early twentieth-century oil boom, Signal Hill is a community of fewer than six thousand people sandwiched between Los Angeles to the north and the port city of Long Beach to the south. It was then a tightly knit, notoriously corrupt little place whose brutal police force had a reputation that smelled like one of the town's depleted oil wells. When you were in the district attorney's office, you quickly learned not to trust anything the Signal Hill police force did. As prosecutors, we treated the city and its cops as if they resided on some distant, lawless planet. But we also knew that outsiders, particularly minority people, avoided the area like the plague. In those days, it was risky even to drive through Signal Hill, especially at night.

On June 2, 1981, however, Settles was late for his part-time job as a student teacher and coach at a nearby junior high school. To make up time, he turned his shiny Triumph sports car onto a shortcut that ran through Signal Hill. The official account of what followed initially went like this: Shortly before noon, a Signal Hill police officer named Jerry Lee Brown claimed he clocked Settles driving forty-seven miles per hour in a twenty-five-miles-per-hour zone. He pulled the young man's TR-7 over. Brown claimed that when he approached the car, Settles became "loud and obnoxious" and refused to get out of the vehicle. Brown called for backup, and, when three other officers arrived, Settles purportedly reached under his seat and pulled out a nine-inch stainless steel knife. The officers drew their guns; Settles allegedly surrendered. A subsequent search of his car, the police said, turned up a "cocaine kit" consisting of a spoon, razor, plastic card, and small vial containing residue of the drug. At first, the officers said the kit was found "around" the sports car's passenger seat. Later, they would claim it was discovered in the trunk.

Settles was handcuffed and taken to the Signal Hill police station, where he was booked on charges of failing to produce an identification card, possession of cocaine, resisting arrest, and assault on a police officer. The last charge was filed because Brown and the other officers alleged that during the course of his booking, Settles kicked them and grabbed at Brown's crotch. Initially, the cops would allege that they subdued the young man by striking him on the legs with their batons. Later, after the examination of Settles' body turned up evidence of numerous blows to his head, face, and upper body, the police would admit they struck him there, too.

According to the police, Settles initially declined to make the phone call to which he was legally entitled and was placed alone in a holding cell. After about an hour, he made a phone call to his mother, who immediately made arrangements to bail him out. Prior to bail being posted, at 2:35 P.M., the police alleged, an officer went to Settles' cell and found him hanging from the bars, the mattress cover from his bunk knotted tightly around his throat.

He was dead.

I sat there in silence and listened as Donell and Helen Settles recited the details of the story they'd been told. They were a handsome couple in their mid-forties, quiet and well spoken. I don't think they had an ounce of self-pity between them, just a deep and wrenching sorrow and an aching sense of loss that they knew would be their companion for the rest of their lives. Helen's hypertension, they told me, had prevented her from bearing other children. Their relationship with Ron had been a close one. Like my own family, they ate together, attended church together, even exercised together. In fact, the three of them had shared dinner and a workout the night before Ron's death. It was clear from what his parents said that Ron had been their entire life. He not only carried a football, he carried all their hopes and dreams. The hardworking, loving young man his parents knew had never been in trouble and had never used drugs. Helen and Donell were sure that the only knife their son had ever owned was the penknife he used to pry his car's broken antenna up when he wanted to listen to the radio. But accusations of drug use and assaulting police officers weren't what troubled Donell and Helen most.

"They say our son took his life, Mr. Cochran," Donell Settles said to me in a voice as raw as an open wound. "We know he didn't take his life. We know our son better than anybody else. He would not take his own life."

One of the things that distinguishes a good civil lawyer is his or her ability to evaluate a case. As I sat there listening and watching Helen and Donell Settles, it was clear to me their case had "loser" written all over it. Their son was dead. Everyone who was in the jail when his body was discovered was a police officer, and they would all lie to protect one another. There were no other witnesses. The Settleses, respectable hardworking people though they are, were still a family of modest means. There would be no retainer for their attorney, no advances to cover expenses. Any lawyer who took this case would be working for a contingency fee and financing all the costs out of his own pocket. And, at the end of the day, the chances that there would be anything to show for it were virtually zero.

I had not spent three years in the district attorney's office and moved out west to Century City to pursue lost causes. My mentors were Marshall and Branton, not Don Quixote. I was not a cynic, but I was a realist. And it seemed to me that the best thing I could do for Donell and Helen Settles was to share gently a little of that realism with them. I explained their problematic legal position, how protracted and expensive any litigation would be.

Finally, I told them, "You must remember that no amount of money can bring your son back. And, at this stage, the tragedy is that money is the only recompense society can offer you for this terrible loss you've suffered."

"Mr. Cochran," Donell replied, "we're not interested in money. All we want is to find out what really happened to our son."

I nodded in silent understanding, then prepared to tell them how unlikely it was that even that simple, decent thing could be accomplished. But before I could get another word out, Helen Settles reached into her bag and withdrew a framed photograph.

It was a studio portrait of a smiling, strikingly handsome young man who had his father's bristling mustache and his mother's level, lively gaze. His own strong features seemed chiseled from the same faultless ebony as his parents'. I recognized him from the sports pages. It was Ron Settles.

No precious jewel, no sacred icon, no fragile babe in arms ever was handled with the loving tenderness with which Helen Settles hugged that photograph to her breast before holding it out to me. As I struggled to frame the words I hoped would send her home with her grief, Helen Settles extended her dead son's portrait across the desk to me and said: "But, Mr. Cochran, he was our pride and joy."

A hard-nosed civil lawyer would have swallowed hard and sent them away. Hattie Cochran's son blinked back his tears and said: "I know that, Mrs. Settles, and I'll move heaven and earth, if that's what it takes, to make them tell us what really happened to your boy. I won't rest a day, not one, until we find the truth."

I was on the case. It was a terrible business decision, and I couldn't have felt better about it. The cause that I had taken as my own all those long years before in the kitchen at Leimert Park had found me once again—even in far-off Century City. And, like David, I prayed, "Lord that delivered me out of the paw of the lion, and out of the paw of the bear, deliver me out of the hand of this Philistine."

"This time, Lord," I prayed with all my heart and in my own words, "let me not fail these good people. Let my stone, like David's, find its mark."

The first order of business was to prepare for the coroner's inquest scheduled to begin in just two months. In the fifteen years since the Deadwyler case, that process had changed profoundly. During my term in the D.A.'s office, I had worked with two progressive young Los Angeles–area legislators—Yvonne Braithwaite Burke and Alan Sieroty—to help rewrite California's law governing coroner's inquiries. Unlike Leonard Deadwyler's, Ron Settles' death would be probed in a full-dress, adversarial inquest in which those of us representing the family would have the right to call and question witnesses and to argue directly to the nine-person jury.

I knew I would need help preparing our case and thought immediately of Mike Mitchell, a young white lawyer with a mop of curly hair, a clipped mustache, and a pugnaciously jutting chin that suggested just what kind of law he practiced. We had met while I was assistant district attorney. Mitchell came to see me about one of his clients, an African American minister from Venice against whom the LAPD had trumped up charges of interfering with a police officer. I took one look at the case, recognized the old 148 trick when I saw it, and suggested that all charges be dismissed. Mitchell and I became friends. He was a brilliant young man who had studied mathematics at the University of North Carolina and law at Harvard, then worked as an attorney for the Securities and Exchange Commission. After a brief time, he'd left federal service to practice as a civil rights attorney. In Los Angeles, he was at the center of a small cadre of lawyers trying to fight police brutality by focusing on the LAPD's misuse of the deadly carotid choke hold. I thought he'd make an ideal partner in the Settles case.

I phoned him not long after Donell and Helen Settles left my office. "Mitchell," I said, "I have this fascinating case." He listened in silence as I ran through the details. "Cochran," he said, "*we* have this fascinating case." Our cooperation cemented our friendship. We went on to work on a number of other cases together as Mike joined my firm, working until the early 1990s in our Los Angeles office. In 1991, he became a partner in our Washington, D.C., office with my other partner, Ralph Lotkin, under the name Cochran, Mitchell & Lotkin.

The differences between Ron Settles' inquest and the one conducted into the death of Leonard Deadwyler went well beyond courtroom procedures. For one thing, Leonard was a simple workingman, unknown to nearly everyone but his family and friends. Ron was a star athlete, admired by his fans and held in real affection by his teammates and coaches, many of them white. In the weeks leading up to the inquest, many of them gave interviews in which they flatly denied that Settles used drugs, was violent or confrontational, or could ever have become depressed enough to commit suicide. The climate in which those interviews were received also was markedly different, in large part, because of an incident that had occurred a few years before. At the height of the Vietnam War, a major peace rally had been staged in Century City. After what the LAPD later would claim was a series of provocations, the officers on the scene attacked the demonstrators in what subsequently became popularly known as a police riot. Hundreds of young people from affluent and middle-class white families—and even some of their teachers and parents—were gassed, beaten, and arrested on flimsy charges. For the first time, a substantial segment of Los

Angeles' majority community had been made to confront the fact that LAPD misconduct was neither rare nor aberrational.

As a consequence of that new wariness, the area's three leading newspapers—the *Times*, the *Herald-Examiner*, and the Long Beach *Press-Telegram*—dispatched investigative reporters to Signal Hill following Ron Settles' death. Their reports were published immediately before and after the inquest, and the portrait they painted was shocking. In the five years before Settles died, scores of people had been seriously injured by Signal Hill's tiny police force. Some had just been beaten; others had been locked in small cells and then subjected to assaults by vicious attack dogs, some of them borrowed for the purpose from the owner of a nearby junkyard. One such man, an epileptic tossed into jail following a seizure, was bitten 116 times. One woman, a Guatemalan immigrant, suffered so many bites in her groin that she required surgery. Among those beaten were a retired white LAPD officer, a black Baptist minister, and a disabled Latino veteran with two artificial legs. Worst of all, another man allegedly had hanged himself in the jail just a week before Ron's death. Moreover, Jerry Brown, the same officer who had arrested Ron Settles, had allegedly used his flashlight to beat a young Latino, Reuben Carrillo, so badly that he had lapsed into a coma and died. As the reporters also discovered, Brown himself had been fired by the LAPD on four counts of misconduct, including drug use and lying to his superiors.

The inquest into Ron Settles' death took eleven days. Nearly thirty witnesses testified. One of them, a white Long Beach attorney who witnessed Settles' arrest, flatly contradicted the officers' account of that event. Another, the only other inmate in the jail when Settles was booked, testified that he heard Ron endure at least two beatings by the police and that he himself was mysteriously taken out of the jail shortly before Settles' body was discovered. Both he and another inmate, who previously had occupied the cell in which Settles died, testified that its bunk did not have a mattress cover, the object Ron purportedly knotted around his own neck.

One of the coroner's forensic pathologists testified that Settles died by hanging, another that the cause of death could have been either hanging or strangulation. None of the coroner's tests found traces of cocaine, alcohol, or any other drug in Ron's body.

Signal Hill's police chief told a variety of stories about Ron Settles' death. He also testified that all tape recordings of the radio traffic surrounding Ron's arrest and booking had inexplicably been erased. He could not explain why his officers, upon finding Settles hanging from the bars of his cell, had waited at least six minutes to summon paramedics, who might have revived him. Furthermore, he could offer no explanation as to why his department had withheld the mattress cover with which Ron allegedly hanged himself from the coroner for more than six weeks.

Most significant, when called to testify, six of the seven Signal Hill officers who were in the jail the night Settles died invoked their Fifth Amendment protection against self-incrimination. All were represented by my old city attorney colleague George Franscell, a fine lawyer who specialized in representing police officers. When asked by the commissioner presiding over the hearing whether there was anything to which he would allow his clients to testify, George replied, "I don't want to be facetious, but you can ask them whether they brush their teeth."

George, an unrelenting advocate, was as good as his word. By that time, the district attorney's SID unit, still headed by my former colleague Gil Garcetti, had begun to take an interest in the case. Acting on Garcetti's orders, prosecutors attempted to interview Jerry Brown and the other officers. Once again, all claimed the protection of the Fifth Amendment.

On September 1, 1981, we argued our case to the coroner's jury of seven women and two men. Four of the women were African Americans; the two men were white, as were two of the women. The seventh woman was Asian American. The foreman they elected, we subsequently learned, was Richard L. Cain, the white minister of a conservative evangelical Protestant church in Glendale.

Mitchell and I previously had demonstrated to the panel just how we believed a police choke hold had killed Ron Settles. We both reminded the jurors of this during our summations. Mike began by quoting Ecclesiastes: " 'To everything there is a season,' " he said, " 'a time to live and a time to die.' This was Ron Settles' time to live—and somebody else caused him to die."

I followed him by reminding our jurors that everything they had heard pointed to the fact that Ron Settles "died at the hands of another. You are the conscience of the community," I told them, "and Ron Settles' voice cries out for justice. I hope you will hear his cry."

"The Signal Hill officers who found Ron's body," I told the jurors, "did not call the paramedics because they didn't want him revived. They killed him."

Three months to the day after Ron Settles was found hanging in his jail cell, following just five hours of deliberation, those seven women and two men returned their verdict. Settles, a majority of the jurors found, had "died at the hands of another and by other than accident." The panel had split almost precisely along racial lines. Our majority consisted of the four African American women and the young white pastor Richard L. Cain, who later would say he simply had "voted my conscience." However, while the racial makeup of our majority was widely commented upon at the time, most observers missed an important characteristic Cain shared with those four black women: They were the panel's only college-educated members.

The very next day, acting on behalf of Helen and Donell Settles, Mike Mitchell and I filed a $50 million claim against the city of Signal Hill for the wrongful death of Ron Settles. I still recall what Helen said when I phoned her with the news.

"All the money in the world will not replace our son," she said. "We've lost everything, and nothing will ever bring him back. Our family is extinct. We can't hope for grandkids, and there is nothing else to hope for. It's very hard to accept that we now have nothing."

Still, Helen told me, she and Donell had begun to include the people of Signal Hill in their prayers. "I feel sorry for them," she said softly. "There's so much injustice and inhumanity there. We're praying for those people every night."

Our case, too, required Helen's prayers. On January 14, 1982, our hopes of a criminal prosecution were dashed when my former boss, District Attorney John Van de Kamp, and my former co-worker, Gil Garcetti, announced that their office was closing the Settles case. Their investigation had turned up massive misconduct in the Signal Hill police force. Three current officers and one retired cop would be prosecuted for felony brutality against other prisoners. Ron Settles' case, however, was over as far as the prosecutors were concerned.

At a press conference explaining his decision not to pursue the matter, Van de Kamp conceded, "We cannot say with absolute finality that a crime was not committed. But there is insufficient evidence to establish the identity of anyone as the perpetrator of any crime directly related to Mr. Settles' death."

In other words, the conspiracy of silence had prevailed once again. Criminal cops were free to pursue their lawlessness behind an apparently impregnable stone wall.

Though he would continue to endorse his boss's decision on Settles, Garcetti, as head of SID, went on to express his particular frustration with the six Signal Hill officers who stopped his investigation cold with their invocation of the Fifth

Amendment. "We should have asked the chief to order them to testify," he said. "If they had then invoked the Fifth, we could have asked for administrative discipline, including dismissal from the force. I think police officers sit in a different position from normal citizens in that there is a greater expectation from the public as to what their responsibilities are . . . and they should come forward and testify."

I welcomed those sentiments at the time. Years later, I would recall them when District Attorney Garcetti and his handpicked deputies stood by in utter silence while LAPD detective Mark Fuhrman invoked his protection against self-incrimination in O. J. Simpson's trial. It never has ceased to amaze me how self-interest and the passage of the years can still the voice of a person's conscience. "I used to know Gil Garcetti," I mused, as I drove home that night during the Simpson case. "Now I wonder if he even knows himself."

As time wore on, our opponents did everything they could to harm Ron Settles' reputation, particularly with allegations of drug use. A second, more sophisticated set of tests had been run on his blood samples, and they purported to find minute traces of PCP. The scientists were quick to point out, however, that the amounts were so small that they could have entered his system if he had simply walked through a room where the drug was being smoked. Still, such allegations were potentially damaging, and they grated harshly on Donell and Helen Settles, who had forbidden anyone even to smoke in their house for fear of harming their athlete son. "Ron couldn't even stand to be around cigarette smoke," Donell told me over and over.

Gradually, almost unwillingly, I came to a conclusion about what our next step would have to be. It wasn't something you could discuss over the phone, so I went to see the Settleses in person. "I know this is extremely painful," I told them, "but I would like you to consider allowing us to exhume Ron's body and have it reautopsied. I would not have it done in our county," I explained. "I want to go as far away as possible and get the very best doctors we can find. In fact, I have two in mind." They were Michael Baden, the country's finest forensic pathologist, and Sidney Weinberg, both of whom were then working in Suffolk County, New York.

I already had spoken to them, and they had agreed to perform the autopsy and all related tests for just $500, the cost of opening their county lab for a day. It was my first encounter with Baden, who later would also play a pivotal role in the Simpson trial, and I liked him from the start. "Look," he said in his unmistakable New York accent, "we'll do it for nothing, but we're going to call it the way we see it. In other words, if we find drugs or anything else that hurts your case, we find whatever we find, Johnnie. That's the way it has to be."

I explained all that to Mr. and Mrs. Settles. They never flinched. "Our son did not use drugs," Donell said with finality. "He did not hang himself. We have no doubts about him, and so we have no fears about what anybody may find."

Helen had a more personal concern. Not long after his death, Ron had been buried in the family plot in Memphis, Tennessee. "Go ahead and take him, if that's what you must do, Mr. Cochran," she said to me. "But promise me this. Whatever happens, you won't leave my son be alone. I want you to be there with his body from the moment he is taken from the ground until he is put back in his coffin and buried again in Memphis. Whatever happens, whatever is done to him, promise me you'll be there. Promise me you won't leave him."

"I promise," I said. "Mr. Mitchell or I will stay with Ron no matter what."

I was about to discover what a commitment like that meant.

I went ahead to New York to finalize the arrangements, and Mike flew to Memphis, where he met officials of the Suffolk

County coroner's office who would take custody of the body the minute it was exhumed. I still vividly recall Mike's call from Tennessee.

"Cochran, I can't believe this," he said through fits of coughing. "Jesus Christ, the smell when they dug the casket up! One of the gravediggers even threw up."

The Suffolk County officials wrapped the coffin in a security seal—the sort of yellow adhesive tape you see around crime scenes—then all of them went directly to the airport and flew on to New York, where the autopsy was to be performed the next day.

I spoke with Helen Settles by phone from my midtown Manhattan hotel, reassuring her that Mitchell was with Ron's body and that both of us would be present in the morning. I promised to call her as soon as the autopsy was over. As routine as it may sound, that brief telephone conversation was a turning point in my education as a lawyer. I dreaded what I knew was coming the next day. I remember sitting there in silence on my bed, the sounds of New York's ceaseless traffic rolling in through the open window.

This, I thought, is what it means to be an advocate. It's not just preparing papers, going to court, or even slugging it out in cross-examination. It's agreeing to be the eyes and ears of two grieving and wounded people. It's accepting *all* the responsibility that comes with their trust in you as a professional and their faith in you as a person.

These two people have entrusted me with all that remains of the most precious thing they ever created together. More than that, they are relying on me to build their son's real memorial on a foundation of justice—and the first stone in his monument is the act of witness I have to perform tomorrow.

I looked down and saw that my hands were shaking, not with apprehension but with the power of revelation. This is what Thurgood Marshall knew, I thought. Being a lawyer means not only sharing the pain of other people's suffering but also accepting the burden of their trust. In the final moment, being a lawyer isn't about winning or losing. It's about keeping faith.

The next morning, Mike Mitchell and I made our way past a crowd of reporters and network camera operators and down into the basement of the Suffolk County coroner's office. Baden and Weinberg already were there, along with Dr. Werner Spitz, the chief medical examiner of Wayne County, Michigan, who had been retained at great expense by Signal Hill, and Dr. Thomas Noguchi, the L.A. county coroner. Signal Hill's lawyer, Inlow "Skip" Campbell, also was present, as were Gil Garcetti and a number of other people from both the Los Angeles County and Suffolk County district attorney offices. All and all, about thirty people crowded into the examining room.

Baden quickly warned us that we ought to change into surgical clothes since the smell would permeate our suits and make them unwearable, probably forever. Everyone but Campbell took his advice, a decision he came to regret. Baden and Weinberg already had warned us that after eight months in the ground, there was no way to tell what sort of shape Ron Settles' body might be in. If it were too badly decayed, they warned us, all this would have been for nothing.

"If any water leaked into that casket," one of them casually remarked to me, "we're going to be looking at nothing but soup."

So, for more than one reason, I quite literally held my breath as the seals were broken and Ron's casket was opened. Inside was a body almost miraculously preserved. Together, the pathologists lifted it out of the coffin and placed it on the table, where their examination began. I had never witnessed an autopsy before, so this was also my first exposure to "forensic humor."

Most of Ron Settles' organs had been removed in the first autopsy, and to stabilize his body the undertaker had filled the chest cavity with sand and newspapers. As one of the doctors began to remove them, he motioned me over to the table.

"Look how well read your client is, Mr. Cochran," he quipped, holding up crumpled copies of *The Wall Street Journal*.

At another point, this doctor slipped and cut himself with a scalpel. "Damn it," he snapped, waving his hand around.

"Don't worry about it, Werner," one of the other doctors said. "Nothing could live in there."

From the outset it was clear to Baden and Weinberg just how sloppy a job the L.A. coroner's office had done. Noguchi's staff simply had taken the Signal Hill cops' word that Settles had hanged himself. They had never done even the most rudimentary things that might have shown otherwise. For example, they never X-rayed Ron's body. When Baden and Weinberg did so, they discovered several broken bones. I still recall watching as they peeled back Ron's skin. The muscle tissue was dark. All the doctors were amazed at his physical conditioning. He had almost no visible fat, which is yellow. What he did have—as Baden quickly pointed out—were dozens of bruises on his face, neck, and upper torso. When a dark-skinned person is beaten shortly before death, the bruises do not have time to show on their skin's surface. Only a meticulous autopsy reveals them. The L.A. coroners had missed most of them.

On and on they cut, peeled, sawed, and probed. At some point, the pathologists sent out for sandwiches, which they ate standing around the table. As the day wore on, the odor became overwhelming. I've never been able to stand the smell of tobacco, but I stood as close as I possibly could to Mitchell, a chain-smoker who lit one cigarette after another. When even that began to fail, we popped ammonia inhalers under our noses.

Finally, Baden and Weinberg found what Mitchell and I had suspected all along—esophageal hemorrhaging. In other words, Ron Settles' windpipe had been crushed against his spine. The compression was "bilateral," meaning it had been applied from one direction. He had been choked to death by a carotid choke hold.

After more than thirteen hours, the autopsy was over. Baden walked up to me and said, "Look, I'm ready to announce the results right now. This man was killed." He pointed out that he had examined the bodies of more than one thousand people who had committed suicide by hanging and that they all exhibited substantial injuries to the tissue around the esophagus. Only a choke hold produces the kind of compression Settles suffered.

Weinberg was equally emphatic. Settles' esophageal injuries, he said, were "never associated with a simple suicidal hanging." He said that based on the day's autopsy, he would list Ron's death as "a probable homicide . . . caused by a combination of carotid and bar-arm choke holds."

Spitz, Signal Hill's paid consultant, denied that Ron's throat injury was the cause of his death. Noguchi continued to insist, "I lean toward hanging."

There was, however, one issue on which the four pathologists completely agreed: Ron's body contained no trace of any drug, including cocaine and PCP.

Mitchell and I showered, then I went to call Mr. and Mrs. Settles. "I'm sorry it took so long," I said. "But we now know what happened to your son. They beat him, then they put him in a choke hold and he died. We may not find a living witness, but because of your courage in letting us go ahead with this, Ron came back from the grave to tell us what happened to him. He never could have done that without you."

Driving back to Manhattan that night, I thought of how right my own mother had been all those years ago in Shreveport. "What's done in the dark will come to the light," she always said. "Truth crushed to earth will rise again."

But for some people, even the risen truth isn't enough.

Garcetti, who had endured the same marathon autopsy as the rest of us and listened to the unequivocal opinions of two of America's leading forensic pathologists, nonetheless decided not to prosecute anyone for killing Ron Settles.

Back in Los Angeles, Mitchell and I prepared to press ahead with our suit. Then Donell called. Helen's hypertension, he explained, was much more serious than either of them had ever let on. More to the point, her condition had worsened dramatically in the months since their son's death. Helen's doctors were concerned about her, and her ability to survive a lengthy trial. "Do you think you can settle this case now?" Donell asked.

"Yes, I think I can," I said, trying to keep the disappointment out of my voice, "but, you know, this really is one where you should think about going all the way." My dream at the time was to win my first million-dollar verdict as a civil lawyer. And to do it in a police misconduct case would be almost too sweet. "Are you sure you don't want to think this over?" I asked.

"No," Donell Settles replied. "We have proved our point."

Suddenly, I recalled that quiet couple in my Century City office and knew they meant it when they told me they wanted the truth and not money.

Still, when I called Skip Campbell, Signal Hill's lawyer, about a settlement, I couldn't help making a $1 million demand.

"Well, Johnnie, I don't want to insult you," he said, "but I think your number is a little high. All we've got is six hundred thousand dollars."

Nobody had ever offered me that much in a civil case. For years, I'd been settling little personal injury suits for $10,000 and $12,000. Furthermore, this offer was for the kind of case that I cared most about. I did my best to remain cool.

"I'm not insulted, Skip," I said, "but I really don't think my clients possibly can go that low."

Eventually, we settled on $760,000, which provoked the only

quarrel Mitchell and I ever had. He was adamant about pushing on. It wasn't just that he wanted the $1 million; he wanted to expose the whole rotten Signal Hill mess in as public a way as possible. So did I, but there were more important issues.

"Mitchell," I said, "this is our clients' case, not ours. They want to settle for seven hundred sixty thousand dollars, and that is what we are going to do."

In fact, in the wake of our settlement, Signal Hill's city government was thrown out of office and a reform slate voted in that hired outside consultants who directed a cleanup of the police department and its relationship with the local city hall. It was a kind of civics lesson on what the civil justice system can accomplish when it is allowed to do its job.

For their part, Helen and Donell Settles were at peace with the result Mitchell and I obtained for them. They had learned the truth about their son's death. More important, they had been confirmed in the knowledge that the son they lost really was the son they knew. And that meant more to them than they could ever say.

It also meant more to me than I could say at the time. Tottering there on the edge of prosperous, respectable conformity, I had listened to my mother's voice and stepped back from the brink. I had done the heart's thing, not the smart thing. I had made an almost impossible promise to Helen and Donell Settles. But God gave me the strength to keep it. His ways sometimes are mysterious, but He is always worthy to be praised.

In keeping faith with Helen and Donell, I had—for the first time—wounded my Philistine. In the process, I also had learned what it really meant to be another human being's advocate. Without that lesson, the struggle that still lay ahead would have been hopeless. But I had also learned that human advocacy—no matter how skillful or principled—always has its limits. Some wrongs simply are beyond our remedies.

Helen Settles, though still a young woman, died a few years after we settled her family's case. I spoke with her not long before her death. I've never forgotten the last thing she said to me: "Anyone who thinks that time heals all wounds is wrong."

No law, however just, no judge, however wise, no lawyer, however able, could relieve Helen Settles of her pain. But, unlike Barbara Deadwyler and Johnie Choyce, she did not have to bear the additional burden of believing her loved one died in vain. Our victory in Ron Settles' case marked a turning point in the fight against police misconduct in Los Angeles. The news media's intense focus on the case had given many in the majority community their first hard look at the problem.

More important, we lawyers were beginning to see in court the fruits of two parallel struggles we had waged for many years. One was the fight we had conducted against the use of peremptory challenges to remove individuals from juries based on their race. Prosecutors in criminal cases and defense attorneys in civil suits traditionally had tried to eliminate virtually all blacks and Latinos from their juries. Beginning in the 1980s, California's appellate courts began to restrict that practice dramatically. They also handed down a series of decisions directing the counties' jury commissioners to adopt practices that would increase the number of minority people in the overall jury pool.

The other struggle was carried out mainly by African American lawyers within our own community. For years, it had been clear to us that many black people simply avoided jury service. In the African American press and in our numerous community speaking engagements, we black lawyers had harped relentlessly on the importance of answering the summons to jury duty. By the early 1980s, our efforts had begun to have an impact. So, too, had the extension of affirmative action programs into both the local civil service and major corporations. For the first time, many African Americans had an equal shot at the kinds of jobs whose benefits included paid jury service. Tom Bradley's critical role in that process is one of his most unrecognized achievements.

The significance of opening jury service equally to citizens of all races and ethnicities has nothing to do with the alleged propensity of African American or other minority jurors to vote in favor of defendants and plaintiffs from their community. For one thing, the allegation is false. Anybody who has been in any big urban courthouse anywhere in this country, for example, knows that every day across this nation, black jurors routinely vote to convict other African Americans of crimes and send them to prison. Throughout the Southwest, juries with Latino majorities do the same to other Latinos.

The important point is that a jury is the conscience of its community. The existence of the jury is the most powerful expression of the American people's ultimate faith in the virtue of popular sovereignty. In these most critical matters—often involving life and death—we trust the interests of our community not to highly trained experts, towering intellectuals, or even elected officials. We entrust our welfare to twelve ordinary American people. We rely on their conscience, their goodwill, and the wisdom of their collective experience to dispense justice—without which liberty itself is a meaningless abstraction.

Juries that include all of a community's people, that allow for the expression of all their informed consciences, and take into account the sum of all their historical experiences simply are more competent to dispense justice. And if that justice is not always perfect—well, neither is anything else this side of the grave.

The Settles case marked a professional turning point for me. When I learned my powerful lesson about a real advocate's commitment to his clients, I came to understand that my craving for professional success could not be satisfied at the expense of my conscience or on terms other than my own. Century City was wonderful, but it was in every sense too far from my roots, my cases, and my people.

Syd and I parted better friends and closer allies than we ever had been, and I moved back to the mid-Wilshire district. I set up shop in a tall building on the edge of the Miracle Mile in a suite of offices whose sweeping views include not only my alma mater, L.A. High, but the tree-lined streets of Hancock Park and, beyond that, the hillside neighborhood where I live. My roots run deep through this neighborhood, and I haven't left.

During the negotiations over Ron Settles' case, I set a new personal goal for myself. The fiercely competitive, highly specialized California trial bar is divided fairly rigidly between lawyers who practice criminal law and those who try civil cases. At the apex of the criminal defense bar are those lawyers who try murder cases. To join the civil bar's elite, you have to win $1 million verdicts for your clients. Few, if any, California lawyers had ever done both. I resolved to become one of the first. And, almost before the Settles case was concluded, I got my chance.

Shortly before we concluded matters for Helen and Donell Settles, I received a phone call from my old friend and UCLA classmate Herbert Avery, the physician who had referred Barbara Deadwyler to me back in 1966. In the intervening years, Herb—a graduate of Howard University School of Medicine—had built an extremely successful practice of his own. He became the "gynecologist to the stars," and his celebrity clients had included the Supremes and quite a number of other Motown recording artists. Herb had joined the staff at Cedars-Sinai, one of Los Angeles' most prestigious hospitals, and purchased a home in the same hillside neighborhood in which I lived.

Then, one day in 1976, his whole world was turned upside down. Early that evening, Herb and his friend Pedro Ferrer, who was married to Mary Wilson, one of the original Supremes, were driving along Franklin Avenue on their way to a tennis match. A short time before, Avery's son, Herb Jr., had borrowed one of his father's cars. Not far from the house, the young man and his companion were stopped by a pair of LAPD officers, allegedly for a "defective taillight." Herb's son produced his driver's license, but was unable to locate the vehicle's registration. Consequently, the officers ordered both young men out of the car and into a nearby vacant lot. Both were told to put their hands above their heads.

That was the sight that greeted Herb and Pedro as they headed west on their way to a friendly tennis match. Alarmed, Herb pulled over, jumped out of his car, and approached the two policemen.

Herb is a tall, light-skinned African American man with a high forehead and a pencil mustache. He has a successful professional's precise diction and dignified bearing. He is always impeccably dressed. But before he could get a word out, according to later testimony, one of the officers sneered, "What have we got here? Here come two pimps."

Herb identified himself as a doctor and said, "This is my car, and that is my son. I'd like to know what's going on here."

At that point, one of the police officers drew his baton, struck Herb in the chest, and ordered him to "get out of the area, now."

"But I live here," Herb replied, which only seemed to further enrage his uniformed assailant.

"I told you to get out of the area," the officer said, using his baton to push Herb off the sidewalk and into the vacant lot. As his horrified son, his friend, and Pedro looked on helplessly, the other officer pulled Herb's shirt up over his head before kneeing him in the groin and kicking his feet out from under him. As the stunned physician crumpled to the ground, the first cop applied a bar-arm choke hold.

"I can't breathe," Herb somehow managed to gasp.

"Good, that's what I want," the officer laughed.

He then planted a knee in Herb's back, handcuffed him, and took him to the Hollywood police station where he was released on $500 bail. No charges were ever filed against him. The experience, however, left him in extraordinary physical and emotional torment. For the next six years, he lived with what he described as "relentless pain" in his neck. Worse, his secure sense of his place in his profession and his community had been destroyed. Depression had been his intermittent companion ever since his mistreatment. He filed a million-dollar damage suit against the City of Los Angeles, which is legally liable for the misconduct of its police officers.

Herb had been through a number of lawyers before he called me, and his suit was already set for trial in December of 1982. Time was short, but you don't turn a friend away.

The city attorney, a fellow named Richard James, called me shortly before the trial began with a settlement offer. I laughed when I heard it.

"Johnnie," he said, "be reasonable. Your guy is only out of pocket eleven thousand dollars for his medical bills. What do you want?"

"This isn't about money," I said. "See you in court."

This time there were lots of living witnesses. And none was better than Herbert Avery himself. As he described the pain and humiliation of his mistreatment at the hands of those two officers, this injured man who had healed so many, who had himself witnessed every variety of human suffering, simply collapsed into tears. There wasn't anyone in the courtroom, including the city attorney, who thought it was a performance. Our judge, a fine jurist named Richard "Skip" Byrne, asked Herb if he needed a recess.

"I'm just tired of it all," Herb said, rubbing at his wet eyes.

"Let's take a break," the unfailingly courteous Byrne said.

Twelve days later, I argued Herb's case to a jury of five

whites, four blacks, and three Latinos. Four of the panelists were women, five were men. I summarized for them the testimony of the more than thirty witnesses we had presented. I reminded them that Herb's lasting emotional and physical injuries had restricted his ability to practice as a surgeon. Then I recalled for them that those injuries were not the product of some harmless practice somehow gone awry.

"The choke hold," I told them, "is deadly. It can kill. These are permanent injuries. He is going to have them for the rest of his life, and he didn't ask for them . . . A father driving past—who among you would see your child stopped by the police and not stop? Any parent would do that," I said. "It is his absolute right. All he wanted to do was find out what he could do to help.

"Dr. Avery never resisted. The conduct of these officers is so negligent it is hard to describe. . . . Dr. Avery's life has been an example of the American dream at work. That's why this event hit him like a ton of bricks. Herbert Avery's story is the story of a man who rises above his beginnings and then, one day, finds himself being treated just as he was when he was poor and downtrodden.

"The one common denominator," I said, dropping my voice almost to a whisper, "is that rich or poor, benevolent or evil, smart or dumb, Herbert Avery is black."

Three days later, the jury returned a verdict in our favor and awarded Herbert Avery $1.3 million. It was my first million-dollar verdict, a landmark in the fight against police misconduct in Los Angeles, and the biggest jury award ever against the LAPD at that time.

Outside the courtroom, I told the press, "I believe this will have an important effect, not just in this case, but in others. This verdict sends a message to the city and its police department that the imposition of these choke holds is not only deadly but expensive as well."

It wasn't quite as expensive as it could have been, though. Exercising his authority under California's civil code, Judge Byrne cut the jury's award to $750,000. "Look, Johnnie," he said to me, "you did too good a job here. With eleven thousand dollars in medical bills, you shouldn't get a million out of this. Take the seven hundred and fifty thousand or face a new trial."

Herb Avery was reluctant, but he ultimately agreed.

By that time, Mike Mitchell and I were hard at work on the case that ultimately eliminated the choke hold as an instrument of police terror on the streets of Los Angeles. This time, the victim was a twenty-year-old African American man named James Thomas Mincey, Jr., a teacher's aide working with handicapped children for the L.A. Unified School District. Shortly before 10 P.M. on March 22, 1982, Mincey was driving to his mother's house in the east San Fernando Valley when he was stopped and cited for speeding by two LAPD officers, who also gave him an additional citation because the windshield of his 1974 Ford Pinto was cracked.

Mincey went on his way, and, a few minutes later, two other officers allegedly spotted the cracked windshield, turned on their patrol car's flashing overhead lights, and began to pursue the young man. For reasons nobody will ever know, he drove without stopping to the house of his mother, Rozella Fowler, who had divorced his father shortly after Mincey was born.

By then, a number of patrol cars had joined the pursuit. When Mincey stopped in front of his mother's house, one of the pursuing officers—Robert Simpach—allegedly grabbed the young man, slammed him against his car, and sprayed him twice with liquid tear gas. The terrified Mincey struggled to reach the sanctuary of his mother's house. Simpach and his partner attempted to handcuff the now blinded young man. Other officers came to their aid. One of them, Rolland Cannon, flipped Mincey, now handcuffed, to the ground and allegedly applied a carotid choke hold.

At that moment, Mrs. Fowler, aroused by the noise, rushed from her modest house shouting, "Please stop choking him. Please don't kill my son. Stop! Please, stop!"

As she approached her still struggling boy, one of the officers raised his baton as if to strike her. Nobody would ever be able to dispute that because one of the neighbors captured the entire scene with his Polaroid camera.

By then, her son's body was convulsing, his eyes rolled back into his head. Cannon, as he had been trained to do, maintained his hold on Mincey's neck until he passed into unconsciousness and then threw the body into the back of a squad car. When the police reached nearby Pacoima Memorial Hospital, James Thomas Mincey was in full cardiac arrest. He died two weeks later without ever regaining consciousness.

In the wake of Mincey's death, Mitchell and I, along with representatives of the NAACP, the Urban League, and the American Civil Liberties Union, appeared before the Los Angeles Police Commission, the civilian panel that theoretically oversees the city's police. We demanded that the commission ban the choke hold. Mitchell and I argued to the panel that not only was the hold intrinsically dangerous but also that the training in its use conducted at the L.A. Police Academy was fundamentally flawed. Recruits were trained, we pointed out, to continue administering the hold until a "suspect" stopped struggling. The problem, we argued, was that a large, physically well-conditioned man being choked might convulse involuntarily well after he had lost consciousness and suffered permanent, perhaps even fatal, damage.

I also contended that the officers' virtual absolute discretion on when to apply the hold was an open invitation to abuse. Citing James Thomas Mincey's death as an example, I said, "This is a case about a guy who was stopped for a traffic violation and was basically given the death penalty—right in front of his mother. He didn't deserve to die."

LAPD chief Daryl Gates bitterly opposed any commission action. After some deliberation, however, the panel declared a moratorium on the hold's use in any but "clearly life-threatening" circumstances.

We filed suit on the Mincey and Fowler families' behalf in federal court, asking for $62 million in damages. In the meantime, more information had begun to emerge about just how the LAPD exercised its discretion when it came to applying the carotid choke hold. Over the previous few years, we discovered, seventeen men had been killed by LAPD–applied choke holds. Twelve of them were African Americans, one was a Latino, four were white. In addition, since our victory in the Avery case, the City of Los Angeles quietly had settled six other such lawsuits for a total of more than $1 million.

In federal court, our suit over Mincey's death was assigned to U.S. Judge Robert Takasugi, one of the finest jurists on the federal bench anywhere in the nation. He took a look at the facts and asked both parties if a settlement wasn't in order. After a six-hour conference behind the closed doors of Takasugi's chambers, we reached an agreement. Though the city's seven-figure offer was far less than our original demand, the family members decided they wanted to settle rather than risk a trial. So we accepted, and Judge Takasugi ordered the terms of the settlement to be kept secret.

That was enough for the city, however, which has extended its ban on the carotid choke hold to this very day. Since that prohibition was declared, not one single person—black, white, or brown—has died at the hands of police officers. The death toll has now stopped. After all those years of struggle and loss, we finally—like Thurgood Marshall—had changed something "for the better." I had brought the Philistine to bay, and, though not yet on his knees, he was wounded.

With each victory I drew additional strength. And I still recall driving home from the office the day we settled the Mincey case. As I turned the facts of the case and its outcome over in my mind, it occurred to me that Dr. Martin Luther King had been right after all:

"The arc of the moral universe is long, but it bends toward justice."

9

All That Glitters

Sometimes, if you're very lucky, you can go home again. And, like a plant restored to friendly soil, the law offices of Johnnie L. Cochran, Jr., flourished after our return to mid-Wilshire. Our successes in the Settles, Avery, and Mincey cases set the tone for my new practice. For a lawyer who never had believed that ambition and idealism were mutually exclusive, it was the best of all possible worlds: We were making money—and a difference.

It also was the moment that my onetime Kappa big brother and longtime mentor, Mayor Tom Bradley, reminded me that when you take your living from a community, you're obliged to give something of yourself back. Actually, Bradley had put me on notice sometime after I departed the district attorney's office for Century City. In August 1981, I received a call from the mayor's aide and confidant E.Z. Burts, now head of the city's harbor, the burgeoning Port of Los Angeles.

"Tom wants to see you," E.Z. said in his casual manner.

I didn't know why the mayor wanted to see me, but of course I was intrigued and promptly arranged to see him at City Hall.

"Johnnie," he said without preamble, "I have a challenge for you." Mayor Bradley explained that what he regarded as a critical vacancy had opened on the commission that ran the city-owned Los Angeles International Airport—LAX, as it's known locally. The mayor wanted me to fill that vacancy. I was interested but slightly perplexed.

"Exactly what does an airport commissioner do, Mayor?" I asked.

"Look, Johnnie," he replied, "you work with the other commissioners to ride herd on the operation. You set policy, and you make sure it gets executed. You'll have a lot of help from the Department of Airports general manager, Clif Moore. But it's still a big job. It's also a prestigious one. You'll learn a lot, go a lot of places, and see a lot of interesting things. But I'm also counting on you to get the job done. I'm bringing you on board because I know you can do that. As I told you, it's a real challenge."

"But, Tom," I mildly protested, thinking of the time involved, "what about my law practice?"

"Oh," he replied, "I don't want you to think we're asking you to do it for nothing. You'll get twenty-five dollars for every meeting."

I can still hear his chuckle. Whoever said Bradley lacked a sense of humor?

I didn't know it at the time, of course, but Tom Bradley was then at the apex of his historic twenty-year tenure in the mayor's office. He was perhaps the most remarkable man in a remarkable generation of African Americans who, like my own parents, had come to Los Angeles in the great migration during and after the war and then stayed on to change their adopted city forever—and for the better. Like me, Tom Bradley was a sharecropper's son. His people had toiled in the cotton fields of Calvert, Texas. Also like me, he went on to UCLA, where he was a track star and excellent student. After graduation, he joined the LAPD, which was the muscular alternative to the post office or teaching for ambitious black men of his generation. Racism was the background noise of Chief William Parker's department, but men like Tom Bradley somehow managed to tune it out, working small miracles of daily humanity in the black neighborhoods they inevitably were assigned to patrol.

After twenty years, Bradley had fought his way up the promotional ladder to lieutenant. He knew he would go no further, so he enrolled in night law school, graduated, passed the bar, and went into politics. In 1963, he was overwhelmingly elected to the city council, representing a district that included Leimert Park, where we both lived. Six years later, Bradley made his first run for the mayor's office. The incumbent, Sam Yorty, whipped the city's mostly white voters—and the all-white downtown business establishment—into a froth of racial anxiety. Anxious white votes and anxious downtown money were too much for Bradley to overcome. He lost.

But there were two things African Americans of Bradley's generation understood better than anyone else—frequent defeats and constant struggle. The day after Yorty beat him, Bradley began working to put together the political coalition that would govern Los Angeles for the next twenty years and reshape it into one of the world's great cities. By law, Los Angeles' city elections are nonpartisan. Fundamentally, however, the Bradley coalition was an alliance between two liberal, Democratic communities, mostly black Central and South Los Angeles and the heavily

Jewish West Side. There were votes and hard workers aplenty in both places and, on the West Side, men and women with wallets to match their social consciences.

Four years later, Bradley's black-Jewish coalition swept him past Yorty and into office. In essence, his program was a simple one: Encourage as much growth and development as the city would support, and make sure that the jobs and benefits that flowed from such expansion were open to as many people as possible. It was a pro-growth *and* pro-equality agenda, and its obvious results soon won the downtown business community over to Bradley's side. It solved some, though certainly not all, of the city's still pressing social problems. But judging on the whole—and, as Winston Churchill said, "It is on the whole that such things must be judged"—the Bradley administration's achievements were remarkable.

Perhaps most remarkable was the way in which the major initiatives he undertook in the second half of his tenure positioned Los Angeles to compete in a future no one could have foreseen at the time. For example, on that day in 1981 when he asked me to join the airport commission, he also outlined his vision of LAX's future. He wanted us to undertake a stunning expansion of the airport's capacity, first for the foreign and domestic passengers who would flow in for the upcoming 1984 Olympics and then for cargo handling. He would shortly dispatch E. Z. Burts to the harbor with instructions to carry out a similar program. By the time we were finished twelve years later, LAX was the nation's third busiest airport, as measured by passenger volume, and its first in air cargo handling. And the Port of Los Angeles in San Pedro was the second busiest harbor in the world.

Like the sparkling-new downtown high-rise district that was also constructed during Tom Bradley's twenty years in office, the dramatically expanded port and airport were critical parts of the infrastructure that positioned Los Angeles as a leader in the foreign trade, financial services, high-tech, and entertainment sectors helping to propel the American economy into the twenty-first century.

Between 1981, when I actually took my seat on the airport commission, and 1993, when I resigned, I served three terms as its panel's president. But in all that time, I never had a prouder day than June 7, 1984, when—less than two months before the opening of the 1984 Summer Olympics—we opened LAX's new $124 million Tom Bradley International Terminal, at 960,000 square feet the largest international airport facility in the United States. The Olympics were particularly dear to ex–track star Tom Bradley, who saw them as a chance to showcase the city of which he was so proud before the world. He also put together the phenomenally able team that made the Los Angeles games not only the best run in history but also the only ones ever at that time to turn a profit.

No Los Angeles city facility had ever been named for a living person, but we Bradley appointees, with me as point person, vaulted that obstacle as he once had the 400 meter hurdles. Then, to put icing on the cake, we commissioned a bronze statue of the mayor and placed it in the front of the terminal's modern entrance. Hundreds of thousands of foreign visitors to the city Tom Bradley built now stream by his beaming face every day. We also made sure our statue was too massive and cumbersome for any future commission to move with ease. From our mayor, we'd learned how to build for the ages.

Tom Bradley was a farsighted man, but I'm quite sure that when he told me that I would "go a lot of places" and "see a lot of interesting things" in the course of my new assignment, he didn't have in mind what happened on my very first trip for the airport commission. Shortly after my appointment was confirmed, I flew to Portland, Oregon, for an annual conference of airport officials from around the country. Such meetings naturally attract people hoping to do business with airport authorities, and, on the first night of the conference, I wandered into a party being given by one of them in a suite at the Benson Hotel. It was a Monday night, and I plopped down on a sofa with a few fellows I knew, keeping one eye on the television—where the *Monday Night Football* game was in progress—while answering my friends' questions about our recent victory in the Settles case. It was also at that time that I met Herman J. Russell, Jr., of H.J. Russell Companies in Atlanta, one of America's premier businessmen, who has become one of my dearest and best friends.

I hadn't been there long when a strikingly attractive young woman made her way into the room. Call it fate, call it chance—whichever you choose says something about your own notions regarding romance—but the only available seat in that crowded, rather overheated room was on the sofa next to me. Our new companion was Dale Mason, and, as it turned out, she was the vice president of marketing for our evening's host, an expanding Atlanta-based company called Gourmet Services.

I am a man who has always enjoyed the company of women in general, but from that first moment there was something special about this particular woman's presence—so special, in fact, that, passionate football fan though I am, I can't recall who was playing that night. It wasn't only her beauty, which was obvious. It wasn't just that she seemed sincerely interested in my stories or that she more than held up her own end of the conversation. It wasn't even her clear professional accomplishment. What I think most attracted me to her was her unique persona, a combination of unforced sweetness and keen intelligence in the service of a personality that was both charmingly cultivated and disconcertingly plainspoken. And, though she was every inch the contemporary career woman, she also seemed to share my instinctive taste for traditional values. A case in point: When it became clear we found each other interesting, we left together and went to the nearby Häagen-Dazs hospitality suite for ice cream. Ah, the life of swinging young professionals!

By the time we parted that evening, Dale and I had agreed to meet again the following day for lunch and then again for her boss's birthday dinner that evening. I'm not quite sure what came over me, but before lunch I suggested a walk through Portland's world-famous rose garden. In that incomparable setting, we exchanged the usual personal histories. She was thirteen years my junior. I learned that she, too, came from Louisiana, though from cosmopolitan New Orleans, where her father was a prominent businessman and her mother a first-rate educator. Like the rest of her family, Dale was a devout Roman Catholic and had been educated largely in religious schools through college, and had earned both her master's and Ph.D. from Atlanta University. She loved her work and her life in the capital of the New South.

Southern culture has a way of producing great ladies—black and white—and it was clear to me that I had met one. After the conference, we returned to our respective homes, though over the next few weeks we exchanged notes and telephone calls. Incurable romantic that I am, I invited her to attend a heavyweight title fight with me. Tolerant woman that she is, Dale graciously accepted, though I later discovered she dislikes boxing.

What followed was hardly a whirlwind courtship. We saw each other with increasing frequency over the next three years. I knew I was not dealing with someone to whom material possessions were an overriding priority when she got off the plane for her first visit to Los Angeles, looked at my waiting Rolls-Royce, and never acknowledged it.

In L.A., she met and liked my children—Melodie, Tiffany, and Jonathan—and the feeling seemed mutual. My parents and sisters hit it off with Dale immediately. I went to New Orleans and met her mother, Daisy, her father, Louis, and her sisters and brothers: Lynette, Louis III, Agnes, Kathy, and Michael. Seeing them all together, I realized the Masons and Cochrans attached an equal importance to family values and obligations. Still, I was a divorced man not uncomfortable with his freedom, and only gradually did I let myself begin to understand that what I was feeling for Dale was neither mere friendship nor deep affection, but love.

Yet I vacillated. My father, who is very fond of Dale and was amused by my indecision, sent me one of his poems. It began:

> Several attractive ladies were quite interested in Handsome
>   Harry
> He was in extreme demand and couldn't decide whom to
>   marry
> One night he dreamt that by waiting so long
> The lady he considered number one was gone.

Shortly thereafter in San Francisco, I presented her with a ring and asked her to marry me. She accepted. We drove to Carmel for the day to discuss the life we foresaw together. Then I went on to New Orleans to ask her parents' permission, which they granted.

On March 1, 1985, Dale and I were married at the Bel Air Hotel in Los Angeles, our contract with one another sealed by vows she wrote herself. It was one contract into which both parties entered gladly and without reservation.

We have our differences, of course. I love to watch football; she plays competitive tennis with zest. I like to end a hard day by giggling through the *Tonight Show* monologue; she can't sleep unless she's checked out *Nightline*. We also have many things we enjoy in common, none more than the nights we spend alone together in conversations where she insists we get closure on a subject. Sometimes, if you are truly favored by fortune, you find someone who is not only your friend and lover but also your equal partner, your one real soul mate. I was lucky enough to find that person in Dale, and without her unfailing kindness, deep intelligence, unstinting loyalty, and fierce candor, the struggles ahead would have been impossible to surmount.

For our honeymoon, we took a trip to Acapulco and then to Europe. Throughout our marriage we have traveled extensively around the world. In our early travels, we continued my practice of adding to my mother's doll collection, which quickly grew to include French, Austrian, Italian, Danish, Swedish, African, Japanese, and Chinese dolls. As often as possible, we've taken my parents along on trips. For a couple born into a world where many people never traveled more than a handful of miles from their birthplace, it's been a wonderful experience. We particularly enjoyed our first trip to Israel, where, among other things, we stayed on a kibbutz. My father, the deacon and Bible scholar, was enthralled at the chance to visit the holy sites in person. We all went away inspired by the energetic, selfless cooperation that characterized life on a kibbutz.

But on those trips, it became clear to us that Mother, though uncomplaining and always good-humored, was in failing health. Coincidentally, it was about this time that I took another piece of advice from Syd Irmas. Now, three things about me always have worried Syd: my lack of what he regards as adequate savings, what he perceives as my law firm's high overhead, and my failure to relax. Syd has always been a person who likes the beach, and he owns a home in an especially beautiful section of Malibu. At his urging, Dale and I purchased a getaway place, a condominium overlooking the ocean in Marina Del Rey.

My parents were our most frequent guests. Mother would stand for what seemed like hours just looking out the window. The peaceful, contented expression on her face reminded me just how much the girl from the piney woods at Robson and Forbings had always loved the sea. She had dreamed of a future for herself—children and a house of her own with palm trees growing in the garden. She and my father had made all that come true themselves. Why not, I thought, give her something she never would have dreamed of for herself, a second home by the sea. So, in 1991, Dale and I purchased an additional condo down the hall from our own. We moved Mother and Father and all their furniture, including the cabinet for her dolls, into their own place.

By then, Mother was in steep decline. She no longer could go out, but she was happy to sit at one of the windows just looking out over the water, watching the sailboats come and go. She often spoke to me about how much she loved that view.

"The ocean is so vast you can't really understand it all, John," she said to me, "and so beautiful that you don't have words to describe it. It's almost heavenly. It reminds me of the glory of God. Just sitting here looking at it is like a prayer."

She had given so much of herself to so many people through so many years. Yet as her strength slipped away like the sun on the water beneath her window, all Mother seemed to feel was gratitude for what she felt she had received.

"God has always been so good to me, John," she said. "I feel His grace more strongly than ever."

Late one Saturday night, shortly after Mother and Dad had moved into their new seaside home, Dale and I returned from a social engagement to find an urgent message: Mother had been hospitalized at the UCLA Medical Center. My father was with her. Irrationally, I reproached myself for having gone out that night. I became quite upset. Looking back, I suspect what I was doing was trying to flood my mind with a manageable feeling to hold at bay the unmanageable—indeed, unthinkable—fear that was beginning to push its way in.

We did not go to church the next morning. I called my pastor, Reverend Epps, at Second Baptist, and asked him to remember

Mother in his prayers that day. Then we joined the rest of the family, which had gathered early at Mother's bedside. Our father was there, of course, along with my sisters, Jean and Pearl, and our brother, RaLonzo. All three of my children, Melodie, Tiffany, and Jonathan, were there, and so were my ex-wife, Barbara, and Jonathan's mother, Patty. Dale's uncle, Dr. Elliott J. Mason, Sr., a minister, led us all in prayer. Though dreadfully weak, Mother was more concerned about us than about herself.

"Oh, thank you all so much for coming," she said, too weak to lift herself from her pillows.

We all prayed together some more; then her attending physician slipped into the room and quietly asked to speak with me outside. Before I could go, Mother clutched at my sleeve.

"I don't want any more surgeries, John," she said. "I don't want to be cut on anymore."

Outside in the corridor, the doctor and I spoke quietly together. "It's really just a matter of time, Mr. Cochran," he said to me. Mother may have been ready to let go, but I was not. Was there any chance, I wondered, that another operation could give us more time together.

"Maybe." The doctor shrugged. "But with a woman of your mother's age and condition, I would have to say there are no guarantees. I really do think it's a matter of time."

Back inside, I kept the doctor's thoughts to myself. Mother was entirely lucid, talking quietly but clearly with everyone in the room. My father, however, was visibly fatigued, just sitting at the foot of her bed. My mother had been taking care of him for a lifetime, and she wasn't about to stop now, even at death's door.

"Now, John, take your father home," she instructed me. "Take him home, and make him get some rest. I'll be here when you get back. Don't worry. You can come spend the evening with me."

Dale and I told my sisters that we'd take Dad home, get a couple of hours' rest, then come back and relieve them. We drove down to our condo. My father went to his condo to take a nap. I lay down in our bedroom and, almost immediately, fell into an exhausted sleep.

Suddenly, I awoke and knew that our mother was no longer with us.

I opened my eyes and found Dale standing silently beside the bed. "Mother's gone," I said calmly.

"Yes," she replied. "Your mother has passed away. The girls just called from the hospital."

I had not heard the phone ring. But I had known it all the same. I rose slowly, put on my clothes, and went down the hall to break the news to our father. My sense of loss was beyond description. I couldn't imagine a world without the comforting sound of my mother's voice, without the soft reassurance of her touch. What would my life be, what would any of our lives be without their loving center? What would my life be without a woman I had spoken to every day of my life?

I went to my father's room, sat down beside his bed, and gently took his hand. He looked at me. "Well," I said haltingly, "Mother's gone on to a better place."

Dad, the man of faith, slowly rose, hugged me strongly, then began to dress. I don't think I've ever seen him quite so composed. "Mother is gone," he repeated. He came from a place and a generation that practiced all the Christian virtues, including resignation to the will of God. "Well," he said at last, "let's go."

We drove to the hospital, where Pearl and Jean were waiting. In her room, now free of all the medical apparatus she disliked so much, Mother was past all suffering at last. Each of us, in turn, said our good-byes. I held her. But her spirit was gone, and the body I embraced seemed almost a kind of reminder of the woman we all loved so very much. Mother was buried in our family crypt after a beautiful funeral service. For months afterward, I would catch myself reaching absentmindedly for the phone to make my nightly call to her. Not a week has gone by since her death that I have not visited her crypt when I'm in town. My sisters and I try to make sure she has fresh flowers, and we spend some time "talking." I always make a special visit on her birthday, July 4th, and on Christmas morning I take her a wreath.

In times of turmoil and stress I visit her even more frequently, and I never fail to find comfort in her counsel and continuing presence. At times, it seems to me that I did not so much lose my mother as gain a guardian angel. Then I think: How could it be otherwise? Nothing, not even implacable death, could ever separate Hattie B. Cochran from her children.

I was also consoled by the pride I knew Mother had taken in my professional accomplishments during the years preceding her death. Soon after I moved back to mid-Wilshire, a brilliant civil attorney named Eric G. Ferrer joined my firm. He was a dapper young ex–New Yorker with a high forehead and a thick and bristling mustache, along with a string of advanced degrees and a taste for island holidays that probably reflected his Puerto Rican heritage.

Together, we prepared and won a string of multimillion-dollar verdicts, suing on behalf of ordinary people who had suffered injury as the result of official misconduct. We secured $2.1 million for a highly regarded young Latino police officer, Ricardo Rose, who was permanently disabled after being mistakenly shot three times by a negligent comrade during a drug raid. We won $2.4 million for the wife and children of Yusaf Bilal, a hardworking thirty-eight-year-old bus driver who was shot in the back and killed by a state highway patrolman during another of those deadly "routine traffic stops." We got $3.1 million for the widow and eight children of a sixty-two-year-old disabled man who had his neck broken by sheriff's deputies while in police custody after having been arrested by LAPD officers for a misdemeanor traffic offense, and then was left alone for five hours in a dark, cold jail cell, where he died. We won $3.7 million for the four orphaned children of a couple killed when a car being negligently driven by a West Covina police officer plowed into their family vehicle as they drove home. We forced the cities of Los Angeles, San Marino, and Pasadena to pay more than $1.5 million to the family of a three-hundred-pound, thirty-nine-year-old barber who died of asphyxiation when police hog-tied him after he was arrested on suspicion of intoxication.

As a consequence of these and other similar victories, I realized a longtime personal ambition when, in 1990, I was named Trial Lawyer of the Year by the Los Angeles Trial Lawyers Association, becoming the first attorney ever to be so honored by both the criminal and civil bars. But among all the civil cases we pursued during those years, three stand out most vividly in my mind as examples of how our much-maligned civil justice system really does serve as the last refuge of the injured and the powerless. In fact, it has always been something of a mystery to me why a society obsessed with victims—as ours has become—takes such a reflexively hostile attitude toward trial lawyers and the civil justice system. Together they maintain the one American institution that actually offers the hope of practical redress to those ordinary people wounded by the callous indifference and wanton misconduct of big government and big business.

Take the case of the sixteen little schoolgirls on whose behalf I sued the Los Angeles Unified School District after they were sexually molested by their teacher, Terry Bartholome, whom school officials knew had a history of deviant conduct. In fact, when the district hired this forty-eight-year-old man, they knew that while serving in the army he had been forced to undergo psychiatric treatment after exposing himself to two military nurses. Nonetheless, he was put to work teaching mostly white students in the San Fernando Valley. When complaints about his conduct were made, he was transferred to the 107th Street School in predominantly black South Los Angeles. When he was accused of molesting two girls there, officials quickly sent him on to another South L.A. school, Sixty-eighth Street, where—even though the principal was instructed to "keep an eye on him"— he was allowed to take charge of a third-grade class composed almost entirely of black children eight and nine years old.

As was later proved in the criminal trial that resulted in Bartholome's conviction on thirty child-molesting charges, he would send the boys out of the room and then stand and masturbate in front of the helpless little girls. School officials, one of whom was convicted of failing to report Bartholome's conduct to police, tried to cover up the whole affair. Yet Bartholome was a man so obviously and dangerously deranged that when police confronted him with evidence of his crimes, he blamed his little black students for "arousing" him with "provocative conduct." The children, he told the investigating officers, "were very, very mature in their knowledge of sexual matters—much more so than girls in other parts of the city. I think my sexual feelings are being caused by my need to leave the inner-city schools," Bartholome said.

It was obvious from the start that the school district would have to settle this case. Had we taken it to trial, any jury, anywhere in the county, not only would have given us whatever we asked but also would have tried to have every official involved horsewhipped, which, frankly, is what they deserved. The district had retained Los Angeles' largest and oldest law firm,

O'Melveny & Myers, the downtown powerhouse whose then managing partner was Warren Christopher, the future secretary of state.

The attorney they assigned to our case, Charles Bakaly, Jr., came right to the point in our first settlement conference. "We don't have enough money," he complained. "We can't pay Mr. Cochran anything like the money he's asking. He's trying to bankrupt the school district."

I had no interest in bankrupting any public institution, but I did have an obligation to obtain just redress for my clients and, as a citizen, to do so in such a manner that the school district would be deterred from future recklessness and deceit. Fortunately, we had a superb judge, Leon Savitch, who prodded us on toward settlement. As the negotiations continued, it occurred to me that part of the solution might be reached by having the district pay incrementally into what is called a "special needs trust" on which the girls could draw as required. For example, they could draw money for the therapy and other treatments they almost certainly would require as the adult victims of childhood molestation.

I'd never structured such a trust, but I knew Syd Irmas had. I phoned him the night after that conference, and he unhesitatingly agreed to drop everything and join us. Together, we reviewed the district's insurance policy and forged a solution. We proposed a structured settlement in which the girls would receive immediate partial payment with the rest to be paid into a trust administered by a major insurance company. The district accepted and agreed to pay out $6,015,000, with approximately $1 million of it earmarked for the special needs trust. The school district was saved from bankruptcy and, ultimately, Bartholome's helpless victims will receive some $25 million.

When I asked the redoubtable Syd what the fee for his timely intervention would be, he declined payment. He did suggest, however, that perhaps I would consider donating a portion of my own fee to one of his family's favorite charities, L.A. Family Housing Corp., which is devoted to helping homeless families, and on the board of which both Dale and I serve. It seemed to me exactly what the situation required, so Dale and I decided to put up $250,000 of what I'd earned on the case. In turn, Syd and his wonderful wife, Audrey, donated some land they owned just south of mid-Wilshire on Redondo Boulevard. On that parcel we constructed ten town-house-style units to house formerly homeless families.

My mother did not live to see the gala opening of the development we dedicated as the Johnnie L. Cochran, Sr., and Hattie B. Cochran Villa. That ceremonial occasion drew not only a panoply of city officials, but also the secretary of housing and urban development, Jack Kemp, who praised Cochran Villa as "a model public-private partnership that deserves to be emulated across this nation." But for me the high point of the day took place during my remarks. It was a deeply overcast morning, but, as I began to speak, the clouds parted and the peach-colored units were bathed in brilliant sunlight.

"I think my mother is pleased," I said.

Another case from that period that stands out in my mind is that of Murphy and Katie Pierson, an elderly African American couple whose mistreatment at the hands of the Los Angeles Police Department virtually defied belief. I can still vividly recall the day they first came to my office in the summer of 1986. He was a tall, light-skinned man, still ruggedly handsome at seventy-four, though as a consequence of his injuries he used a cane and could no longer stand upright. His hearing was not as it once was. She was seventy-one, carefully dressed, and precise in her speech. They had been married for forty-five years and were devout Roman Catholics.

They had lived for many years in the house they had purchased in South Los Angeles. By the mid-1980s, their street, like so many in the neighborhood, had become a haven for drug dealers, some of whom insisted on plying their trade right on Murphy's carefully tended front lawn. One evening around 7:30 P.M., when he had made one of his frequent trips out onto the front porch to order the thugs off his property, one of them sneeringly asked Murphy if he "wanted to buy some cocaine."

That was too much for the old man, who ducked back into the house and came out with an unloaded shotgun. That got the drug dealers' attention, and they scurried away. But as Murphy turned to go back into his home, an LAPD patrol car came cruising up the street. The officers inside, Brent Jones and John Pearce, spotted the old man on the porch with his shotgun and jumped out of their car, sidearms drawn. In complete violation of all established LAPD procedures, Pierce—gun in hand—advanced on the old man, whose back was turned. The officer shouted at him. The confused, hard-of-hearing Murphy turned, the shotgun pointed skyward. Over the next few seconds, the cops shot at him eleven times, wounding him in the chest, buttocks, and right hand.

When the sound of gunfire boomed through the neighborhood, Katie was on her knees in a back room, doing something she did every night at that time, praying with her rosary along with Father Peyton, the radio priest who operates under the motto "The family that prays together stays together." She rushed—rosary beads still in her hand—to the front porch, where she discovered her husband bleeding.

I can't imagine what went through those officers' heads when they saw her there—"Look out, she's got a rosary!" In any event, they grabbed her, literally dragged her across her husband's bleeding body, and took her to the front lawn, where they forced her to kneel on the ground and be handcuffed before throwing her into the back of their patrol car. Murphy was taken to Cedars-Sinai Medical Center, where able doctors and his own iron constitution saved his life. Katie was held at the Wilshire Division Police Station until 2:30 A.M., when she was released without charges. In all that time, despite her repeated entreaties, nobody would tell her whether her beloved husband was dead or alive.

All of this had happened in daylight in full sight of the Piersons' neighbors. And, when we interviewed them, they corroborated every iota of the old couple's story. Neither officer involved was ever charged with any crime or subjected to any departmental discipline. When I approached the city on the Piersons' behalf, the city attorney offered us $50,000 in compensation. "See you in court," I replied. Three years later, a jury awarded Murphy Pierson $1.8 million. Mrs. Pierson was additionally awarded $430,000 for being falsely arrested and detained, bringing their total to $2,230,000. Murphy has since passed on, but Katie remains an honored guest at all our firm's celebrations.

At the time, our verdict in the Pierson case was the largest ever awarded in a case growing out of the LAPD's misconduct. But something even more substantial was in the offing.

One night in Hollywood, a thirteen-year-old Latina named Patty Díaz was fast asleep in her family's apartment. At 3 A.M., Stanley Tanabe, an LAPD officer in full uniform and wearing his sidearm, knocked at the apartment door and demanded admittance. He claimed he was responding to a report of a woman screaming and he said he would not leave until he had thoroughly searched the Díaz apartment. He went to the back bedroom, where he sexually assaulted little Patty in the presence of her ten-year-old brother and two-year-old sister. He then left the apartment but returned within five minutes carrying what he purported was a composite drawing of a suspect. He then left, telling the terrified, stunned thirteen-year-old girl that he would return.

The very next morning, Patty and her mother went to the Hollywood police station and filed a complaint. However, the sergeant's log of that complaint, which contained an accurate description of Tanabe, was withheld from detectives subsequently assigned to investigate the matter. Moreover, the detectives were instructed by their superiors to keep their probe "hush-hush."

One evening a month later, while Patty's mother was out, Tanabe made good on his threat. Once again in full uniform, he forced his way into the apartment and attempted to assault the girl. At that moment, Patty's mother returned and the girl seized the opportunity to run to a neighbor's apartment and telephone police. Tanabe was arrested as he tried to get in his unmarked police car and flee the scene. He was subsequently tried and convicted of sexual battery and burglary and sentenced to two years in prison, of which he served just a little more than twelve months.

For Patty Díaz, the months that followed were a nightmare. She was diagnosed as suffering from post-traumatic stress disorder with psychotic features. Three times she tried to take her own life by slashing her wrists. The last attempt took place on her *quinceañera*, or fifteenth birthday. Traditional Latino families, such as the Díazes, regard that as their daughter's "coming-out" day and mark it with a celebration in her honor second only to her wedding. Patty's *quinceañera* coincided with the day of Tanabe's release from prison. She spent it alone, sobbing in her room before attempting, once again, to end the life she had come to regard as a source of torment to herself and shame to her family.

Eric Ferrer and I took her case. From the start, it was a cause that engaged every fiber of our moral and legal beings. The police department's conduct had been unconscionably reckless and deceitful, and the city's response had been callous. The injury done to poor Patty Díaz and her mother was so clear. Moreover, as we began to investigate, we discovered that there had been ample warning of Tanabe's problems. He initially had entered the police academy in 1980 but was unable to complete his training. At the time, two of his training officers noted what they believed was mental rigidity on his part and predicted that if Tanabe were ever allowed to become a police officer, he might subject himself and the city to civil and criminal liability. He subsequently applied to three other police departments and was rejected on psychological grounds. Finally, he reapplied to the LAPD and was accepted.

We demanded that the city pay Patty Díaz and her mother $750,000. The city offered them only $150,000. We went to trial. While cross-examining the LAPD captain in charge of the case, I forced him to admit that the sergeant's log had been withheld from the investigating detectives and that the investigation had been flawed and negligent. I can still hear the jury's collective intake of breath when we compelled that admission. I also recall the tears in their eyes when Patty Díaz, a pained but courageous witness on her own behalf, displayed for the jurors the still vivid scars on her wrists.

Eric and I knew that much would ride on my final argument, and we labored over how to make it equal to the demands of the case. The entire trial had been tape-recorded, so we devised a simple but forceful stratagem. I would argue, and, as I returned to each critical piece of testimony, I would signal Eric. He would have the tape keyed to precisely that moment in the trial so that the jurors could hear it once again for themselves. It worked flawlessly.

Then, as I brought my argument to a close, I experienced one of those moments of intuition that veteran trial lawyers learn to trust. I could feel the jury was with me. I needed to hold them there, and I improvised. I turned away from them for a second, then quickly turned back, making eye contact with each of the four Latinos on the panel. Without preamble, I spoke to them in Spanish. *"Sólo quien mueve con el saco sabe que pesa,"* I said.

This is an old Spanish maxim that translates, "Only he who carries the sack knows the weight of the burden." The Latino jurors nodded their heads in agreement, and I knew they shortly would explain the sentiment to their colleagues in the jury room. I continued in English:

"This girl, who showed you her wrists, who tried to kill herself because she didn't feel she could go on—she knows what that saying means better than anyone here. Understand what it is to be fifteen years old and living with this pain in your head for the rest of your life. You've got to do justice for her. Not ten percent justice. Not fifteen percent justice. Full one hundred percent justice.

"We owe her that. For you are the conscience of this community and your verdict will send a strong message to the City of Los Angeles."

As I returned to my seat and sat down, I looked over at Eric. He just looked back and nodded. The jury was instructed and began its deliberations.

While they worked, I left for Italy, where I was to meet Dale and my best friend, Ron Sunderland, and his wife, Diane, at Villa d'Este in the lake country of northern Italy. We planned to celebrate Dale's birthday there before going on to the Barcelona Summer Olympics together. We were still in Italy a week later when, at 1:30 A.M., the phone in our hotel room rang. I answered—groggily. At the other end, I could make out Eric's excited voice, one word spilling out after another while in the background people seemed to be shouting in Spanish.

"Please speak slower, Eric," I mumbled, still trying to shake off a deep sleep.

"Nine million," he kept repeating like a mantra. "Nine million. The jury just awarded Patty nine million dollars!"

I sat bolt upright in bed.

Actually, the full award was $9.4 million plus attorney's fees, and it remains the largest single award in a case resulting from the LAPD's chronic misconduct. My Philistine was still on his feet, but we were making him bleed badly.

Best of all, that money allowed Patty Díaz to obtain appropriate help and start life anew. She is now happily married and a young mother. That was a result worth working for.

Another of the ambitions I'd carried with me on our return to mid-Wilshire remained only partially fulfilled: establishing a real entertainment division. But, inspired in part by the example of Leo Branton, and perhaps in part, by the view of the Hollywood sign from my office window, we pushed on, building a client list that included such wonderful artists as Aretha Franklin, Chaka Khan, Stevie Wonder, and George Clinton. In those years, however, our brushes with celebrity clients came most often when one of them had a brush with the law.

When former professional football great Jim Brown was falsely accused of assaulting a thirty-three-year-old schoolteacher with whom he occasionally played tennis, he sought me out. Jim was vulnerable. His prickly temperament had somewhat eroded his popularity, and he had allegedly been involved in incidents of domestic violence. But these latest charges were false and malicious. At his preliminary hearing, I mounted a vigorous defense. We had investigated the crime scene ourselves and turned up evidence that contradicted the charges, all of which we turned over to the prosecutors. When I cross-examined Brown's accuser, she told a conflicting and confused story, different in many significant details from the one she had told police and prosecutors. My opponent in Jim's case was an extraordinarily talented deputy district attorney named Dino Fulgoni, now a judge. He was a tough and relentless advocate but a highly principled prosecutor. I could see he was not happy with what he was seeing and hearing.

On the morning we were set to conclude the evidence in the preliminary hearing before Judge Candace Cooper, Dino, after consulting with Judge Cooper and me, stood up and stunned the packed courtroom by moving to dismiss all charges against Brown "in the interests of justice."

"I would not wish anyone to be forced to stand trial with the contradictory nature of the proof that came forth before this court," Dino said. He also credited me with "uncovering evidence that tends to negate allegations that there was an assault with intent to commit rape."

Afterward, Jim Brown told the assembled reporters, "I'm glad to be an American because we have a chance in our system, if we're innocent, for the facts to come out."

I seconded his sentiments but tried to draw the journalists' attention to the fact that justice had been done not only because Jim had had the benefit of a vigorous defense but also because he had been prosecuted by a D.A. strictly attentive to his ethical obligations. "Justice was served," I said. "Mr. Fulgoni kept an open mind, and when the charges could not be proved to a moral certainty, they were dismissed."

Dino Fulgoni was a prosecutor indifferent to the political impact of decisions he felt were required of him by law and morality. Unfortunately, that kind of prosecutor has become a rare breed in our politicized, win-at-any-cost criminal justice system. At least that is true in Los Angeles, where the average deputy D.A. now proceeds through even the most routine matter with the political calculation of a Chicago alderman.

In 1989, I won an acquittal for former child television star

Todd Bridges, whose tragic addiction to crack cocaine had led to charges of attempted murder and voluntary manslaughter. His jury also deadlocked eight-four for "not guilty" on the lesser charge of assault with a deadly weapon. In a second trial, I secured his acquittal of that charge as well. Those back-to-back trials allowed me to renew acquaintance with a prosecutor I had hired in 1978 during my days in the D.A.'s office, an excellent star prosecutor by the name of Bill Hodgman. Undeterred by his loss in the Bridges cases, Bill went on to secure the conviction of the financier Charles Keating in the biggest prosecution growing out of the nation's savings and loan debacle. Bill and I would be seeing a lot more of each other in the not-too-distant future.

Like so many other Americans in late 1993, I was following with interest the growing controversy surrounding musical superstar Michael Jackson. The parents of a boy Michael had befriended alleged that Jackson had betrayed their trust and molested their son. It was a shocking, potentially devastating charge against an entertainer beloved by tens of millions of fans around the world. The allegation fell with particular force in the African American community, where Jackson had long been admired.

Like many superstars, Jackson basically was a prisoner of his own overwhelming celebrity. He relies for advice on a tiny circle of intimate advisers, one of whom is actress Elizabeth Taylor. On December 1, 1993, I received a call from an old friend, Neil Papiano, one of the country's leading trial lawyers.

"Johnnie," he said, "I think you're going to get a call from one of my clients—perhaps my most famous client, Elizabeth Taylor. She's very concerned about Michael Jackson, with whom she's very close. She's very worried about this whole molestation mess and has asked me who I think would be the best lawyer to represent him. Johnnie," Neil said, "I told her you would be my choice, that I know you can help this young man. I just didn't want you to be surprised if she calls." Neil also was at pains to inform me that his client was to be addressed as "Elizabeth," never as "Liz."

I thanked him profusely and tried to pretend I wasn't anxiously waiting for that call. My blood was up. It wasn't just the prospect of representing so well known a celebrity. The obvious glee the tabloid press was taking in a superstar's potential downfall struck me as not just mean-spirited but also dangerous.

A few hours later, Jan Thomas, our receptionist, buzzed me. Now calling Jan a "receptionist" is like calling Michael Jordan a "basketball player." She is our firm's indispensable one-woman nerve center; she cheers our victories and pricks our pomposities. But that afternoon, even she sounded at least somewhat impressed.

"Boss of mine," she said in her familiar salutation, "Elizabeth Taylor is on the line, and it's *the* Elizabeth Taylor."

Ms. Taylor was charming, but businesslike, obviously very worried about her friend. "I've heard a lot about you," she said, "and I was wondering if you could come to my house on Friday so that we and some other people involved can confer in person."

I took her address and agreed to be at her house in a neighborhood overlooking Beverly Hills the following Friday. When I arrived, I was shown into a beautiful living room. Michael's manager, Sandy Gallin, already was there, along with long-time Jackson confidant Bob Jones, as were attorney Bert Fields and a raft of public relations specialists, including one Washington heavyweight who had flown in for the day. I also spotted both Neil Papiano and my friend Howard Weitzman, who had been representing Michael in the matter. We milled about and made small talk for a few moments before we were joined by Elizabeth Taylor.

"I want you to represent Michael," she said to me.

I began asking questions about the case's posture. However, to my utter astonishment, no one could tell me whether or not a warrant had been issued for Michael Jackson's arrest. We talked for the next two hours, and it was clear to me that my perspective differed dramatically from that of almost everyone else in the room—except, perhaps, Elizabeth Taylor. What I wanted to know was: What is the status of the criminal investigation, if there is one? Finally, Elizabeth looked at me and said: "Johnnie, I think your question about this warrant is a good one. Can we go back to that?"

"I think we should," I said. "Look, guys, the first thing I have to do is find out whether there's a warrant for him and whether I can give him any assurance he won't be arrested when he steps off the plane in this country."

"How do we go about finding that out?" Elizabeth asked.

"Well," I replied, "at three this afternoon, I'll be meeting downtown with Gil Garcetti, the district attorney, on another matter. I'll just ask him."

Elizabeth, who obviously relished a direct solution, smiled, and I knew my position on the case had become a little more solid. An hour later, I spoke with Gil Garcetti and explained that I had been hired to represent Jackson and asked him whether any warrant had been issued. He told me none had. I then asked that, if a warrant ever were obtained, he would contact me and allow me to arrange a dignified surrender, rather than simply arresting Michael. Gil agreed.

Early the next morning Michael Jackson, who was in Europe, telephoned my house. He obviously was relieved, and we hit it off immediately. It was the first of many long telephone chats we have had since. But what impressed me most was the very first thing he said to me.

"I am innocent of these charges, Johnnie," he said emphatically.

I told Michael of my plans to involve my associate Carl Douglas, a former federal public defender, in his case. Carl and Eric Ferrer are two of the best trial lawyers in our firm. Carl is a terrific lawyer with an astonishing capacity for hard work and a willingness to put himself on the line emotionally for his clients. I felt sure he and Michael would like each other, and so they did.

A couple of days later, Carl and I drove to the Santa Monica airport, where Michael's private helicopter was waiting to fly us to his famous Neverland retreat in Santa Barbara County north of Los Angeles. It is, as the name suggests, a consciously magical place with its vast mansion, private zoo, and dazzling amusement park. There is music everywhere, and, the minute I stepped out of the helicopter, I understood that this whole enchanted environment had been designed to reinforce and maintain the childlike sense of wonder so crucial to Michael's art.

I remember turning to Carl and saying, "We can't let this young man be taken down. He's told us he's innocent."

I also knew that by then the parents of the alleged victim had fired their first attorney, a strident, part-time radio talk show host by the name of Gloria Allred, and hired Larry Feldman, one of the finest trial lawyers in the country. Feldman is a tall, slender, slightly balding man with chiseled features and a legendary touch with juries. If you want to imagine his courtroom style, picture what Abe Lincoln might have been like if he'd been bar-mitzvahed. Larry is a more than formidable opponent, but I also know that he is a strong practitioner of the same sort of client-centered advocacy in which I believe.

Shortly thereafter Michael appeared at the NAACP's Image Awards, where his surprise appearance provoked a five-minute standing ovation. Busy with his own career, he had not previously involved himself much in the affairs of the black community. I thought it essential that he see for himself the reservoir of pride and goodwill his people maintained for him. He was touched and, I think, a little surprised. I know that support was a source of comfort and strength to him during his ordeal and, perhaps more important, something for him to ponder afterward.

From a lawyer's standpoint, Michael was—and is—an ideal client. He is intelligent, articulate, and decisive. Best of all, he solicits counsel when he feels he needs it, listens carefully, and follows reasonable advice to the letter.

Larry Feldman and I sat down to negotiate under the auspices of a retired judge we had retained, as California law permits. I've never faced a tougher, smarter, or more able adversary. Both Larry and I agreed that it would be in our clients' best interests to put this matter behind them and allow them to get on with their lives. It was Martin Luther King's birthday.

We held an outdoor press conference in Santa Monica to announce the settlement. Howard, Larry, Carl, and I all were there. So were more than 250 reporters. As Carl and I were walking to my car, I recall looking up and seeing news helicopters overhead filming us.

I turned and whispered to Carl, who seemed slightly dazed by the whole scene, "Take a look at this, my boy, you'll never see anything like it again in your life."

As we both were about to discover, I've never been so utterly wrong.

10

"Does He Need Your Help?"

THERE ARE DAYS OF SUCH CONSEQUENCE THAT THEY stand like bookmarks in the story of your life, irrevocably dividing all that came before from everything that happens thereafter. For me, June 13, 1994, was such a day, though what I recall most vividly about it was its routine beginning.

It was a Monday. I rose at 6:15 A.M. and prepared for the arrival fifteen minutes later of Marc Vahanian, the personal trainer with whom I work out four times each week when I'm in town. In the early 1990s, Dale and I renovated our hillside home along crisp modernist lines. It is now a series of soaring, light-filled spaces whose gleaming white walls provide an appropriate backdrop for our collection of African and African American art. But perhaps the smartest thing we did was to install a state-of-the-art gym in a glassed-in gallery overlooking the two-story den and media room at the rear of the house. The telephone's ring, the hum of incoming faxes, and the sound of television news are a nearly constant presence in much of our house, but we consciously decided to maintain the gym as a kind of sanctuary in which we could remain blissfully—if only fleetingly—focused and out of touch with the rest of the world.

So it wasn't until Marc and I finished and I returned to our bedroom that I found Dale deeply engrossed in the *Today* show, which, like every other news program that day, was dominated by a story out of Brentwood, an affluent neighborhood on Los Angeles' fashionable West Side. Shortly after midnight, just outside a condominium on busy Bundy Drive, Nicole Brown Simpson, the ex-wife of former football star O. J. Simpson, and an as-yet-unidentified young man had been found stabbed to death. Neither Dale nor I had ever met Nicole. I knew O.J., however, and we were very concerned about his two youngest children, who, according to the reports, lived with their mother. The television remained on as Dale and I dressed and breakfasted. Something about the sheer volume of the news coverage and the frenzied pace at which the story was unfolding made me uneasy. I knew from experience that media attention inevitably increases the pressure on police investigators, and, when they're working under pressure, investigating officers—particularly in the LAPD—make more than their usual quota of mistakes.

Driving south through Hollywood on my way to work, I kept the car radio tuned to an all-news station. Between the bulletins, which seemed to be coming with increasing frequency, I thought about O. J. Simpson. We weren't really close friends, though we certainly were well acquainted with one another. In fact, our daughters shared their Cotillion Debut in 1986, when their official "coming out" ball was sponsored by the Los Angeles

Chapter of the Links. We were proud fathers with our beautiful and talented daughters. I escorted my baby Tiffany, and O.J. was beaming with joy as he presented his lovely Arnelle. It was an extraordinarily happy evening. In June 1992, we had spent a delightful evening together in Washington, D.C. That June, Musanna Overr, the daughter of my old friend Elaine Matthews Overr, and O.J.'s daughter Arnelle had graduated from Howard University. Elaine and I had been friends since high school. Over the years, I had watched Musanna grow into a charming and accomplished young woman, and I think I may have been the proudest guest at her commencement.

That evening, Simpson and I had hosted a dinner party for the girls at the Paper Moon restaurant in Georgetown. The onetime Heisman Trophy winner was a genial, easygoing presence, very much at ease not only with his daughter but also with her mother, Marguerite, from whom he was divorced. It had been years since O.J. had made his incomparable way up a football field, but I have never forgotten the constant stream of strangers—mostly white—who came to our table in hopes of a photo, an autograph, or merely a handshake. Nobody—no matter how intrusive—went away disappointed. And I remembered being struck not only by the unforced good nature with which O.J. handled it all but also by the intimate quality of his celebrity status. People felt free to approach him. He, seemingly without effort, somehow managed to send them away happily confirmed in their admiration for him. I am by trade a student of people and their reactions to one another. But I had never seen anything quite like it. In the intervening years, Simpson and I had bumped into each other several times at professional football games. We'd exchanged enthusiastic greetings but not much more.

When I reached the office, I discovered that most of my

associates and staff had turned on their television sets to follow the developments in the case. We learned that the young man whose body had been discovered along with that of Nicole Brown was Ronald Lyle Goldman, a waiter at a nearby Italian restaurant where Nicole and her family had dined the night of the murders. We also discovered that O.J. was on his way back from Chicago, where he had arrived from Los Angeles only hours before being informed of his ex-wife's death.

At that point, events began to take a turn that transformed my unease as a friend into the alarm of a lawyer. Shortly after arriving back at his own Brentwood estate, not far from the scene of his ex-wife's murder, O.J. was briefly handcuffed by waiting police officers, acting on the orders of LAPD detective Philip Vannatter, who, along with his partner, Tom Lange, was in charge of investigating the killings. Apparently, Vannatter and Lange had searched the grounds of O.J.'s home without a warrant earlier that morning.

Simpson's attorney, my old friend Howard Weitzman, was on the scene, along with O.J.'s personal lawyer, Leroy "Skip" Taft. Howard convinced Vannatter to remove Simpson's handcuffs, but my alarm mounted as I watched Weitzman and O.J. prepare to drive downtown for a police interrogation. I recall shaking my head and turning to one of our firm's young lawyers, Shawn Chapman, a former public defender, who by then was wearing her own look of incredulity.

"I don't care what the cops want," I told Shawn. "You don't let a traumatized client who hasn't had any sleep and has made two flights across the country in less than twelve hours talk to anybody."

"I don't get it," Shawn replied.

At that moment, a grim-faced O.J. looked back at us from the television screen and, as he slid heavily into a waiting police car, said: "I know nothing."

"Then why in the world are you going downtown," I muttered to no one in particular.

And, then, silently to myself: "My God, they're letting him ride down there alone with the cops." As it later turned out, O.J. answered questions without reservation all the way downtown, while the accompanying officers made notes and his lawyers, Weitzman and Taft, followed in a second car.

In fact, as I subsequently learned, Howard had tried to dissuade O.J. from talking to the police that day. But Simpson, a proud man used to being very much in charge of his own affairs, sometimes has difficulty taking advice. He kept insisting that if he simply explained things to the police, they would accept his word and set about finding the killers. But once they arrived at Parker Center, the LAPD's downtown headquarters, things got even worse.

"We want to talk to O.J., but we really want to talk to him alone," Vannatter told Howard. "If he wants a lawyer present, we won't talk to him right now."

Weitzman resisted. Vannatter persisted. O.J. broke the tie. He had nothing to hide and, therefore, nothing to fear, he said. He went in to talk with the detectives alone. After insisting that the interview at least be tape-recorded, Howard and Skip went off in search of a good cup of cappuccino. Inside the LAPD's elite Robbery-Homicide Division—from which they both would soon retire—Lange and Vannatter were usually described as a "salty" duo. To outsiders, detectives usually say that word means "well-seasoned" or "veteran." To insiders, it also connotes a kind of laziness, a certain cynicism about the criminal justice system, and a willingness to bend inconvenient rules. For the next thirty-three minutes, this "salty" pair was left alone to question a stunned, sleepless, grieving O. J. Simpson as they wished. Their interview completed, they called in a department nurse, Thano Peratis, who took a sample of Simpson's blood.

When they finally finished, Howard made a brief statement to
the crush of reporters gathered outside Parker Center. "We are
done for the day," he said. "We came here to cooperate. We did
that. There is a continuing investigation. If we are asked to come
back, we intend to cooperate." O.J., he said, was "in shock.
He is devastated. He had a tremendous amount of feeling for
Nicole. . . . It's a tremendous loss."

In the next morning's papers and news broadcasts,
Weitzman's comments inevitably were followed by some mention of the fact that O.J. had pled no contest to spousal battery
charges in 1989.

By that afternoon, Los Angeles' rather tightly knit legal community was awash in rumors that Howard Weitzman, who had
done very little criminal work in the years since he won John
DeLorean's stunning acquittal, had withdrawn from the
Simpson case. His replacement, as the telephonic rumor mill had
it, was Century City attorney Robert L. Shapiro. That immediately struck many people as significant, since Shapiro—an
affable man with a wide circle of entertainment industry contacts—was known primarily as a deal maker. The large number
of minor cases he had resolved in that fashion for celebrity
clients, including Johnny Carson, led many of Bob's friends to
refer to him affectionately as "the drunk-driving lawyer to the
stars." We knew each other only slightly, and the only serious
case I could recall him handling was that of Marlon Brando's
son, Christian, who was charged with murdering his sister's
boyfriend. In that instance, Shapiro had arranged for the young
man to plead guilty to voluntary manslaughter.

In fact, as I later learned, Simpson and his principal advisers—
Taft and Robert Kardashian, a businessman and lawyer—had

retained Shapiro at the suggestion of Roger King, one of the owners of the company that syndicates such television shows as *Wheel of Fortune, Jeopardy*, and *Oprah.* Initially, King had also offered to defray part of O.J.'s legal expenses. He never did so, however.

Shapiro's selection was "Topic A" among my associates when I returned to the office from a meeting that afternoon.

"I don't get it," Carl Douglas muttered to me. "They can't really be planning to deal this thing, can they?"

"Well," I replied, "nobody's been arrested yet, so there's no case for anybody to deal."

Carl eloquently rolled his eyes.

By then, I was beginning to field telephone calls of my own from a different, though related, direction. During the televised trial of the police officers accused of beating Rodney King two years before, I had frequently served as an on-the-air commentator. I enjoyed the work, and a number of news executives apparently had taken note. All the networks were gearing up to cover what already was being called "the Simpson case." Everyone was talking about the murders, and the news reports were disquieting.

"Simpson was a winner of the Heisman Trophy."

"He was a commentator on NBC."

"He was a spokesman for Hertz."

"He was highly regarded."

The news readers used the past tense. For some reason—my instincts as a lawyer no doubt—this disturbed me. I thought it was premature. It was like it was a done deal. But O. J. Simpson wasn't dead. The stations were running synopses of his life. As though it was already over. As though, in essence, he was already convicted.

I had not yet spoken to Simpson and there had not yet been

any attempt from anyone in his camp to contact me. But the media's full-blown obsession saddened me, made me wary. I knew the tactics of the LAPD. I knew the media sometimes jumps the gun. Although my only plan was to remain an observer, at the moment I was observing with a certain amount of exterior detachment and interior dread. On my desk that Wednesday afternoon was a stack of phone messages from various producers. I looked at them and thought, "Why not?" By the time I left that day, I had been booked on the next night's *Larry King Show* on CNN and on ABC's *Nightline* the evening after that.

Thursday's evening news was dominated by footage of a grieving O. J. Simpson and his young children, Justin and Sydney, at their mother's funeral. But the tone of King's show, though balanced as usual, was a clear signal of things to come. The other panelists were a magazine journalist and former prosecutor Vincent Bugliosi. King asked me what I would do if I were Simpson's attorney.

"The first priority is putting together a team," I replied. "You can only anticipate that charges will be filed at some point in the near future. It is incumbent upon the defense to anticipate a double homicide filing. He'll want to line up some experts and somebody who is really good at trial, it seems to me. And he has to start combating . . . this trial by press."

To his credit, Shapiro had already begun assembling a top-notch team. He had immediately engaged two of the nation's finest pathologists, Dr. Michael Baden, who had helped perform the autopsy for me in the Ron Settles case, and Baden's colleague, Dr. Barbara Wolf. They had encouraged Bob to sign up Dr. Henry Lee, director of Connecticut's Forensic Science Laboratory and America's most respected criminalist. Thereafter, he also had been in touch with the country's two finest experts on

DNA evidence, Barry Scheck and Peter Neufeld in New York. Bob also had retained a pair of leading legal scholars, Gerald Uelmen, the retired dean of the Santa Clara Law School and California's foremost authority on the U.S. Constitution and Bill of Rights, and Alan Dershowitz of Harvard Law School fame. Recruiting a team of this caliber on such short notice was Bob Shapiro's single most crucial contribution to O. J. Simpson's defense, and its importance should not be minimized. The cast included everyone but a trial lawyer, a fact that would shortly come to preoccupy the client.

Early the next morning, Friday, June 17, Detective Tom Lange telephoned Shapiro and told him that O. J. Simpson would be charged with two counts of first-degree murder. He gave Bob until 10 A.M. to surrender his client to the police at Parker Center. What happened next is the sort of thing that has led many commentators—not unfairly—to suggest that Los Angeles and not Paris is surrealism's natural home. Simpson had spent the night after Nicole's funeral at his friend Bob Kardashian's sprawling ten-thousand-square-foot home in the Encino Hills section of the San Fernando Valley. Shapiro immediately went there, along with his forensic experts and a physician and psychiatrist who were treating the distraught O.J. Together, they rushed Simpson through a series of tests, obtaining blood, hair, and tissue samples, while O.J. and his friends and girlfriend, Paula Barbieri, frantically tried to put his affairs in order. As the hours trickled by, the police became impatient, finally declaring their intention to come to Kardashian's house and take O.J. into custody themselves. Shapiro elected not to tell his client this. When he subsequently went into Simpson's room to inform him that the police had arrived, he discovered O. J. Simpson and his lifelong friend and former teammate, A. C. Cowlings, had fled.

Like much of the rest of the country, I followed these events by radio and, when I reached the office that morning, by television. There was Shapiro, standing in front of a bank of cameras and making his appeal to O.J. to surrender. There was Kardashian, whom Shapiro had convinced to read aloud the rambling, ambiguous letter with its intimations of suicide that a clearly distraught O.J. had left behind. Around me, my associates Carl Douglas, Shawn Chapman, Cameron Stewart, Eddie Harris, Brian Dunn, and Eric Ferrer buzzed with perplexed anxiety at what appeared would be an unfolding tragedy.

They were looking to me for answers, but my deepest thoughts on the matter were increasingly dark and personal. All this was great theater—of a terrible sort. But theater for whose benefit? As far as I could see, nothing that was being said or done had O. J. Simpson's welfare as its central preoccupation. Shapiro's ability to conduct his criminal practice depended mainly on the goodwill of the police department and the district attorney's office. Failure to deliver on a promised surrender under such heavily scrutinized circumstances could easily leave those former good feelings in tatters. All this public hand-wringing, it seemed to me, was intended to make sure that nobody blamed him for this unprecedented mess.

It certainly wasn't my style of advocacy, but I decided to keep my thoughts to myself. At a moment when many of us believed Simpson might well be dead by his own hand, they seemed a secondary consideration. But in less time than I imagined, I would be forced to confront them again.

Because of the three-hour time difference between Washington, D.C., and Los Angeles, *Nightline* guests have to check in with ABC News's local studio in the early evening. So by the time O.J. and A.C. were spotted heading north on the 405 Freeway on the homeward leg of their now celebrated low-speed chase, I was watching it all unfold on a monitor in the main studio at the network's sprawling production facility just north of Sunset Boulevard in East Hollywood. Since my days on the Deadwyler case, I've always had a great respect for the serious news media and number many of its members as my friends.

But sitting there that night, I was acutely aware of the distance between Johnnie L. Cochran, Jr., the advocate, and the bright-eyed, adrenaline-pumping news professionals all around me. In my heart, it was impossible to subsume my personal concern for O. J. Simpson, the desperate, even suicidal man, in the excite-ment of "the story." Moreover, I'd had too much hard experi-ence with the LAPD to trust completely in its ability to bring this whole bizarre incident to a peaceful conclusion.

And yet, a short time later, there was ABC's Ted Koppel introducing me as "a Los Angeles attorney and friend of O. J. Simpson" and asking me to comment on just such a result. "Now this quite extraordinary behavior of today—how would you deal with that in the context of the case?" Koppel inquired.

"Very carefully," I replied. "There is a real problem here. One of your concerns is that the district attorney is going to argue that because there was flight, that showed consciousness of guilt. One of the things one has to deal with is the fact that he did, ulti-mately, turn himself in."

Suddenly, the analyst in me receded and the advocate moved unbidden to the fore: "You know, this is a person not used to being arrested, not used to having a warrant, and I'm not sure he was altogether clear on what was going to happen to him. The good part is he is now in custody without major incident. But one does have to try and explain this. In that connection, the question of his emotional state may play heavily. I think he was confused; I think he was frightened; I think he was very fragile—and, perhaps, suicidal."

Driving the short distance home, I wondered whether I had

ventured too far across the line that delineates analysis from advocacy. As I made my weary way into the house, I looked at Dale and asked simply, "How'd I do?"

"You did a good job," she said with one of her patented half smiles.

There are some reviews that count more than others, though unbeknownst to me, I was collecting other good notices in quarters nearly—but not quite—so important.

THE NEXT MORNING, I WENT TO THE OFFICE TO CATCH UP on all the work I had neglected through the previous two days of turmoil. There was nothing I would have liked better than to end the day with a quiet evening at home. But Dale's sisters, Agnes and Kathy, were our houseguests, and we'd all made plans to spend the afternoon at the Hollywood Bowl, where Bill Cosby had invited us to be his guests at the Playboy Jazz Festival, which he was hosting. From there, we were to go on to the wedding of our close friends, Lisa Gray and Jacob Arback. They were not the kinds of plans you change on a whim.

Bill is a valued friend and adviser of mine. Like all great comic geniuses, he can dissect even the most serious topic, using laughter to lead you where you might otherwise fear to go. Backstage, though, it was clear that even Cosby was fighting to stave off the gloom that O. J. Simpson's predicament had cast across our party. There were jokes, a great deal of mutual kidding, and some photographs. Then, suddenly, Bill draped his arm around my shoulder and guided me to a private corner.

"Johnnie," he said to me, "don't touch it. Don't touch it with a ten-foot pole."

"I think I know what you mean, Bill," I replied, knowing perfectly well what he had in mind.

It was on my mind, too. The lovely wedding pushed these thoughts from my mind. But only temporarily. To this very day I remember the look on my father's face when Dale and I walked through the door at home about eleven-thirty that night. Dad, now retired, lives with us. And by the look on his face I knew that O. J. Simpson had called. Not just once, as Dad quickly informed me, but four or five times. This first call from O.J. came in on June 18, 1994. I had not seen O.J. for more than a year before that. I had not discussed his case with anyone and knew nothing about the details of this case and would not for months.

Inmates in the county jail have access to a phone at specified times during the day. Dad had allowed O.J.'s calls to be recorded on our voice mail.

Dale and I stood together, playing them back. They began with a variety of the halting, somewhat stilted introductions people inevitably use when they resign themselves to talking with a machine. Each message, however, ended with virtually the same words, spoken urgently but clearly in O.J.'s low, strong voice: "Johnnie, I am innocent of these crimes. Please come and see me, man. I need to talk to you."

"Are you going to take it?" Dale asked in a voice that seemed tinged with both anticipation and apprehension.

"Innocent." How many times has my stomach churned at that fearsome word's sound? O.J. always maintained his innocence, from his first tape-recorded call on June 18, 1994, to the day of the verdicts on October 3, 1995. I must say that I have never told anyone, friend or foe, that I believe that O. J. Simpson is guilty or that he should plead guilty to a lesser charge.

And how many times have I done precisely what I did that night—turn to the man who is the father of my conscience as well as my body.

"Well, Chief," I said, employing the affectionate nickname by which Dad has been known by generations of insurance agents, "what do you think? Do you think I should take it?"

My father is an older man with a younger man's eyes, and he fixed them directly on mine. "Does he need your help?" he asked. "If another man needs help and you have it to give, then what is there to decide?" With that, he clamped his large and reassuring hand on my shoulder. My father's manner is mild, but his hands are rough. His mind is fixed on the twenty-first century, but those hands still carry the memory of the cotton fields and their toil, as his heart still cherishes the simple decency that allowed so many in his generation to transcend their time and place. I thought that night that God had never favored any son with a better teacher than the Chief.

And yet the prudent part of me, the man of affairs and substance, remained unsure. O.J.'s calls became a nightly ritual.

"Man," he said to me one night, "everybody says I should be talking to you about this case. I need you. I think I need you on this case. I'm innocent. I did not do this."

I took a deep breath. "Look, O.J., I just don't know at this point. You've got Bob Shapiro. There's so much media attention focused on you right now that if I come down to the jail, it will cause all kinds of talk. You don't need that right now. And before I do anything, I'll need to talk to Shapiro."

O. J. Simpson is not an easy man to put off. It wasn't just that our civil practice was booming, but we were also doing the kinds of cases into which I'd always put my heart—the ones that really make a difference. A criminal case, especially a murder in which the death penalty might be an issue, is a lawyer's highest calling. But, on a personal level, it is also a gut-wrenching emotional roller coaster. I simply didn't know whether I really wanted to make that kind of commitment at this stage in my career. Moreover, I had signed an agreement with NBC News to provide legal commentary on the Simpson case. It was an interesting, challenging new line of endeavor and a terrific source of visibility for our firm. Finally, I had the lingering sense that my acquaintance with O. J. Simpson was just close enough to preclude a strictly professional relationship, which was what this case would require.

APPROXIMATELY TWO WEEKS AFTER THE BODIES OF Nicole Brown and Ron Goldman were discovered, I telephoned Shapiro and told him that his client had contacted me. I told Bob that I was not particularly interested in the case but that before I did anything I thought we should meet and talk. He agreed, and we made a date to get together in a private room at the Beverly Hills Tennis Club on Maple Drive, where Dale is a member. What stands out most in my mind about that meeting is Bob's unusual dress—black shirt, black pants, and a gleaming silver metal belt.

We chatted briefly about strategy for Simpson's upcoming preliminary hearing and agreed that the defense team still lacked the right trial lawyer. Then I told Bob again of O.J.'s repeated requests that I come down to the jail for a meeting.

"Well, gee, Johnnie." He grimaced. "O.J. is also talking to Gerry Spence." He, of course, is the well-known Wyoming defense attorney easily recognized by his trademark Stetson hat and fringed buckskin coat. Somehow, I found it hard to picture Gerry in front of a jury in downtown L.A., where the case by then had been moved. As it turned out, however, things didn't work out between Spence and Shapiro. I've never heard Gerry's side of the story, but Bob subsequently told me that Spence said he just couldn't "be part of an orchestra." Shapiro and I talked a while longer, then parted on amicable terms. I went away somewhat reassured.

But as O.J.'s calls continued, I began to cast around for other trial lawyers to recommend. It would have to be someone with heart *and* moxie. So one of the first people I thought of was my longtime friend Leslie Abramson, who has offices in the same mid-Wilshire building as mine. I knew that she sometimes worked with her close friend Gerald Chaleff, the superb defense attorney who had saved Angelo Buono, the so-called Hillside Strangler, from the gas chamber. Together, they might be the trial team Simpson needed.

About that time, Dale and I flew back to Washington, D.C., where my friend Ron Brown, the secretary of commerce, had invited us to attend a White House summer concert at which Aretha Franklin and Lou Rawls—two of my clients—were the featured performers. I had appeared on that morning's *Today* show to discuss the Simpson case. And, as we made our way through the receiving line, First Lady Hillary Clinton shook my hand and said, "Well, we saw you on television this morning." We chatted for a bit, and it was clear that, as an interested and knowledgeable lawyer, she was following the case.

So, too, were our tablemates for the evening, Ron Brown and Congressman Julian Dixon, an old friend and mentor. Since the case seemed to be on everyone's mind anyway, as the evening wore on I stole away to make a phone call. Why not find out what Leslie's thoughts are? I asked myself. Now, when Leslie and I talk, it's warrior to warrior with a lot of kidding thrown in.

"Les," I said when she picked up the phone in her home, "this is Johnnie and you'll never guess where I'm calling you from."

"Where are you?" she inquired suspiciously.

"I am speaking to you from the White House—"

"Jesus, Johnnie," she said, "is there anyplace you don't do business? Don't you ever relax? Oh, don't tell me, the President's your client now."

"No, no, not yet, anyway," I said. "Besides, you know the defense never rests."

"Is that why I'm always tired? Okay, what's up?"

We spoke seriously for some time. She said that she and Gerald would be interested in principle, assuming the appropriate arrangements could be made. I told her I would get back to her. But when the evening broke up and Dale and I returned to our hotel room, there were more messages from O. J. Simpson. The need for some sort of decision was coming closer.

BACK IN LOS ANGELES, THE AGGRESSIVE MEDIA COV-erage of Simpson's situation had become a major source of concern among many African Americans. District Attorney Gil Garcetti had already moved the case from the county's Santa Monica Courthouse to the downtown Criminal Courts Building. In part, that was because he wanted the prosecution to remain firmly under his thumb. But he had also told a columnist for the *Los Angeles Times* that he feared a guilty verdict handed down by one of the nearly all-white juries common on the West Side would not be accepted in the African American community. Memories of the rioting that followed the acquittal of the LAPD officers accused of beating Rodney King were still fresh in people's minds. But many black leaders were also concerned that the virulent campaign against Simpson being conducted in the tabloid press would lead the D.A.'s office to do something it seldom did in this kind of case—seek the death penalty.

I agreed to accompany a group concerned with the issue that included Connie Rice of the NAACP Legal Defense Fund, John Mack of the Urban League, the Reverend Cecil Murray of the First AME Church, and Joe Duff of the NAACP and others to a meeting with Garcetti, who met us in the Urban League's conference room. We made our case to him, and, shortly thereafter, the district attorney's office announced that it would not seek the death penalty for O. J. Simpson.

Simpson's calls continued. In California, people accused of felonies can either be indicted by a grand jury or given a preliminary hearing, or "prelim," at which a municipal court judge determines whether the prosecution has sufficient evidence to warrant a trial in superior court.

On June 28, the eve of Simpson's preliminary hearing, another voice joined the chorus. I returned home after a long day to find a voice mail message that began: "Johnnie, this is Bob Kardashian. Sorry to call you so late, but we've got a problem and I need to talk with you. It's very important. So if you could call me . . ."

As I watched the six-day preliminary hearing, I knew at least part of the problem Kardashian had on his mind. Like Carl, Shawn, and the other experienced criminal defense lawyers in our firm, I was mystified by some of what the defense did. It seemed ill prepared to really examine Mark Fuhrman, the LAPD detective who seemed to have discovered most of the key evidence implicating O.J., including the bloody glove recovered on the grounds of his Rockingham estate.

Gerry Uelmen argued incisively and cogently that all the evidence collected at Rockingham ought to be excluded because no warrant had been obtained for the search, a clear violation of the Fourth Amendment. But as any experienced California lawyer knows, that is an issue you may raise only once. A negative ruling precludes you from opening the question again. No municipal court judge—subject to popular election and hopeful of gubernatorial elevation to the superior court—would ever suppress evidence of that sort in so highly scrutinized a case. There's little justice in that, but it is the reality in California's intensely politicized criminal justice system.

And, as I subsequently discovered, there was a reason Gerry, one of the state's finest legal scholars, had raised the issue in the preliminary. He had been told to do so by Shapiro, who not only was convinced that Judge Kathleen Kennedy-Powell would grant the motion because she had studied constitutional law under Uelmen but also because he believed that this case could be won at prelim and that Simpson would go home free.

The preliminary hearing concluded on July 8, 1994. O. J. Simpson was held over for trial, with his next court appearance set for July 22, two weeks hence.

The next weekend, Dale and I flew to Chicago for a meeting of NAACP Legal Defense Fund lawyers, at which I was the guest speaker. Simpson tracked us down from his jail phone, and we spent two days collecting his messages. "I at least have to talk to this man," I told her. That Monday, after the preliminary hearing, I phoned Shapiro and informed him of the continued calls.

I began to poll my friends for advice. Ted Alexander, a close friend since junior high school, urged me to take the case. Syd Irmas and Ron Sunderland argued that I should walk away.

"What do you need this for?" Ron asked. "You've worked so hard to build your practice, and this isn't going to help one bit."

There was also another client whose interests I had to consider. While we all believed Michael Jackson's situation had been resolved, the district attorney's investigation into his case still had not been closed. Some of Michael's business associates had told me he was concerned that if I took the Simpson case, I might not be able to give his affairs the attention they deserved. I flew to New York, where Michael was recording a new album at Studio One. Wayne Nagin, his longtime security person, met me at the door and led me into the soundproof room where Jackson was working.

"Michael," I told him, "O. J. Simpson has asked me to become involved in his defense. I don't know what I'm going to do, but it's important to me that you know that this will in no way diminish the sense of responsibility I feel toward you. I don't want you to doubt our office's abilities to act on your behalf, whatever happens. We know your matter is still not fully resolved, and all of us will be completely available to you at all times, no matter what I decide about O.J."

"Look, Johnnie," Michael said in his soft voice, "I want you to do what you have to do. But I want you to be there for me. If you can do that, then okay. Tell O.J. I love him. Tell him it's all right."

"Thanks, Michael," I said. "And don't worry. I'll always be there for you. You've got my word."

As my cab took me back to my hotel, I thought: There are a couple more pieces I need to put in place.

THAT NEXT SUNDAY, I WAS AT SECOND BAPTIST A LITTLE early. I needed to talk with my pastor, the Reverend William Saxe Epps. We spoke quietly together there in the light of the stained glass windows of our historic church.

"Pastor," I began. Then, thinking better of it, I just asked, "Please pray for me."

He knew what was on my mind and heart. "See, Johnnie, to thine own self be true," he said. "Just say what you want and the Lord hears. Sometimes, you're in a place where everybody loves you and there's nothing like it. When folks love you, you can do no wrong. But when they don't love you anymore, it seems you can do no right."

Emboldened, I said, "Pastor, you know I have this decision to make, and I'm still not sure what to do. Will you pray for me?"

Without hesitation, he bowed his head and prayed: "Lord, lead this man in the way that is best. Let him be honest with himself about what he is doing and why."

There was nothing to say but "Amen."

After church, I had one more stop to make. At my mother's crypt, I knelt, offered her my love—and waited. It was a wonderful, ineffably peaceful silence. And there, deep in my heart, I heard Hattie Cochran's voice repeating the same question the husband she loved so much had asked me: "Does he need your help?"

I went home that night and talked the matter out with Dale— "brought it to closure," as she likes to say. As always, she was supportive, though as an experienced marketing professional, she had a far clearer idea, I think, of what a burden the public scrutiny we were about to undergo would impose. On balance, taking O. J. Simpson's case would be a "bad" business decision in much the same way my decision to pursue the Settles' lawsuit had been. But at the end of the day, you decide certain questions with your heart rather than your head.

I called Ron Sunderland and told him of my decision. "Look," I said, "the guy needs me. Besides, the old criminal lawyer in me is starting to stir. I don't want to sit this one out as a commentator on the sidelines. Now that I've made up my mind, it would upset me greatly if somebody else won the case."

The next night, O. J. Simpson called. "Please, you have got to help me," he repeated. "I need you on this case. I have nobody else to try the case. I understand you're the best trial lawyer I can get for this. I want you to come and do it."

This time I answered. "Well, my brother," I replied, "you've got me."

Bob Shapiro could read the handwriting on the wall. When we spoke the following morning, he informed me, "Johnnie, I've decided you're the guy we need on this team."

"Thank you, Bob," I replied dryly.

We met shortly thereafter in his rather cramped Century City office to finalize our arrangements. I informed him that Carl

Douglas and Shawn Chapman would also be working on the case.

That Friday, July 22, 1994, I entered the lockup behind Department 100 in the Criminal Courts Building. It was the first time I had seen O.J. in at least a year and a half. He appeared tired and haggard but brightened immediately when he caught sight of me. He jumped up and approached the wire mesh that separated us. Simultaneously, as if on cue, we raised our hands and pressed them together against the wire.

O.J. looked into my eyes and almost sighed. "Man, am I glad to see you. Thank you."

I breathed a silent prayer that he would say the same when our long ordeal was through.

My children and I on Christmas Day, 1994. That's Jonathan, Melodie, and Tiffany.

Dale's uncle, Dr. Elliott J. Mason, Sr., the former pastor of Trinity Baptist Church in L.A., is very special to me for many reasons, not the least of which is that he prayed with us on the morning of my mother's death. Here, the two of us are pictured at a happier point in time in 1988.

Dale and I celebrating Christmas in 1993.

One of my favorite people in the whole world, my mother-in-law, the lovely Daisy Mason.

All photos, unless otherwise indicated, are from the Cochran family archives.

Relaxing with Michael Brown, Ron Brown's son, Julian Dixon, friend and Democratic congressman from California, and the late Secretary of Commerce Ron Brown. We lost a great leader and an extraordinary person in Ron.

Ron Sunderland has been my best friend since my days at Loyola Law School. In the middle is friend and premier business-man Herman J. Russell of Atlanta.

Four of my oldest and dearest friends gathered at the Charles R. Drew dinner. They are the Reverend Paul Martin, pastor of Macedonia Baptist Church in Denver; Dr. Ted Alexander, assistant superintendent, Los Angeles Unified School District; Bill Baker, Sr., retired inspector, Los Angeles County Sheriff's Department and husband of my sister Pearl; Dr. George F. Jackson, Jr., cardiovascular surgeon, who helped save my mother's life in 1971.

I was deeply honored to receive the Man of the Year Award from the Brotherhood Crusade in 1994. The Brotherhood Crusade is one of the finest philanthropic organizations in Los Angeles. Its mission is to fund deserving community programs throughout L.A.

Malcolm Payne Sr.

Malcolm Payne Sr.

Ed Lewis, publisher and CEO of *Essence* magazine, poses with me along with Michael Jackson and Attorney Carl Douglas at my office in January 1995 .

Conferring with my client, O. J. Simpson, during a pretrial hearing.

Despite what the press wanted people to believe about O.J.'s past relationships, Marguerite Simpson-Thomas, O.J.'s first wife, was a major presence supporting O.J. at the trial. In the middle is O.J.'s daughter, Arnelle Simpson, and to her left is his sister Carmelita Durio.

An informal gathering on January 11, 1995, prior to opening statements. From left to right that's me with Gerald Uelmen, Robert Shapiro, Judge Lance Ito (partially obscured), Marcia Clark (back to camera), Bill Hodgman, Cheri Lewis, and Christopher Darden.

My opening statement on January 25, 1995. Despite the many objections by the prosecution, I persevered.

Early in the trial, Marcia Clark, Christopher Darden, and I were able to enjoy a few moments of levity. This one was during a brief recess before the jury joined us in the courtroom.

My cross-examination of Detective Tom Lange. By this point, Lange had been on the stand for almost a week. The strain is beginning to show.

The defense goes on the offensive: Two of the most effective cross-examinations during the trial were conducted by two lawyers with vastly different styles. F. Lee Bailey's cross of Detective Mark Fuhrman (top photo) had elements of high drama, while Barry Scheck's methodical, relentless questioning (bottom photo) of LAPD criminalist Dennis Fung was something to behold. Different styles, same result—the systematic dismantling of the prosecution's version of events.

At a work session in my office in early June 1995. By this time the prosecution had been presenting its case for nearly six months. Bob Blasier, our master of technology and graphics, is at the laptop. Robert Shapiro, Carl Douglas, F. Lee Bailey, Dr. Henry Lee, and yours truly round out the cast.

A very revealing photo of my colleagues and their contributions. To my right is Barry Scheck making a point, and to my left is Robert Shapiro.

Judge Lance Ito. Despite enormous personal and professional sacrifices, Judge Ito performed capably under those heavy burdens. I say that despite the overwhelming number of rulings he made in favor of the prosecution.

Sometimes you try to give advice and it goes unheeded.

American Airlines passenger Steve Valerie's testimony proved quite valuable. He flew with O.J. on the June 12th flight to Chicago and had clear recollections of carefully scanning O.J.'s hands and looking for a championship ring. Like the ring that O.J. never won, there was also no cut on either of O.J.'s hands.

LAPD officer Don Thompson provided us with a damning bit of testimony. He was the officer who was told by Detective Vannatter to handcuff O. J. Simpson as soon as he set foot on the Rockingham property. If he wasn't already a prime suspect, why were they handcuffing him?

Here we see some of our best expert witnesses in action. In the photo at the top, Herb MacDonell explains the mystery of the blood on the socks. In the middle photo, Dr. Henry Lee gives one of his patented demonstrations to the jury. In the bottom photo we see Dr. Michael Baden on the witness stand actually enjoying cross-examination.

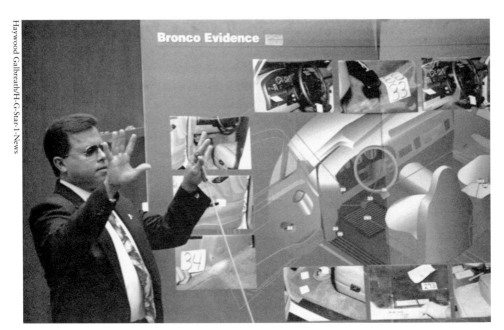

Sometimes you get help from the strangest sources. "Bloodhound" William Blasini took it upon himself to check out O.J.'s impounded Bronco for signs of blood. Here he's demonstrating how he put his hands on the Bronco's window to peer inside and leave his fingerprints to verify that he was there. He saw no blood.

Midnight hour for the prosecution, when all their chariots turned into pumpkins. At 4:35 P.M. on June 13, 1995, with glove expert Richard Rubin on the stand, Christopher Darden's nightmare begins. O.J. is seen clutching the pen he was asked to pick up, a demonstration that was supposed to show that the gloves did, in fact, fit. As we now all know, the gloves didn't fit.

Kathleen Bell showed remarkable courage in coming forward with her testimony regarding racist remarks she heard Detective Mark Fuhrman make at a Marine Corps recruiting station. She faxed my office on July 18, 1994, and also contacted the prosecution. Merely wanting to set the record straight, she was disregarded by the prosecution.

One of the greatest days of my life in court. David finally slays the Philistine. Standing behind his constitutional protection against self-incrimination, Detective Mark Fuhrman, flanked by his lawyer, Darryl Mounger, pleads the Fifth Amendment. September 6, 1995, the day this man's silence spoke volumes about the level of deceit and doubt that plagued the prosecution's case.

That same day, Mr. Darden's abortive attempt to cross-examine Laura Hart McKinny, possessor of the vile so-called Fuhrman tapes, continued his antagonistic questioning of witnesses. Ms. Hart McKinny asked Darden, "Why are we having this hostile conversation?"

Closing argument, September 27, 1995. If you had asked me days, hours, or even seconds before I began my close, I would not have told you that I would have put on that watch cap. Sometimes things just happen. The expression on the faces of the two lead prosecutors says it all.

The defense team gathers at my office (from left to right): Robert Kardashian, Alan Dershowitz, Barry Scheck, Leroy "Skip" Taft, F. Lee Bailey, Peter Neufeld, Carl Douglas, Robert Shapiro, William Thompson, Bob Blasier, Ralph Lotkin, and Shawn Chapman.

Our team's expert witnesses (from left to right): Chuck Morton, Dr. Henry Lee, Dr. Robert Huizenga, Larry Ragle, Dr. Herb MacDonell, me, Dr. Michael Baden, and Dr. Bertram Maltz. Seated is Dr. Barbara Wolf.

Here after court, F. Lee Bailey, Robert Shapiro, and I face the media.

Back in my offices following the verdict on October 3, 1995. From left to right that's me, Shawn Chapman, Carl Douglas (standing), Gerald Uelmen, and Chuck Lindner.

The staff at the law offices of Johnnie L. Cochran, Jr. No superlative is too good for this team. From top left to bottom right: Excel Sharrieff, Marc Dobbs, Charlesetta Williams, Patsy Henry, Clara Hill-Williams, Clarence Daniels, Fred Sherrard, Akida Mushaka, Rolanda Carter, Jennifer Darien, Irma Castellanos, Jan Thomas, Toni Adams, Carmen Qualls, Eloise McGill, Johnnie L. Cochran, Jr., Jentry Collins, Carl Douglas, Shawn Chapman, Cameron Stewart, Dion Raymond, Tammy Wayne, Eddie Harris, Sonia Davis, Eric Ferrer, Debbie Daniels, Maria Arciniega, Don Wilson, Brian Dunn, Kamau Omowale.

Members of the Simpson jury join us at our Christmas party along with Mr. and Mrs. Benny Baker and their daughter Terri.

In August of this year, I got a chance to renew acquaintances with the Reverend C.A.W. Clark, former pastor of Little Union Baptist Church in Shreveport. Though many years have passed, the Reverend Clark has retained much of his fiery spirit.

Here I am with my current pastor, the Reverend Dr. William Saxe Epps. We're pictured at his father's church in Jersey City, New Jersey, where I spoke in August 1996. Pastor Epps has been a source of inspiration and great support.

Among the many cases we will be pursuing in our search for justice is the Reginald Denny civil trial. Here, Reginald and I are flanking Larry King.

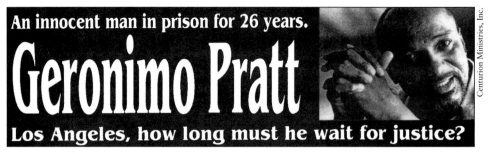

An innocent man in prison for 26 years.

Geronimo Pratt

Los Angeles, how long must he wait for justice?

This billboard went up in Los Angeles in August 1996. The answer to the question posed is: If I have my way, the waiting is over.

Elmer "Geronimo" Pratt was unjustly convicted of murder in 1972. Because of the FBI's Counter-Intelligence Program, this innocent man has spent more than twenty-five years in jail. The defense will not rest until he, a man about whom I care deeply, goes free.

11

Thirty Pieces
of Silver

MINUTES AFTER O. J. SIMPSON AND I HAD TOUCHED
hands there in the lockup, we were all standing in front of Judge
Cecil Mills, then the presiding judge of the Los Angeles County
Superior Court's Criminal Division.

I was somewhat surprised, though flattered, at O.J.'s sudden
ebullience. Nor was I the only one to take notice. As the Associated Press's Linda Deutsch, America's premier trial reporter,
noted in her account of that morning's proceedings:

> It was a reborn Simpson at Friday's arraignment, no longer the
> dazed defendant who could barely utter his name at his first court
> appearance a month ago. Here was the O.J. his fans had known
> and loved for decades—a man who looked like a winner.

Whatever lingering doubts I might have felt about the wisdom of my decision to enter the case vanished as I listened to my new client's response when Judge Mills asked him, "How do you plead?"

"Absolutely, one hundred percent not guilty," O.J. said with as much conviction as I have ever heard in a courtroom. There are those, of course, who ascribed his delivery to his actor's training. I can only assume they never saw any of his films.

The morning's major surprise came when Mills announced he was sending our case to Judge Lance A. Ito, whom I had come to know when he worked in the Hardcore Gang Unit of the district attorney's office during my tenure. Prior to the trials of particularly serious or high-profile cases in Los Angeles County, it is not unusual for both prosecutors and defense attorneys to meet informally with the presiding judge to give them some sense of which, if any, of the available judges are most acceptable to their side. It's a subtle dance, but those who learn its steps can often gain an important advantage.

As an attorney who had never tried a murder case before, Shapiro essentially was ignorant of this process. He had told me he believed our case would be sent to Judge Paul Flynn, a wealthy former federal prosecutor. At the last minute, however, the court administration apparently had second thoughts about transferring the case to Judge Flynn, who was said to be lukewarm to the notion of presiding over such a high-profile case. Ito was the assistant presiding judge and a popular figure among his fellow judges, the overwhelming majority of whom were also former prosecutors of one sort or another. It was later learned he had waged a quiet but determined political campaign among the court's administrators to get the Simpson trial.

I don't like surprises in court, but I wasn't at all unhappy with Ito's selection, even though his wife, Captain Peggy York, was the LAPD's highest-ranking woman, shortly to be placed in command of the department's Internal Affairs Division. In fact, in accepting Lance Ito as our judge, we formally waived our client's right to assert any conflict of interest growing out of his wife's position. At the time, no one could have anticipated the controversial role Ito's marital situation would come to occupy in the proceedings. Still, I knew Lance to be a highly intelligent, widely read, extraordinarily hardworking judge. He has an impish sense of humor and, as a jurist, is about as fair-minded as his exclusively prosecutorial experience permits. To my mind, he also has another saving grace, one we Californians are perhaps more conscious of than other Americans. As the son of loyal Nisei who suffered inexcusable mistreatment by our government during the Second World War, Ito has firsthand knowledge of racism's corrosive impact on American society. His conservative, former deputy D.A.'s political instincts may sometimes war with that consciousness, as they did during the Simpson trial's later stages, but nothing can totally erase what his heart knows.

The potential significance of Ito's sensitivity to such issues was clear from all the news reports filed from the courtroom that day. Without exception they noted not only that I was an experienced trial lawyer whose clients had included Michael Jackson, but also that I was the first black attorney to join Simpson's defense team. Linda Deutsch's report noted that on this, my first day in court as Simpson's attorney, my presence was "important because race could become an issue in the case." A few also remarked on my close ties to Los Angeles' African American leaders and reported that I had been part of the delegation that had met with Garcetti to discuss whether or not O.J. would face the death penalty. Many also pointed out that "sources" among Simpson's defense lawyers already had signaled their intention to try to prove that the glove recovered at Rockingham had been planted by a white LAPD officer.

Since I had just taken up Simpson's cause that day, the defense sources alluded to did not include me. In fact, the source of the information concerning the possibility of a white detective—Mark Fuhrman—planting evidence at O.J.'s Rockingham home was Bob Shapiro. Earlier that week, *New Yorker* correspondent Jeffrey Toobin, a reporter for whom I have little respect and do not trust, had published a piece quoting from legal documents Fuhrman had filed in connection with his failed attempt to obtain a disability pension from the LAPD. In those documents were reports of psychiatric examinations during which Fuhrman had not only professed profound hostility toward blacks, Latinos, and other minorities but had also described incidents of violence directed against nonwhites. He further alleged that his racial animosity stretched back to his service in the U.S. Marine Corps, before he joined the police department.

According to Toobin, Simpson's defense would attempt to use this evidence of Fuhrman's racism to explain his unusual role in the events that followed the discovery of the bodies of Nicole Brown and Ron Goldman. Fuhrman, a detective assigned to the LAPD's West Los Angeles Division, had made the first thorough investigation of the murder scene, pinpointing many key items of evidence. He was unwatched and unsupervised for various periods of time during those early-morning hours. When Lange and Vannatter arrived at the Bundy site to take charge, it was Fuhrman who guided them to Rockingham, allegedly to inform Simpson of his ex-wife's death. Since he had visited O.J.'s residence earlier, Fuhrman insisted on leading the way. At Rockingham, it was Fuhrman, again alone, who claimed to have spotted minute traces of blood on O.J.'s white Ford Bronco, which was parked on the street. When nobody inside responded to Lange and Vannatter's repeated soundings of the gate's buzzer, it was Fuhrman who climbed the wall and admitted his colleagues, who commenced their warrantless search of the grounds. During that search, it was Fuhrman—once again utterly alone—who purported to have found a bloody glove matching the one at the murder scene in a narrow passage behind the guest house.

It was quite a night for an ambitious young West Side detective who had been rebuffed in repeated attempts to gain admission into the elite Robbery-Homicide Unit to which both Lange and Vannatter belonged. But what advanced this prodigy of detection from the unusual to the curious was the fact that Fuhrman's name appeared nowhere in the Robbery-Homicide detectives' report of the night's activities. That, of course, aroused the suspicions of defense investigators Bill Pavelic, himself a former LAPD detective, and Pat McKenna and John McNally, both of whom had long worked with F. Lee Bailey. Once they began to uncover evidence of Fuhrman's dubious past, his role moved from the merely puzzling to the possibly sinister.

At the very least, it was obvious that critical items of evidence seeming to link O. J. Simpson to the murders of his ex-wife and Ron Goldman had been gathered by a detective who, according to his own account, was a virulent racist. Or perhaps he was, as the police officials who denied his disability claim seemed to believe, not really a violent racist but merely a colossal liar.

It is upon such threads that successful defenses often hang. Shapiro had chosen to begin spinning his by giving the *New Yorker*'s Toobin an off-the-record briefing on what was known about Fuhrman. In the course of that conversation, he let drop that the detective's incriminating comments were contained in the public record of his disability suit against the city. It didn't take much imagination to suspect that Toobin—himself an inexperienced lawyer and former federal prosecutor—wouldn't have much trouble obtaining the information directly.

One of the consequences of Toobin's article and a similar piece that appeared simultaneously in the *Los Angeles Times* was that important witnesses with firsthand knowledge of Fuhrman's racist inclinations came forward. All in all, it was a fairly successful exercise. And during my first weeks on the case, Shapiro several times smugly recounted the whole sequence as further evidence of his dexterity in handling the media. But fifteen months later, when Bob Shapiro accused the rest of us of "dealing the race card," he had conveniently forgotten that he was the one who first shuffled the deck.

As I soon discovered, my presence had been a matter of serious note not only in the media but also on the other side of the courtroom aisle. By the time O. J. Simpson's trial actually began in January of 1995, the Los Angeles County district attorney's office would have more than forty-two deputy D.A.'s and dozens of clerks working on the case. But at O.J.'s arraignment, we faced just two prosecutors, Marcia Clark and Bill Hodgman. I knew Bill from my own days in the D.A.'s office and had faced him as an adversary when I won Todd Bridges' two acquittals. He is a bright, even-tempered, almost doggedly civil man. Marcia I knew only by reputation as one of the office's rising young stars. She had run up a string of successful homicide prosecutions and had been the D.A. personally called to the scene by Phil Vannatter the night the bodies of Nicole Brown and Ron Goldman were discovered. A passionate and zealous advocate, she sometimes seemed to have difficulty maintaining her stamina and deciding when not to fight. Still, as the trial went on, my regard for Marcia increased, and I felt she was the one member of the prosecution team who could hurt us if given the chance.

But I wonder how she and Bill would have felt if they'd had the opportunity to listen in on the telephone conversation I had with their boss, Gil Garcetti, just prior to the arraignment. I'd been out of the office most of that afternoon, so as I drove down the Harbor Freeway on the way to my next appointment, I phoned in to pick up my messages. At the top of the stack was a call from Garcetti.

When I phoned his office a few minutes later, Gil quickly came on the line. Despite our differences over the Settles and other cases, we had remained friends since our days together in the D.A.'s office. When Gil ran for district attorney, I raised money for his campaign and, more important, personally introduced him to the congregations at Second Baptist and First AME, churches that are centers of political activity in Los Angeles' African American community. We briefly exchanged pleasantries, then Gil came to the point.

"Johnnie," he said, "there's no need to take this thing to trial. We can get it settled and behind us right now."

"What have you got in mind?" I asked. Though I had no intention of bargaining away the freedom of a client who unwaveringly asserted his innocence, I wondered just how far Gil was willing to go.

"Well, suppose we let your guy plead to a second?" he replied.

I decided to see how eager Gil really was. At the very least it would give me a hint of his confidence in his prosecutors and their case. "A second!" I said, feigning amazement. "What about a voluntary manslaughter?"

"Look," Garcetti said, "I think a second is more than fair, but if you want to come in, we can talk about it. Things can be worked out."

"Gil," I replied, "there really isn't anything to talk about. My client says he is innocent. So unless you're willing to cut him loose, there's no point in our meeting about this."

I drove on down the Harbor Freeway trying to decide which was more preposterous—Garcetti's attempt to deal away a case his office claimed was ironclad or his willingness to discuss the proposal over a cellular phone hookup on which God knows who could be listening in. From the first moment I had spoken with him after his arrest, O. J. Simpson had unceasingly maintained his innocence to me. As far as I was concerned, that meant there would be no deals no matter how good the offer. I take my clients at their word or I don't take them as clients. As I was about to discover, other members of the defense team had other ideas.

Four days after the arraignment, on Tuesday, July 26, the defense team held its first general meeting. From the outset, it was clear to me that the case had already outgrown both the resources of Shapiro's modest staff and the ability of his cramped physical facilities to accommodate it. Even allowing for the rapid pace at which Bob—quite correctly—had elected to proceed toward trial, the disarray was troubling. Bob rented space from a large Century City law firm, and there just wasn't enough room to accommodate everything and everyone we needed. Files were spilling across the floor, phones were constantly tied up, and Gerry Uelmen, our team's most distinguished member, was forced to work on critical and sensitive motions at a table in the firm's law library while clerks and other attorneys streamed in and out. Even parking was a problem. Since Shapiro had no assigned spaces or the ability to validate our tickets, it cost each one of us sixteen dollars every time we had to go to his office.

We met that day in one of the conference rooms. Uelmen and

I were there, along with Carl Douglas and Shawn Chapman, as well as the three investigators, Pavelic, McNally, and McKenna. Sara Caplan, a very capable associate of Shapiro's who would ultimately leave the team, was present, as was Barry Scheck. Shortly after we began, Dr. Henry Lee joined us, while Michael Baden and Alan Dershowitz participated by speaker phone. But nothing had quite prepared us for the way in which Bob began the meeting: "How many people here think O. J. Simpson is guilty?" he asked, looking around the table. It was an astounding way to begin organizing the defense of a client who never once ceased to assert his innocence of the crimes of which he was accused.

"What the hell was that about?" Carl demanded nearly three hours later as he, Shawn, and I made our way back to our car. Carl often plays the role of devil's advocate when we discuss cases. I suggested to him that perhaps Bob simply was doing the same. But from the looks on their faces, I could see neither he nor Shawn was buying it. And the truth was I couldn't even convince myself. Still, we had signed on as members of a team, and—as I reminded them—we owed it to our client to try and make it work.

But it wasn't going to be easy. At the close of our meetings—whose numbers seemed to grow in inverse proportion to their productivity—Bob on occasion would ask Carl, Shawn, and the investigators to leave the room so that he could discuss some "sensitive" item with the team's "senior" members. It was deeply insulting, especially to my associates, who were used to functioning in an office where work, information, and trust were shared equally. Carl quite rightly resented the whole business and would wait outside for me, seething somewhere between rage and tears.

The whole charade was pointless anyway, since the minute I emerged, I would brief them both on whatever had been discussed. Usually, it was nothing more than one of the tidbits of Hollywood gossip that seemed to cling to Bob like lint. Once, for example, he breathlessly informed us that he had "obtained information that Nicole had carried on a lesbian relationship" with her friend Faye Resnick. The rest of us just looked at each other—and then at the floor.

On another occasion, while the rest of the team scrambled to keep abreast of the case while preparing for jury selection, Bob confided that he had been preparing a list of films in which "courageous" juries acquit the accused.

"We have to be more concerned with the climate of public opinion," he explained, "so I plan to use my contacts with network and cable executives to get them to program as many of these movies as we can get on before jury selection starts."

"Well," I thought, "it's a dirty job, but . . ."

I continued to chalk much of this up to Bob's inexperience with murder cases. Moreover, I was adamant about tuning everything else out so I could prepare for jury selection, my first task for the team. It is a commonplace of legal commentary to note that cases are won and lost when their juries are picked. It's one of those commonplaces that happen to be true. Like most successful trial lawyers, I have a great deal of confidence in my ability to select jurors. This time around, however, I would be working with an extraordinary jury consultant named Jo-Ellan Dimitrius, whose record of success with Los Angeles juries is virtually unmatched in her field.

Her initial public opinion surveys revealed a number of heartening facts. For one thing, fully 46 percent of those surveyed said they "would like to believe O.J. didn't do it." That is an extraordinary reservoir of goodwill in a society in which little more than lip service is usually paid to the presumption of innocence. The polling also found that majorities of every ethnic group felt the LAPD frequently treated African American suspects unfairly.

While more than nine out of ten of those surveyed had followed the case closely through the media and had an unusually detailed knowledge of the physical and scientific evidence likely to be presented, a whopping 66 percent of all respondents did *not* believe O.J. had had enough time to commit the murders. All these sentiments and a willingness to entertain the notion of O.J.'s innocence were strongest among middle-aged black women.

These findings—many of which cut across ethnic and gender lines—were not a product of some reflexive racial attitude but of historical and cultural experience. America's African American communities are places where the vitality of oral history remains strong. Black women are the primary repository of their community's collective memory. In Los Angeles, that means they recall not only the lives of their immediate families and neighbors but also the outcome of legal cases that stand as landmarks in their community—like *Deadwyler* and *Settles*. They have had to assume that role because blacks for so many generations were denied any real access to the media through which the larger society formalizes its history—newspapers, magazines, and books. The persistence of such orally transmitted memories does not render African Americans of either sex unwilling to convict criminals who happen to be black. They hand down such convictions every day in courtrooms all across the country. In fact, as our pretrial survey found, 65 percent of all the blacks polled felt African Americans usually received justice from Los Angeles' legal system. But because they do possess those unclouded historical memories, African American jurors, particularly in Los Angeles, are less likely to assume the police are always well-meaning and infallible, and these jurors are more stringent than those of some other ethnic groups in demanding the state meet its burden of proof.

Through polling and the use of focus groups conducted in a

separate Santa Monica facility, Jo-Ellan and I continued to work on the questionnaire we would present to prospective jurors. The document we finally compiled was seventy-six pages long and contained 294 questions. They ranged from the standard inquiries about familial and residential history to questions about education and attitudes toward domestic violence, ethnic prejudice, DNA, and expert witnesses. We asked about their exposure to media coverage of the case as well as their familiarity with the Brentwood area. We probed not only their religious and political views but also their preferences in hobbies and entertainment. We asked how often they watched *Monday Night Football* and whether simply filling out the questionnaire itself had caused them "to form an opinion about this case." At the end of the day, Jo-Ellan promised, we would have a more detailed and systematic understanding of our prospective jurors than they did of themselves.

As our work on this critical phase of the proceedings continued, I struggled to maintain a friendly, collegial relationship with Bob Shapiro. With Carl's encouragement, I began riding to court with Bob and his longtime driver, Keno Jenkins, in Shapiro's black sport utility vehicle. Bob would leave the gated, West Side community where he lives and swing by our mid-Wilshire office to pick me up so we could chat on the fifteen- or twenty-minute drive downtown. Unfortunately, in my mind these sessions just reinforced the differences in the way we approached our client and his situation.

Bob had made careful calculations about how much money he intended to make from the case. The figure he cited most frequently was $5 million, which he planned to use to wrap up his criminal law practice and move into sports and entertainment representation, perhaps even movie producing. He repeatedly chided me for giving free speeches to churches, schools, and community groups—something I have always done.

"There's real money to be made in this stuff, Johnnie," he said. "It's crazy to give it away."

Frequently, he would share the tips he'd received from his expanding circle of show business friends. At one point, for example, he informed me that Michael Ovitz—then head of Creative Artists Agency, Hollywood's most powerful talent agency—had advised him he was "on camera too much." I tried to suppress my increasing irritation with what seemed to me a preoccupation with everything but our client's welfare. With jury selection looming before us, I forced myself to focus on a process that I knew could be as decisive as it was intricate.

On Tuesday, September 26, we began choosing the twelve ordinary people who would decide O. J. Simpson's fate. With a capacity of 250, the room where potential jurors assemble is the largest in the Criminal Courts Building. At precisely 1:30 P.M. we entered in procession—a bailiff in the lead, followed by Judge Ito in his robes, O.J., Shapiro and me, then Marcia Clark and Bill Hodgman. Ito mounted the dais at the front of the room and began his remarks by saying: "This is the case of the *People of California versus Orenthal James Simpson.* Will you please stand, Mr. Simpson."

As O.J. rose, a collective gasp escaped from many of those 250 throats. Ito then introduced each of the lawyers and gave a brief but eloquent talk on the constitutional responsibilities of jurors. He explained that they would be given our questionnaire, which they were to fill out completely before leaving that day. He also estimated that Simpson's trial would last four months. A year later, I would wonder in passing whether any of the remaining panelists even remembered Ito's hopeful prediction.

Based on the polling and focus-group data, Jo-Ellan and I had an ideal juror in mind, preferably a woman in her thirties or forties with some personal or familial experience with law enforcement. Such familiarity usually breeds not contempt but realism. We wanted jurors who were able to bring to bear that element of real-world experience as they weighed the credibility of the testifying officers against that of O. J. Simpson, who we then expected would take the stand on his own behalf. To our way of thinking, African American women who met these criteria would be the ideal jurors, but women of any ethnicity or race probably would be preferable to men.

After carefully reviewing *all* the questionnaires, we assigned each of the prospective jurors a numerical rating—the most desirable panelists got a "1," the least acceptable a "5." With that behind us, we began the actual questioning of our candidates in the process called "voir dire." Downtown L.A. is my "home court." I have picked hundreds of criminal and civil juries from its pool. Questioning them is, for me, a relaxed, almost conversational exercise. These are the people of all races and backgrounds with whom I grew up and alongside whom I have worked all my life. We speak to each other with understanding.

Prosecutors, who lack that background and traditionally harbor an ideological suspicion of minority jurors, lack that sense of comfort. And in this instance, it showed. In his questioning of one elderly black man, Watson Calhoun, Hodgman stumbled so insensitively through his voir dire that the old gentleman snapped, "You're riling me up. This reminds me of when I lived in the South."

Bill retreated in confusion, and Mr. Calhoun ultimately was seated as an alternate juror.

Prosecutors, particularly in Los Angeles, also have been slow to adopt the scientific analytic principles Jo-Ellan employs. In the Simpson case, for example, they had been offered free the services of Donald Vinson, president of Decision Quest, one of the country's top jury consultants. Vinson's pretrial polling had yielded virtually the same results Jo-Ellan's had. He, too, believed that the "ideal" defense juror would be a moderately middle-aged woman, preferably black, with some contact with law enforcement. The prosecutors, however, ignored his findings, in part because Marcia Clark believed African American women would give particular weight to evidence of prior spousal abuse. In fact, the available scientific evidence suggests the contrary, but Marcia was confident of her instincts.

When voir dire began, she and Hodgman tried to hide their adviser in the back of the courtroom. We introduced Jo-Ellan to the panel as a member of our team and then informed the prospective jurors that the D.A., too, had such an expert but that he was in the back of the courtroom in their midst. That afternoon, Vinson—who basically had donated to the state a critical service for which our client paid dearly—disappeared from the courtroom, never to return.

Now, every trial attorney has his or her personal quirks when it comes to picking juries. I, for example, excuse any man who shows up wearing either white socks or a string tie. It's not rational, but that's just the way I feel. But from the very first day, it was clear to us that Bill and Marcia were particularly at sea when it came to questioning black panelists. It was as if they were speaking across some great divide. In fact, as the process continued, they sought help from one of their African American law clerks, David Wooden. He's an intelligent young man—now a promising lawyer—but there was something both revealing and chilling about their reliance on someone with so little experience when so much was at stake.

I pursue jury selection with relentless intensity. The U.S. and California supreme courts, for example, have both ruled that prosecutors may not exercise their peremptory—that is, unexplained—challenges to jurors based solely on the prospective panelist's race. So as Bill and Marcia used their first ten or so peremptories to excuse eight or nine black panelists, I was on my feet in protest over every one. The perception grew that O. J. Simpson might be denied a jury that reflected a cross section of our community. Shortly thereafter, we heard that Garcetti, who was monitoring the whole process, had sent down instructions for his deputies to ease up. Gil continued to micromanage the case from jury selection to final argument.

When they made a halfhearted attempt to claim we were excusing Caucasian panelists without cause, we were able to use our detailed questionnaires to demonstrate that the excused candidate had revealed actual bias, as was the case of one man who said he believed DNA testing "always was 100 percent accurate."

By November 3, we had a jury of eight women and four men. Eight of the panelists were African American, one was white, one was Latino, and two were of mixed racial background. Within a little more than a month, we had also selected our alternates, something I regarded as critical if, as I believed even then, this would be a much longer trial than anybody imagined. Nine of the alternates were women; three were men. Seven were black, four were white, and one was Latino.

I clearly recall driving home the night we finished and thinking, "I've never picked a better jury." Much later that same evening, in fact, I spoke with one of the Los Angeles Times reporters with whom I was to speak frequently during the trial.

"What sort of jury have you got?" he asked.

"These are my people," I replied. "I know their hearts, and they know mine. And when the time comes, that's how I'm going to speak to them—heart to heart."

I wasn't the only one to take note of what we'd accomplished. As he did throughout the trial, O.J. spoke frequently by telephone with Alan Dershowitz at Harvard. "Whatever you do," Alan told O.J. that night, "make sure you keep Johnnie Cochran between you and that jury."

Jury selection did not end Jo-Ellan Dimitrius's involvement with our team. She continued to conduct focus groups for us with panels matching the composition of our jury at the time. Her advice would prove critical months later, when we agonized over the question of whether O.J. should take the stand.

The satisfaction I felt about our collaboration with Jo-Ellan could not eclipse my growing disillusionment with Bob Shapiro and my anxiety about where he might be taking our client. Other members of the team, including the unfailingly kind and courteous Gerry Uelmen, had begun to grumble about the amount of time Bob spent on the phone chatting during the day and all the evenings and weekends he seemed to find free for social events. Early in the process, for example, I had erupted when he announced that a *Life* magazine photographer would be attending our meetings at his office "to preserve them."

"Bob," I said, "there are inviolable issues of attorney-client privilege here, and we just can't have this." When the other attorneys seconded my sentiments, Shapiro reluctantly agreed.

Then, one Sunday, in the very midst of jury selection, he announced that we all were to gather at his office to pose for a group portrait for *Vanity Fair* photographer Annie Leibovitz, a wonderful artist in her own right.

There was no time. I phoned Bob and told him I wasn't

coming. He protested that all the arrangements had been made and that Leibovitz had flown in from New York just to take this picture. "Bob, we've all got too much to do. Go ahead and take the photo without me," I said and hung up.

Coincidentally, Simpson phoned me from the jail a few minutes later. "O.J.," I said, "they want me to drive all the way out to Century City for some magazine picture. I just don't have the time for this. I'm working, and so are Shawn and Carl."

"You're absolutely right," O.J. replied, a note of what I thought was relief creeping into his voice. "I don't want you to go. I'm glad you're not doing it."

One morning a few days later, when I climbed into the backseat of the car alongside him, Bob suddenly announced, "I've got it."

"Got what?" I asked gingerly, hoping he was not about to describe some kind of health problem.

"I've figured out what happened. O.J. went to Nicole's house to key [scratch] her car. He found her with Goldman, flew into an uncontrollable rage, and killed them both before he knew what had happened."

"Bob, those people were murdered with a knife, not a key," I pointed out.

"Okay," he said brightly, "he went there to key her car *and* slash her tires."

"Bob," I said, struggling to sound more patient than I felt, "our client has told us he is innocent. He says he did not kill those people. He has never told me anything else. Has he told you something different?"

"No, of course not," Shapiro replied.

"Then what are we talking about?" I said with some exasperation.

But I knew exactly what we were talking about—the kinds of

facts that might have set up a manslaughter plea if they happened to be true.

Undeterred by my lack of enthusiasm, Shapiro later tried out his theory on O.J. himself, while other team members listened in horror.

Simpson's response was the appropriate one: "You've got to be out of your mind."

It's fair to say that as my good opinion of Bob Shapiro declined, the esteem in which I held F. Lee Bailey—with whom I had never worked before—increased. Lee had done a masterful job analyzing the time-line evidence during the case's early days, flying out from his home in Florida to focus on that soon after O.J.'s arrest. He had piloted his own helicopter over Brentwood, while his technical assistant, Howard Harris, took aerial photographs, which they then assembled in an overhead map. By driving and walking every possible route between Bundy and Rockingham and then correlating the times and distances with their aerial survey and the witness statements, Lee became convinced that the prosecution's time line would never stand up in court. As it happened, our jury concurred. Lee was also a valuable continuing source of memos on trial strategy.

Unfortunately, his relations with Shapiro, who had once been his close friend, rapidly deteriorated. There were quarrels over money. McKenna and McNally, Lee's investigators, grew increasingly hostile to Bob. Throughout November and December, we were plagued by leaks, many of them to the tabloid press, which was prepared to pay well for any story about O.J. Bailey and his people believed they had proof that Bob was the source of at least one leak—the transcript of O.J.'s interview with Lange and Vannatter—to the *Star*. Shapiro was equally insistent that Bailey's staff was doing the leaking. It was a mess that deepened when Lee, who was not being paid at that point, discovered during a visit with our client that Shapiro had told O.J. that Bailey would remain in Los Angeles throughout the entire trial. Lee, who dislikes California courts and the pace of our trials, was stunned.

As we broke for the holidays, it was becoming increasingly clear to everyone, including Simpson, that something would have to be done to resolve the situation. And, with the actual presentation of evidence looming, I was becoming even more anxious about the posture of our case and our ability to respond to the unpredictable demands of a high-profile murder trial.

On December 18, Bailey and I met in New York, where we each happened to have other business. "Look, here's where we are," Lee said. "O.J. had made it clear to me that he expects me to stay. I'm not talking to Shapiro anymore, but clearly he shouldn't be trying this case. O.J. doesn't want him to. And he is indicating to me that he wants me to do at least some of the work with you in charge. You have to tell me how you feel. I'm not happy about being in California, but I have a chance to make a pretty good deal on an apartment. But I have to decide quickly."

Knowing how both O.J. and I felt about Lee, the answer was easy. "I would like you to come," I said.

By then, events were moving rapidly, primarily at the behest of our client, who even in custody remained very much on top of his affairs, particularly when money was involved. He had become especially incensed, for example, when he discovered that Shapiro's landlords were charging him $4,000 every time they turned on their conference room air-conditioning for one of our weekend meetings. He was also alarmed by what he perceived as the continuing disorganization of our case files and evidence.

On December 27, O.J. called Carl Douglas, whose long hours and attention to detail had won his admiration. Simpson told

Carl he wanted him to take over management of the case materials, even if that meant shifting everything from Century City to our mid-Wilshire offices. At the request of O.J. and Skip Taft, we faxed Shapiro, who was vacationing with his family in Hawaii, and informed him that all future meetings would occur at our offices and all future travel and housing arrangements for witnesses would be made by our secretaries.

On the morning of January 2, 1995, O.J. asked me to come to the jail early so that he and I could talk with Shapiro. The time had come, he said, for me to assume formal control over the case. Time was too short, the presentation of evidence too near for further bickering and confusion. O.J. had become particularly alarmed based upon a telephone conversation that Lee Bailey had had with Shapiro. According to Lee, Bob had said, "Cochran should just get out of there. I am the perfect person to try this case." That, O.J. said, was the furthest thing from his mind.

When Bob arrived, he took the news badly. "I've been stabbed in the back," he said. "You just want me to sit there like window dressing. Well, I'm not going to do it. I'm going to quit."

That, as I'd learned a few minutes before, was precisely what the ever-shrewd O. J. Simpson wanted to avoid. He was wise in the ways of the Hollywood circles in which Shapiro paddled, and he feared what an embittered former defense attorney with a fondness for the press might do. He had been advised by his friends to keep Shapiro on board, and that's what he set about doing.

About that time, Bailey arrived and the atmosphere became even more tense. For a man with a football background, O. J. Simpson has an almost visceral dislike of confrontation. He began to smooth the whole thing over with the sort of sports analogies of which both he and Shapiro are so fond.

Bob could be the coach, he suggested, while Lee and I carried

the ball and the other lawyers functioned as specialty players.
Shapiro was having none of that.

"You're benching me, that's what you're doing. And I'm
going to quit."

"Okay, okay," replied O. J. Simpson, the Heisman Trophy
winner. "Johnnie will be the running back. Lee will be the
fullback, and you, Bob, can be the quarterback—only from now
on, there's no more passing."

Actually, I never believed Bob Shapiro—the $5 million man—
had any intention of leaving the case. We all sat through a somewhat tense meeting at my offices that afternoon. But whatever
Bob's unhappiness, it was clear that the rest of the team was
relieved to be in a place where there were a secure war room,
private offices, multiple conference rooms, and a large and
helpful support staff.

But, when the meeting broke up, Shapiro and Dershowitz,
who had flown in that day, headed back to the jail. When we
reconvened the next morning, Bob stormed in and took the seat
at the head of my conference table.

"Everybody sit down now," he ordered. "I have had a
meeting with O.J. I am in charge. There is no question about it."

"Damn it," Lee Bailey exploded, "you've been down there
threatening the client. Even I don't believe it. You know, Bob, I
have a lot of trouble with this."

"I was there," Dershowitz interjected. "I heard O.J. say that."

"Alan, I don't care what you heard O.J. say," Bailey snarled.
"He certainly was forced into any statement putting Bob Shapiro
back in charge. He told me personally that he didn't want that."

I had prepared myself for this scene and sat silently until the
angry mutterings around the table ceased. "Tell the truth, Bob,"
I said. "O.J. called me right after you guys left the jail. He was
beside himself at your behavior. He's going to call here in a
minute. I am going to put him on the speaker phone and let him

tell everybody for himself who's in charge. I'm going to put an end to this."

As if on cue, the phone rang. O.J. spoke quietly, but firmly, for a few minutes and then concluded: "I want Johnnie to be my lead attorney, and I want the rest of you to do what he tells you."

As he spoke those words, there were audible sighs all around the table. Mine was a prayer of thanksgiving. Nearly five months after I had accepted the responsibility of becoming O. J. Simpson's advocate, I finally had the opportunity to do all I believed needed to be done for him.

It felt like a victory, and I prayed it also was an omen.

12

"By Their Fruits Shall Ye Know Them"

As SOON AS A TRIAL BEGINS, I START THINKING ABOUT my final argument. I keep a yellow legal pad on the night table beside our bed, and on it I jot down what I call "points for argument."

To my mind, the first thing you say to a jury and the last things said are all of one piece. When I'm trying a case with another attorney, I will frequently call him or her just before retiring for the night. We'll spend a few minutes chatting about our case, and something that is said will usually spark a thought worth noting on my pad. During O. J. Simpson's trial, for example, I often called Barry Scheck and Peter Neufeld at Le Bel Age Hotel up on San Vicente Boulevard, where they lived for more than a year. No matter how late I rang their rooms, they were always working and, invariably, had something optimistic and stimulating to say. I've always had a fond spot in my heart for folks from Louisiana—where I was born—but working with Barry and Peter taught me that they raise them extra smart, tough, and honest in Brooklyn.

Quite often, though, the best points come to me suddenly in the middle of the night. And no matter what the hour or how tired I am, I force myself to sit up and write them down. There's a reason for this. Whatever the commentators may say, a trial is not really a struggle between opposing lawyers but between opposing stories. Over the course of the 265 days they were sequestered, for example, the jurors in O. J. Simpson's double murder trial watched nineteen different lawyers present them with 1,010 evidentiary exhibits and the testimony of more than 100 witnesses. No one, no matter how intelligent or diligent, could possibly assimilate that much information—much of it highly technical—on his or her own. What juries require is a story into whose outline they can plug the testimony and evidence with which they are relentlessly bombarded. It is through that process that they form their systematic understanding of the case. And it is that understanding that, ultimately, informs their verdict.

Telling that story is the trial lawyer's real task—and it isn't easy. First of all, the story you present cannot simply be concocted out of wishful thinking. It must be a clear, coherent, credible framework into which the actual evidence and testimony presented will plausibly fit. Second, your tale must be told according to rules of law as precise and intricate as the most demanding literary convention. Just as Shakespeare had his sonnet and Dante his terza rima, so the trial lawyer must look to the Constitution for his structure and to the case law for his cadence.

To succeed, your story must not only conform completely to

those legal intricacies but also be more credible and plausible than the other side's version. The jurors, then, must trust the lawyer as a "storyteller." For me, that trust is a thread that runs through the entire trial process. It begins in voir dire, when I use eye contact to establish an implicit bond of faith with the jurors; it continues into the opening statement, when I promise them certain things; it extends through the presentation of evidence, when I try and deliver what I've promised; then it ends in the final argument, when I remind them of their promises and the promises I've kept and explain those things on which I have been unable to deliver.

If I have successfully accomplished each of these steps, those twelve people will go into the jury room and use my client's story to piece all the puzzling things they've been told into a coherent picture that satisfies both their sense of legal duty and their human curiosity about what really happened.

Clearly, then, the next link in our narrative chain would be the opening statement, which I decided to deliver myself. Through the months leading up to that point, we had fought out a series of pretrial motions, most of which Judge Ito decided in the prosecution's favor. He denied us access to Fuhrman's LAPD personnel and military service records, for example, and refused to reconsider the question of suppressing the evidence obtained during the warrantless search of O. J. Simpson's estate. But on that issue, Gerry Uelmen did force Ito to concede a critical point. Vannatter, the judge agreed, had acted with "reckless disregard for the truth" when he completed the sworn search warrant affidavit by saying he believed the people inside the Rockingham compound might have been in danger.

This judicial assessment of Vannatter's integrity was critical for us because it strongly supported the case theory we were preparing to put before the jury. Our theory was based not only on the facts before us but also on what our experience suggested to us about their meaning. In this connection, it is worth noting that we *never* believed or argued that some shadowy cabal of Los Angeles police offices set out to frame O. J. Simpson for murder because he is a black man. "Absurd" would be too charitable a description for such a contention—and it was never ours. O.J. is one of those rare figures in contemporary American life whose achievements and personal charisma transcend conventional racial categorizations.

To put it bluntly, nobody thought of him as black. He was a stupendous athlete, a successful corporate spokesman, a competent television sportscaster, a minor actor, and an extremely well-liked celebrity-about-town—more or less in that order. His social ambit, much of it centered around the high-stakes golf and card games at his beloved Riviera Country Club, was almost entirely white. He was a generous participant in many charitable endeavors and, as is too frequently overlooked, had many friends in law enforcement, including the LAPD, where his football career is still widely admired.

What we did believe—and what a competent, unbiased analysis of the evidence supported—was that a process far more complex and amorphously malevolent than straightforward conspiracy had led the LAPD to charge him with the murders of Nicole Brown and Ron Goldman. None of us on O. J. Simpson's defense team believed that any of the officers who arrived at Bundy Drive the night of June 12, 1994, went there with the predetermined intention of framing our client. Nor did they sit down together later in those dark hours—or at any other time—and say: "Let's do it."

But if you look carefully at the facts, then weigh them against the culture and history of the LAPD and the district attorney's office, as well as against the political climate in which they were then operating, another possibility presents itself. What happened that night and over the succeeding days resulted from the unplanned interaction of the sloth, carelessness, incompetence, dishonesty, bias, and ambition of the police and prosecutorial authorities involved.

The problem began with the officers who first went to the scene. As any competent defense lawyer who has ever tried a case in L.A. will attest, the Los Angeles Police Department is notorious for its poor management of crime scenes, which are seldom properly secured and almost never adequately combed for clues. That night at Bundy Drive was no exception. The evidence is clear that the officers who responded initially trampled all over the site of the murders and Nicole Brown's condominium, contaminating much evidence and, in all likelihood, obliterating a great deal more. It also is well documented that despite its reputation as the nation's most "modern" police force, the LAPD for decades has spent far too little money training and equipping its forensic technicians and maintaining the laboratories in which they analyze evidence. Thus, much of the work those officers performed at Bundy Drive and Rockingham was, to say the least, substandard.

Then you have Detectives Tom Lange and Phil Vannatter, two salty old Robbery-Homicide veterans easing into retirement. They'd been around and knew that when a woman turns up murdered—as Nicole was—on some occasions the husband or ex-husband did it. Knowing that, they fixed immediately on O. J. Simpson as their suspect and simply ignored anything that might have deflected them in another—perhaps more arduous— direction. Having rushed to that judgment, Vannatter decided to "improve the case," to make sure things came out the way he thought they should. Tell a couple of small lies and adjust the physical evidence slightly, and even a criminal justice system blinded by legal technicalities would reach the same conclusion he had. Lange, his partner, well schooled in the department's traditional code of silence, simply looked away, as he doubtlessly had many times before.

Detective Mark Fuhrman was something else entirely. He was not incompetent nor slothful; he was neither careless nor misguided. He was a living remnant of the LAPD's dark past, an active, vocal, hate-filled bigot whose violent—even murderous—impulses were, by his own account, barely under control. Lange and Vannatter, like most of their Robbery-Homicide colleagues, thought Fuhrman was an unstable troublemaker, and privately derided him as "that squirrel." But, like some cunning rodent, he somehow managed to touch nearly every significant piece of evidence that conveniently assisted the two senior detectives in their rush to link O. J. Simpson to the murders.

Finally, there were the prosecutors. Marcia Clark, who had worked with Vannatter on an earlier case, was the deputy district attorney he personally called from the scene of the crimes. Marcia was one of the office's ambitious rising young stars. She knew that the way to achieve an even more visible place in the firmament was to attach herself to a high-publicity case. The trial of Nicole Brown and Ronald Goldman's killer would be such an opportunity, but only if O. J. Simpson was the defendant. Marcia's boss, my former co-worker Gil Garcetti, had problems of his own. His two immediate predecessors in office—Robert Philibosian, a skilled career prosecutor, and Ira Reiner, a career politican—had been defeated by voters unhappy with their office's performance in the McMartin Preschool and Rodney King cases. Gil's own term in office had begun with a stunning defeat, the hung jury in the first trial of the Menendez brothers. He did not feel he could afford another such loss if he hoped to remain in office.

The more my talented colleagues on O.J.'s defense team analyzed the evidence, the more I became convinced that all these personalities and forces—both historical and political—had combined to put our client in the dock. There had been no concerted plan. But the criminalists' ignorance and incompetence, the detectives' habitual sloth and deceit, Fuhrman's racism, and the prosecutors' ambitions had come together with terrible effect.

It would have been far easier to tell our jury a simple, straightforward story of conspiracy. But all of us were sure that was not the case. With its access to the country's most sophisticated private and public crime labs, including the legendary FBI facilities, the prosecution—whose own case was entirely circumstantial— would try to bury O. J. Simpson under what Marcia later called "a mountain of evidence."

We, on the other hand, would have to tell our jury the story of how that mountain ultimately had to crumble because it had been piled atop a foundation that was—in Barry Scheck's brilliantly concise phrase—"contaminated, compromised and corrupted from the start."

To TELL ALL OF THAT STORY, WE OBVIOUSLY WOULD need the freedom to probe and place before the jury the issue of Mark Fuhrman's racial bias, the full extent of which was still unknown to us at that point. Under a United States Supreme Court decision in a case called *Davis v. Alaska*, we were entitled to that line of inquiry. The prosecutors, of course, opposed us. So, on Friday, January 13, we went into court to argue the issue. The initial phase of the prosecution's argument was made by Cheri Lewis, a deputy D.A. whose brittle, abrasive manner always seemed to irritate Judge Ito considerably more than it did us. She also happened to be Fuhrman's designated handler for the prosecution, and the two of them apparently had developed a friendly relationship. She was the D.A. who looked after his feelings and often vouched for his credibility to her more skeptical colleagues.

The other prosecutor who would speak to the issue was the newest addition to an ever-growing team. He was someone I knew rather well, a thirty-eight-year-old African American named Christopher Darden. In the previous months, he had conducted the grand jury investigation into whether or not A. C. Cowlings had illegally aided and abetted O.J.'s flight from arrest. That probe failed to produce an indictment, though it did give the prosecutors an opportunity to grill several of our expert witnesses, including Michael Baden and Henry Lee. When the process concluded, Darden joined Simpson's prosecutors.

Prior to being assigned the Cowlings grand jury, Darden had served in one of the units I had supervised as assistant district attorney—the Special Investigation Division, or SID, which is charged with prosecuting police misconduct. Eric Ferrer and I had dealt with him frequently in that post. From the start, Chris had attempted to cultivate me as a kind of mentor, sometimes even addressing me affectionately as "stepdaddy." He professed admiration for the work our firm was doing, obtaining compensation for the victims of police misconduct. I strongly believe in encouraging young African American lawyers. So when the supervisory spot in SID became vacant and Darden called asking me to recommend him to his superiors for the job, I did so. He didn't get it, and I can't say I was particularly surprised.

The truth was that despite his carefully cultivated reputation as a buster of rogue cops, Darden pursued extraordinarily few of the complaints filed with him. As far as I know, he personally tried only one such case, a misdemeanor growing out of the police riot that took place during an abortive drug sweep at Thirty-ninth and Dalton, in one of the city's poorer black neighborhoods. Chris lost.

I had been particularly troubled by his role in a case Eric and I

had settled only the previous August. In early September of
1991, police officers in West Covina, a suburban community in
the San Gabriel Valley east of Los Angeles, were investigating a
string of shopping mall robberies. In the course of those
inquiries, they sought permission to search the apartment of
Darrell Stephens, a twenty-seven-year-old African American
who had no part in the crimes. When Stephens demanded that
they produce a warrant, the officers left, vowing to return and
"kick ass."

Shortly after dawn two days later, ten members of the West
Covina Police Department SWAT team used a battering ram to
shatter the door of Stephens's apartment. Seconds later, neighbors heard a hail of automatic weapons fire. Darrell Stephens lay
dead in his underwear, facedown on the floor of his own bedroom. He was shot twenty-eight times—all in the back.

Stephens's anguished parents went to the Los Angeles County
district attorney's office, and Darden was assigned to investigate
the case. While he ultimately told the parents he felt great sympathy for them, he also claimed he had been unable to develop
sufficient evidence of misconduct to warrant any criminal prosecution of any of the officers involved. Our firm took the parents'
civil case and filed suit in federal court. While we were preparing
for trial, we received a telephone call from Chris Darden. There
was one piece of evidence, he said, of which he thought we
should be aware. One of the SWAT officers who had burst into
Stephens's bedroom that morning had left on the radio microphone attached to his flak jacket. The incident had been
recorded. The last words you could hear the officer saying before
he emptied the magazine of his AR-15 into the helpless Stephens
were: "Don't move, nigger."

Chris said he was sure the epithet was on the tape since he had
heard it himself while conducting the investigation.

We obtained the recording, and it was one of the key pieces of

278

evidence that led the city of West Covina to settle with Stephens's parents for $875,000.

In the course of reviewing the case, however, Eric and I noticed something very troubling. The official report on the incident Darden had prepared for the district attorney's office contained no mention of the tape or its contents. I had always been slightly troubled by the aura of an adolescent Hamlet that always seemed to surround Darden. Everything about his life and profession seemed to leave him in a state of unresolved conflict. As a former prosecutor myself, I was not unaware of how powerful the pressures to conform could be within the city attorney's and district attorney's offices, particularly when you hoped for advancement, as Darden did. But there were times during our acquaintance—as in the Stephens case—when it seemed to me that Chris felt he was always free to make the most self-serving choice so long as he looked sufficiently anguished over it.

Some of that I attributed mainly to the difference in our ages. As a beneficiary of the civil rights struggles waged by previous generations, Chris Darden seemed to me to be one of those young blacks who had had the luxury of assimilating the narcissism so common among Americans his age. "Nobody understands my pain but me because only I have suffered it" could be their motto. Like Frederick Douglass, W.E.B. Du Bois, Dr. King, and Malcolm X, they understand the anger discrimination engenders. But their self-involvement forever forestalls them from experiencing the liberation those great men found in selfless commitment.

As I was about to discover, Chris Darden's reticence in the Stephens case apparently reflected a much deeper emotional distress than I had suspected.

When Cheri Lewis's argument shambled to a halt, Darden took the podium. He was concerned about what the impact would be when the jurors—eight of whom were black at that point—heard that Mark Fuhrman had employed the epithet "nigger."

"It is a dirty, filthy word," he told the court. "It is not a word that I allow people to use in my household. I'm sure Mr. Cochran doesn't, either. And the reason we don't is because it is an extremely derogatory and denigrating term, because it is so prejudicial and extremely inflammatory."

I had expected a legal argument about relevance, but this was something quite different. If I understood where Chris was heading, he was about to argue that black jurors were somehow peculiarly unfit to hear this word, even if it in fact had been used by a participant in the case. Sure enough:

"It will upset black jurors," he continued. "It will upset the black jurors . . . it will become a test . . . and the test will be: Whose side are you on? The side of the white policeman or the side of the black defendant and his very prominent and black lawyer? That is what it is going to do. Either you are with the man or you are with the brothers. . . . No one, no African American can hear that word without getting upset."

As Darden continued, my mind suddenly jumped back to an afternoon some years before when, during a business trip to another city, I had wandered into a secondhand bookstore while killing time between appointments. As a small boy in Shreveport years before, the *Encyclopædia Britannica* had been my first window on the wider world. But, as you might imagine, the volumes to which I had ready access were hardly up-to-date. They were, as I have never forgotten for some reason, part of the 1911 edition. Imagine my happy surprise then, when in this bookstore that afternoon, I stumbled across that very version of my treasured encyclopedia.

I couldn't help but pick up a volume. And as I lovingly thumbed through it, my eye fell on an entry I'd never glimpsed as a little boy. Under the heading "The Negro" it read: "Mentally the negro is inferior to the white." Various pseudo-Darwinian explanations were offered for that observation, concluding with: "the arrest or even deterioration in mental development is no doubt very largely due to the fact that after puberty, sexual matters take the first place in the negro's life and thoughts. . . . The mental constitution of the negro is very similar to that of a child, normally good-natured and cheerful, but subject to sudden fits of emotion and passion during which he is capable of performing acts of singular atrocity, impressionable, vain, but often exhibiting in the capacity of servant a dog-like fidelity." As I subsequently discovered, that entry was written by Walter Francis Wilcox, chief statistician of the United States Census Bureau.

Discovering that slander in a book that had meant so much to me was difficult but, sadly, unsurprising given the era in which it was written. What was surprising—stunning, in fact—was hearing a fresh version of the same old calumny coming from the lips of a Los Angeles County deputy district attorney.

"When you mention that word to this jury or to any African American, it blinds people," Darden said. "It will blind this jury. It will blind them to the truth. They won't be able to discern what is true and what is not. It will affect their judgment. It will impair their ability to be fair and impartial. . . ."

In the prosecution's view, our eight black jurors were children, so emotional and fragile, so easily influenced and led, that—despite everything else they had suffered and overcome—a single word could cause them to take leave of their reason and abandon any notion of duty, justice, or moral obligation. Were there similar words to which white, Latino, or Asian jurors would respond in kind—or was this a uniquely black characteristic? The whole thing reminded me of former police chief Daryl Gates's insistence that the reason his officers' choke holds killed more blacks than whites was because blacks were "built differently."

I don't think I've ever been quite as angry in a courtroom as I was when I rose to respond to Darden's remarks. It was one of the few times during the Simpson trial that I acutely felt the presence of the cameras in the courtroom. I could not allow these vile sentiments to go unrefuted before so many people.

Darden's remarks this morning, I told Judge Ito, "are perhaps the most incredible remarks I've heard in a court of law in the thirty-two years I've been practicing. . . . His remarks are demeaning to African Americans as a group. . . . And so I want to apologize to African Americans across this country. It is demeaning to our jurors to say that African Americans who have lived under oppression for two hundred-plus years cannot work within the mainstream, cannot hear these offensive words. . . . African Americans live with offensive words, offensive looks, offensive treatment every day of their lives," I said, "and yet they still believe in this country."

Darden continued to argue that certain facts were just too inflammatory for black jurors to hear. As an example, he claimed that O.J. "has a fetish for blond-haired white women," but that the prosecutors would not try to bring that up because it "would inflame the passions of the jury." Shades of 1911 and Walter Francis Wilcox, I thought.

"How outrageous is this?" I responded. "If this man loves somebody who is purple, he has the right to get married. . . . His first wife was African American. That's the beauty of America. That's what people have fought and died for."

I then insisted on reading into the record a sworn statement by Kathleen Bell, one of the selfless white witnesses who had come forward with evidence of Fuhrman's continuing bigotry. At their first meeting at a social gathering, Bell said Fuhrman told her, "If I had my way, they would take all the niggers, put them together in a big group, and burn them."

Darden slumped in his chair, pointedly turning and staring away from me, toward the back of the courtroom. Judge Ito looked legitimately pained. "This is the one main unresolved problem of our society," he said. "And for those of us who grew up in the sixties and had hoped this would kind of go away, it's a big disappointment to still have to read this stuff."

Fair enough, I thought, but it's worse to have to try cases in which evidence may have been tampered with by police officers who still believe this stuff. Ito subsequently ruled that we could introduce "relevant" evidence of Fuhrman's racism.

A LITTLE MORE THAN A WEEK AFTER OUR CONFRONTA-tion over Fuhrman, Marcia Clark and Chris Darden delivered their opening statements. As expected, Marcia graphically laid out the trail of blood drops whose DNA, she claimed, "matched" O. J. Simpson's and which led, she said, from the scene of the murders on Bundy Drive to our client's bedroom at Rockingham. It all sounded utterly damning, but during the weeks of preparation leading up to this point I had been assured by Barry Scheck and Peter Neufeld, America's leading authori-ties on the forensic application of DNA, that the term "match" was scientifically inaccurate and legally inappropriate. Further-more, they stressed, it did not matter what the results of tests run at the prestigious California Department of Justice and the pri-vate Cellmark Diagnostics in Maryland had shown. Any sample that had been collected at that anarchic crime scene and then been passed through the LAPD's crime lab was hopelessly com-promised and, therefore, unreliable, they said over and over.

I can still see Scheck in jeans and leather jacket, his mop of hair bobbing hypnotically with each emphatic gesture. "Don't worry about this, Johnnie," he would say. "We've been in this L.A. lab; our experts have been in there. It's unbelievable. The place is a cesspool of contamination. We can prove it, and we will." I knew little of DNA technology when O. J. Simpson's trial began and had never met Scheck and Neufeld before. But from the first moment we spoke, it was clear to me that they not only had real experience but also the instincts of accomplished trial lawyers. As time went on, I also discovered their astonishing work ethic. They immediately gained my complete confidence, and there has never been an instant in which I regretted giving it.

As I prepared my own opening, Lee Bailey was similarly confident and helpful with his analysis of the time-line evidence. "It just doesn't wash," he would boom with conviction, rolling up on the balls of his feet and thrusting that impressive head of his forward. "This case can be won on the basis of the time line alone because the one they've offered just doesn't work." Meanwhile, because Peter Neufeld had been forced to return briefly to New York to try another case, our team was joined by yet another technical wizard, Bob Blasier from Sacramento. Blasier was an expert not only on DNA but also on computers, and I quickly found that he had the ability to generate the professional graphics and charts I would use to illustrate my opening statement and the testimony of key witnesses that followed. In fact, Blasier's mastery of the computer was so complete that Ito and the prosecutors would turn to him whenever they needed instant citations from the trial record. Good citizens that we are, we never charged them for the service.

When I finally rose to address our jurors for the first time, I ran through a few introductory remarks, then moved to those sentiments I hoped would lay the groundwork for all that would follow in the long months ahead: "You hear a lot of talk about justice," I said. "I guess that Dr. Martin Luther King said it best when he said, 'Injustice anywhere is a threat to justice everywhere.' And so, we are now embarked on this search for justice, this search for truth. . . . Each of you made a number of promises in the course of voir dire examination. . . . Cicero said that 'he who violates his oath profanes the divinity of faith itself.' And, of course, we know that you will live up to your promises and be fair and keep an open mind and decide this case not on speculation, not on conjecture, not on surmise, but based upon the facts.

"You, then, as jurors, are the conscience of this community. . . . You have the rare opportunity, it seems to me, to be a participant in this search for justice and for truth, and, in the final analysis, I'm optimistic that you will be able to render perhaps the most important decision of your lives. And so we want you to keep your minds open and fresh so that you can render that decision impartially to both sides so that people all across the world can say this system works, this was a fair trial, these were fair people."

From there, I moved on through a kind of laundry list of the witnesses we intended to call and a brief summary of the testimony each would offer, along with a thought or two on its significance to our case. The process took much longer than I had anticipated because of the repeated objections—most of them overruled—lodged by Bill Hodgman. Some of these objections appeared to be merely tactical, designed to throw me off stride, an unusual maneuver for Bill, who—like Gerry Uelmen—is one of the courtroom's authentic gentlemen. Others, however, had a firmer basis since, according to the prosecutors, they had never been given the statements of some witnesses I mentioned, as California's so-called reciprocal discovery statute requires. In essence, that law, which was enacted by popular initiative, requires both sides in a criminal trial to exchange most witness statements before the trial.

When Carl had taken over management of the case files from Bob Shapiro's office late in December, he had been assured that the prosecutors had received all the discovery to which they were entitled up to that point. As it turned out, statements and tape-recorded interviews with potentially important witnesses, like Rosa Lopez and Mary Anne Gerchas, had not been turned over. Ito, as the law requires, took a dim view of this and subsequently slapped both Carl and me, as the lawyers now in charge, with $950 fines.

Not one word of apology ever crossed Shapiro's lips about the embarrassing position in which he had left us. But he did confess sometime later, "You know, I just don't understand those discovery laws."

He was, however, well schooled in self-preservation. Within a few days, we watched him scuttle in and out of Judge Ito's chambers by himself before court convened. "What were you doing in there, Bob?" I asked suspiciously.

"Oh," he said, "I found a few more things we hadn't turned over. So I gave them to Ito."

"You did what?" I demanded. "Bob, don't you think before you go off covering your own backside, you ought to tell us and our client what you have before you turn it over to the prosecution? What was it? What did you give them?"

"I'm not quite sure. There were a bunch of things," he said, hurried and rattled, as he always seemed to be whenever push came to shove during the trial.

I looked over at the long-suffering Carl, whose eyes were wide with helpless horror. Fortunately, whatever Shapiro turned over that day, it must have been of little consequence because we heard nothing more about it.

There was a great deal of discussion in the days that followed about what transpired on the eighteenth floor of the Criminal Courts Building on the evening following the first day of my opening statement. My friend Bill Hodgman had appeared unwell all through his uncharacteristically contentious performance that day. I knew how carefully Garcetti was monitoring the proceedings and that nearly every evening he and his senior assistants insisted on meeting with their trial team. The group, as several of the prosecutors repeatedly complained to us, invariably included Gil's media adviser, a former television news personality named Suzanne Childs. She was known by some in the office as "Deputy Bubbles."

That night, the entire prosecution team was ordered to Gil's private conference room, where a tense and apparently angry discussion ensued of the team's performance that day. At some point, Hodgman, by then visibly ill, excused himself, went to another office, and collapsed. Some accounts have alleged that when we were informed officially of his illness the next day we congratulated each other. That is false and grotesque. Bill Hodgman was and is my friend; he is the only Simpson prosecutor to whom I still regularly speak. I tried to reach his wife as soon as I learned of Bill's collapse, and our office sent him flowers as soon as we learned where he was recovering. Thankfully, his illness—apparently induced by stress—passed quickly, though he never really returned to the courtroom during O. J. Simpson's trial.

After a delay, I wrapped up my opening statement with a blaze of the wonderfully illustrative charts and visual aids Bob Blasier had so skillfully prepared. Displayed together, they gave the jury a schematic view of the story we were about to unfold for them. I was accustomed to trying complex civil cases where such "demonstrative evidence" is a normal part of one's presentation. In criminal trials, only the most accomplished advocates tend to employ such powerful storytelling props, and even they are frequently constrained by their client's finances. In this case, we labored under no such limits, primarily due to Bob Blasier's ability to turn out these amazing charts and graphs. Those graphics seemed to have an even bigger impact on the prosecutors than they did on the jury. As the chart came down and I turned from the podium to walk back to my seat, I glanced at the prosecutors, and for the first time I saw fear—real fear—in their eyes.

"Maybe, guys," I chuckled silently to myself, "this isn't going to be a slam-dunk after all."

The first phase of the prosecution's case dealt with the tumultuous, sometimes abusive, nature of Nicole Brown and O. J. Simpson's relationship. It was difficult testimony through which we proceeded gingerly. We believed that the incidents described were very much a part of O.J.'s past when the murders occurred and that the feelings were not part of those tragic events. But he clearly was in distress throughout those weeks in court. And I am not sure that he has ever come to appropriate terms with that phase of his life.

Clearly, the most disturbing of the testimony concerning the abusive incidents in O.J. and Nicole Simpson's relationship came from Sharyn Gilbert, the 911 operator who took a call from the Simpsons' home on New Year's Day, 1989, and from Denise Brown, the murdered woman's sister. At the time, we believed that the most significant thing about their testimony was that it involved events that had occurred years previous to the killings. As we later discovered, that point also was clear to O.J.'s jurors. In the course of preparing Simpson's defense, we had retained Dr. Lenore Walker of Denver, the nation's leading authority on the "battered woman syndrome." Dr. Walker, who braved intense criticism from many of her usual allies for her work on O.J.'s case, not only examined our client in the jail, but also helped us understand why his behavior did not match that of the abusive spouse who kills.

In such instances, Dr. Walker told us, there almost invariably are two readily identifiable things: a pattern of escalating violence and an obvious situational trigger for the homicide. Obviously, there had been no escalation of violence in the Simpsons' relationship, which was over at the time of the murders. Moreover, everything about O.J.'s behavior on the afternoon and evening of the killings belied the notion that he was somehow a ticking bomb. The best illustration of that fact was the videotape of his good-humored visit to his daughter Sydney's dance recital just hours before the bodies were discovered on Bundy. Nothing about that footage suggests a man sliding toward some sort of murderous rage. Moreover, as Dr. Walker and other psychiatric experts with whom we had consulted pointed out, there was nothing in O. J. Simpson's life history that suggested a resort to violence when under stress.

Why, then, didn't we call Lenore Walker or other experts as witnesses to refute the prosecution's testimony regarding domestic violence? The answer simply was that all our pretrial research led us to believe that the jurors we had selected would not be inclined to attach an exaggerated significance to the testimony, however emotionally wrenching it appeared. Had we put our witnesses on the stand, they would have been extensively cross-examined by the prosecutors and their interviews with him opened to scrutiny. Given what we believed would be the transitory impact of this phase of the state's case, we saw no reason to give the state license to trample through our client's psyche in that fashion.

Looming before us, however, was the testimony of three witnesses whose cross-examination would definitely play a critical role in the case at hand. First among them was Mark Fuhrman. Virtually from the time we began riding to court together,

Shapiro had urged me over and over to cross-examine Fuhrman myself.

"The guy's made for you, Johnnie," he said to me. "Think about it, a black lawyer confronting a racist white cop. It's got to work with this jury."

Actually, what works best with juries is truth, and the more I thought about it, the more convinced I became that the best way to pry the truth from Fuhrman was to have another member of the team examine him. To Shapiro's horror, I assigned the job to F. Lee Bailey, who almost from the moment he joined the case had had what can only be called a trial lawyer's intuition about Fuhrman. Most of the country had watched the preliminary hearing and thought that if you called central casting and asked for the ideal cop, you'd probably get someone a lot like Mark Fuhrman. Bailey had seen something very different.

Shapiro, who was anxious about his ability to handle the hearing, had asked Bailey to watch it on television each day, then meet with him that night to advise him. When Fuhrman took the stand, Lee didn't wait for evening. He paged Sara Caplan, Bob's associate, and asked that Shapiro phone him as soon as possible. "There's something very wrong with this guy's testimony," Bailey said when Shapiro finally came on the line. "I'm telling you there's a flaw in there. And it's a bad one. We've got to take a look at it as soon as possible." In the months that followed, we learned just how right Lee's instincts were.

I did not know Detective Mark Fuhrman. In fact, for all the people I did know in law enforcement in L.A., I had not even heard of Mark Fuhrman—and I prided myself on knowing everybody worth knowing. But I knew the Fuhrman *type*. I was still unconvinced that the prosecution would actually call him, but if they did make that tactical blunder, I knew who would do the cross-examination for us and it wouldn't be me—much to the chagrin of Bob Shapiro, who kept telling me, "But he's made for you, Johnnie." It wouldn't be Bob Shapiro, either. I told Bailey, "I want you to take Fuhrman, Lee, because everybody will expect that I'm going to do it. I think I like the picture better with you up there cross-examining. Go after him if they dare to call him. Kick his ass."

We had absolutely no knowledge of the taped interviews Fuhrman had made with the screenwriter Laura Hart McKinny. Absolutely no idea whatsoever. That came later and that came from God. But we had enough.

And as the evidence mounted that Mark Fuhrman was poison, I became increasingly uneasy about the role into which I thought the district attorney's office was trying to thrust Chris Darden. He may have been willfully confused and insufficiently in control of his emotions. But on a purely human level, he did not deserve to have people he trusted play upon his sense of loyalty and use him to launder the testimony of this despicable false witness. Several times during that period, I gave Chris as much warning as my duty to our client permitted.

"Don't let them saddle you with this guy," I urged him during private moments in the courtroom. "Let these other lawyers argue about this man."

During the course of a mock cross-examination through which a panel of deputy D.A.'s put Fuhrman immediately before he took the stand, the detective confided to Chris that his hobby was collecting Nazi war medals. "The workmanship is fantastic," he said admiringly. Later that day, according to Darden, he told Marcia Clark she would have to question Fuhrman.

For my part, there was nothing I would have liked better than the chance to question Mark Fuhrman myself. He was the living embodiment of the social evil against which I had struggled for so much of my career. We had never exchanged a word, but I knew him and his kind. Because of them, I had given up a job I loved in the city attorney's office and the security for my young family that went with it. Because of them, I had sat across the desk from one grieving parent after another, and said, "I'm sorry about your boy, but there's nothing more we can do." Because of them, Barbara Deadwyler raised her children alone and Johnie Choyce never read another of her hardworking son's poems. Because of them, we had been forced to snatch the truth about Ron Settles' death out of his own grave. Because of them, my friend Herb Avery had seen the career he worked all his life to build shattered, and James Thomas Mincey had lost his life.

Oh, I knew him.

But I also knew that this case was about O. J. Simpson and not about me. No matter how great a sense of satisfaction I might have gained by exposing Mark Fuhrman to the world, what mattered was what O. J. Simpson's jury saw. And what really mattered about Fuhrman was the fact that he was a liar. If he was willing to perjure himself about his bigotry, then clearly he was willing to testify falsely about other things— things like blood and gloves.

Credibility, not race, was the issue in this cross-examination, and it was critical that we maintain that focus so that it could be communicated to the jury. The best way to do that, I was convinced, was to confront Fuhrman with a white lawyer. So, I put my history and my feelings aside and turned over the witness I'd wanted to confront all my life to Lee Bailey. I'm not sure I've ever made a more difficult decision nor been more certain that I was right.

Lee Bailey's cross-examination of Fuhrman was almost as widely panned as it was misunderstood. Lee's sense of courtroom theater may occasionally lurch uncomfortably close to melodrama, but on this occasion he knew exactly what he had to accomplish. It is also worth noting, by the way, that while the commentators scoffed at Bailey's performance that day, the jurors subsequently told us they loved it.

"He was just like a lawyer in the movies," one of them later said with obvious pleasure.

More important, he did just what O. J. Simpson's defense required him to do. Playing on Fuhrman's arrogance and obvious disdain, Bailey danced him around until he stated two things without qualification: He had "never" spoken the word "nigger" in the past ten years, and he had "never" planted evidence.

"Do you use the word 'nigger' in describing people?" Bailey asked.

"No, sir," Fuhrman replied.

"Have you used that word in the past ten years?"

"Not that I recall," Fuhrman said.

"You mean"—Bailey in stentorian astonishment—"if you called someone a nigger, you have forgotten it?"

"I'm not sure I can answer the question the way you phrased it, sir," Fuhrman replied smugly.

"Are you therefore saying you have not used that word in the past ten years, Detective Fuhrman?" Bailey demanded.

"Yes, that is what I'm saying," Fuhrman said, a note of caution creeping into his voice.

"And you say under oath that you have not addressed any black person as a nigger or spoken about blacks as niggers in the past ten years, Detective Fuhrman?" Bailey said.

"That's what I'm saying, sir," responded Fuhrman, his voice firming.

"So that anyone who comes to this court and quotes you as using that word in dealing with African Americans would be a liar, would they not, Detective Fuhrman?" said Bailey.

"Yes, they would," the detective replied.

"All of them, correct?" wondered Bailey, who could hear what others could not, the sound of a very large door opening.

"All of them," Fuhrman said.

It would be months before we would discover screen-writer Laura Hart McKinny's tape-recorded conversations with Fuhrman, and even longer before the jurors would hear the detective impeach himself in his own voice. But, the truth was, it really did not matter. Lee Bailey had accomplished what our client required of him, and, if the pundits missed it, the jurors did not. As several of them told us after the trial, they never believed Fuhrman.

"I could tell by the way he twisted around in his seat and clenched his hands in his lap, that he was lying," Armanda Cooley, the forewoman, would tell us. From her vantage point in the first seat of the jury box's front row, she had seen all she needed to see.

It was Lee's finest moment in the trial.

A few days later, Shapiro—a blue ribbon signifying support for the LAPD wistfully fixed to his lapel—cross-examined Phil Vannatter. Deferential though he may have been to a veteran of a department whose goodwill he was desperate to retain, Bob nonetheless extracted two absolutely key facts from Vannatter. On the early morning of June 13, he had spent far more time at the Rockingham estate from which Simpson then was absent than he had at the Bundy Drive condo, where two people lay murdered. The only reasonable inference to be drawn from that was that Vannatter had already fixed on Simpson as the primary suspect. Moreover, when Simpson's blood sample was taken at Parker Center later that day, Vannatter did not book it into evidence as required by procedure. Instead, he placed it in his pocket, where it remained for the next three hours until he turned it over to LAPD criminalist Dennis Fung back at Rockingham. The significance of that inexplicable interval would shortly loom still larger when it emerged that the LAPD could not account for all the blood its nurse had taken from Simpson that afternoon. How much of it had disappeared during those mysterious three hours, and where had it gone?

If every trial is in some sense a drama, then I suppose it must have its interludes of comic relief. Kato Kaelin was ours. Many adjectives have been employed to describe America's most celebrated houseguest; perhaps "feckless" would be the kindest. He told Mark Fuhrman one story about O.J.'s demeanor and movements on the night of the murders and about the mysterious thumps he claimed to have heard in the passageway where the Rockingham glove was found. On the stand, he said other things, leading Marcia Clark—at Judge Ito's suggestion—to have him declared "a hostile witness." Later, in other forums, he told other stories. His only real purpose seemed to be to make sure nobody was mad at him, no matter what that might cost other people, including O.J., from whom he had been freeloading.

At one point, while Kato was on the stand, I leaned over to O.J. and inquired, "Simpson, why in the world did you let this person live at your house?"

"Look," he said, shaking his head, "I was just easygoing. I didn't think it was appropriate for him to live in the same condo with Nicole and the kids, so I just sort of let him stay at the house."

It may not have been entirely fair, but somehow Kato and Shapiro began to merge in my mind.

When the prosecutors called LAPD criminalists Dennis Fung and Andrea Mazzola to the stand, they surely must have anticipated that they would be on and off in a matter of hours. Of course, at that point, they had not dealt with Barry Scheck and Peter Neufeld, nor, I think, were they entirely clear on just how serious a challenge we intended to mount on the LAPD's scandalously slipshod methods of collecting and analyzing the sort of scientific evidence with which they were attempting to convict O. J. Simpson.

More than a week later, they could have no doubt. Scheck's meticulously prepared, relentlessly pursued cross-examination of Fung is one of the most brilliant courtroom performances I have ever witnessed. Using their own manuals, reports, and even crime-scene videos, Scheck impeached Fung and Neufeld impeached Mazzola on their lack of training, their fidelity to their department's own procedures, and their collection, preservation, and handling of the evidence. Barry used their own notes and crime-scene videos not only to show them contaminating evidence but also to contradict Vannatter's account of how Simpson's blood sample had been transferred to the criminalists. As it turned out, that crucial reference sample—after hours in the detective's possession—had just been tossed into a plastic garbage bag with other key items of evidence, then left to sit on the front seat of the criminalists' truck.

Scheck's cross-examination was so devastating that I would not be surprised if—on his deathbed—the last thing Dennis Fung hears is the sound of Barry Scheck demanding: "What about that, Mr. Fung?"

Ito clearly shared my assessment. At one point late in the process, he called us to a sidebar conference. "He's like a deer caught in the headlights," he said of the criminalist. "When are you going to let him go, Mr. Scheck?"

By shredding the credibility of the LAPD's forensic technicians, Barry and Peter left us well positioned for the battering we knew would follow over the coming weeks as the prosecutors put on a parade of sophisticated, polished scientific witnesses who testified that the results of their DNA tests linked O.J. to the murder scene. Barry and Peter, whom Shapiro—a conservative Republican—increasingly took to describing as "the junior Kunstlers" in a derisive reference to the famed left-wing defense attorney, fought a dogged rearguard action on cross-examination. When there appears to be less than one chance in a billion that this material did not come from your client, the obstacle appears insurmountable. But we believed Barry Scheck's contamination argument would take us over this hurdle.

We also worried about what the impact on the jury would be when we lost the battle to prevent them from being shown dramatically oversized color photos of Nicole Brown and Ron Goldman's hideously wounded bodies. We worried less about the extended and preposterously speculative testimony of the coroner, Dr. Lakshmanan Sathyavagiswaren, as we were confident that his overreaching theories about how the murders had been accomplished could be dealt with more than adequately by our own forensic scientists, Michael Baden and Henry Lee.

Throughout this period, we also kept up a quiet psychological struggle with Marcia Clark and Chris Darden. I appreciate Marcia's qualities as a prosecutor. Moreover, I appreciated the fact that when my ex-wife, Barbara, and Patty, my son's mother, began earning extra money by peddling concocted stories about our relationships to the tabloid press, Marcia made a point of expressing her concern to me.

"I think what they are doing to you is awful," she said with unmistakable feeling.

I felt the same when her disgruntled ex-husband not only began talking to the tabloids but actually went into court to try to wrest custody of Marcia's children from her. I thought it was an appalling thing to do to a single professional woman who obviously loved her children very much and evinced constant concern for their welfare. She asked if I would testify on her behalf and I told her if it became necessary, and did not conflict with my responsiblities to O. J. Simpson, I would do it. I was glad things never reached that point. But it was clear to me that the rigors of enduring all this alone and the stress of this trial were taking a toll.

No matter how deeply wounded I was by Barbara's and Patty's betrayals, I had Dale's support and loyalty and the love of my father and three children to sustain me. My daughter Tiffany, a television anchorwoman with an ABC affiliate in South Carolina, took it upon herself to defend me in an article for a newsmagazine. In another instance, when Patty's decision to go on a particularly sordid TV talk show on the very eve of Jonathan's university finals left him terribly upset, Dale insisted that he come and stay with us. Meanwhile, Dale maintained not only her own professional commitments but also the stable, well-organized home that left me free to focus completely on my client's welfare. Marcia apparently had no one to do these things for her.

It also was clear to me that Chris Darden had developed something more than a collegial attitude toward his co-counsel. Marcia enjoys pointed kidding; so do I. She has a flirtatious manner; I let her indulge it. She had a particular antipathy toward Shapiro, whom she called "the empty suit." She would slide up beside me, put her hand on my shoulder, and whisper into my ear, "You guys are having too good a week, Cochran. Give us a break, huh? Let the 'empty suit' do a witness or two."

"Marcia," I would exclaim in hushed tones during the weeks of scientific testimony in which she took no part, "are you still on this case? I thought Brian Kelberg [their forensic specialist] was in charge now. Is Gil going to let you do anything else?"

All this passed in the form of whispered exchanges, and it

clearly drove Darden to distraction. "Stay away from my woman," he growled at one point, only half in jest.

Marcia, I could see, was simply wearing down under the strain of an unsettled personal life. Darden's temper was wearing thinner. We began to look for ways to exploit that, and one soon presented itself.

On June 15, 1995, the prosecution called to the stand a man named Richard Rubin, who had been an executive with the firm that had manufactured the gloves recovered at Bundy Drive and Rockingham. The D.A.'s were essentially jumping through hoops trying to show that those gloves belonged to O. J. Simpson. Obviously, the first step would be to ask O.J. to try them on, and Darden appeared to be flirting with the idea. Both Shapiro and I had already tried on the gloves—with the requisite latex liners to prevent contamination—and then put our hands up against Simpson's. Obviously, the pair of gloves they had didn't fit O. J. Simpson. He himself had repeatedly told me he was perfectly willing to try on the gloves, since they weren't his. Knowing that, we didn't want the prosecutors to talk around the point. We wanted them to ask O.J. to put the gloves on because it would have more impact than if we staged such a demonstration as part of our cross-examination of Rubin.

I made a few conversational feints at Darden over the issue to put him on edge. It was one of those days when he clearly seemed rattled. But I knew the one person he couldn't stand taking anything from was Lee Bailey. Lee and I huddled. "One more push and that young man might just go over the edge," I suggested.

During a recess in the testimony, Lee walked casually over to Darden and said, "You've got the balls of a stud field mouse."

"What are you on my back for now," Chris replied with one of his patented snarls.

"If you had any nuts at all," Bailey sneered, "you'd make O.J.

try on that glove. If you don't have him try on the glove, we will."

And so he did. At Chris Darden's demand, O.J. stood in front of the jury and futilely attempted to pull the obviously under-sized gloves onto his decidedly oversized hands.

"They don't fit," Simpson turned to Darden and said, "They don't fit. See? They're too tight."

The jury, all eyes and ears at that point, took the whole thing in. It was one of the worst humiliations I have ever seen a prose-cutor suffer in front of a jury. Darden had allowed himself to be bullied into making the mistake every first-year law student is warned not to make: Never ask a question to which you do not know the answer or conduct an experiment of which you don't know the results.

As we drove to the office that afternoon, I thought to myself, We just may have won this case.

It was, I told my jubilant colleagues back at the office that night, perhaps "the most expensive piece of remedial legal edu-cation I'd ever seen." They all laughed and then laughed again when someone quipped that, all things considered, "Darden has helped the defense more than Shapiro."

13

"And David Took
a Stone"

O<small>N</small> J<small>ULY</small> 6, 1995, O. J. S<small>IMPSON'S</small> <small>PROSECUTORS</small>—
visibly weary and dispirited—wrapped up their case. The legal
term for such a moment is "rest," but most observers
felt "slumped to a halt" better described the district attorneys'
posture.

We had always been slightly puzzled over why all the commentators who insisted on calling us "The Dream Team" never
seemed to notice "The Thundering Herd" on the other side of
the courtroom. In terms of human and financial resources, we
were ludicrously overmatched. The Los Angeles County district
attorney's office had never deployed as many prosecutors on a
single case as they did prosecuting O. J. Simpson. At any given
moment, more than forty deputy district attorneys and more

than a dozen clerks were working full-time against us. They also could draw on the resources not only of their own investigative staff, but also of the LAPD and the Los Angeles County Sheriff's Department. They had the technical services of the FBI's crime laboratory—the world's finest—as well as the services of the California Department of Justice, Interpol, and the private facilities at Cell Mark. By the time the trial was through, the prosecutors would have spent an estimated $8 million, a sum O. J. Simpson never could have matched. The prosecution's overwhelming material advantages allowed them to screen, prepare, and call fifty-eight witnesses during their case-in-chief and to put before the jury 488 individual different evidentiary exhibits.

They had taken nearly six months to put their evidence before the jury. We planned to tell O.J.'s story in less than half that time in a presentation bracketed by the testimony of two of America's most distinguished forensic scientists, Michael Baden and Henry Lee. What sets both those men apart from their colleagues is not just their technical skills, which obviously are superb, but also their independence. That is what allows them to testify for both prosecution and defense attorneys with equal frequency. Michael had agreed to participate in the Simpson case on precisely the same basis on which he had agreed to reautopsy Ron Settles: "We find whatever we find." Henry's approach was equally rigorous.

There is another critical quality they share as well. In these days of on-camera courtroom commentators, you will often hear the term "professional witness." Many police detectives become such witnesses solely through experience. The FBI actually sends its agents to class to school them on how to appear in court. The professional witness's hallmark is his habit of turning slightly in the witness chair and looking directly at the jurors while he answers questions. All the federal agents who testified against O. J. Simpson employed that technique. So did LAPD detectives

Tom Lange and Phil Vannatter. Lee and Baden—perhaps because of their experience as teachers—represent a different kind of witness. They are unforced, natural communicators and explainers, an invaluable quality given the highly technical, often quite gruesome subjects about which they are asked to testify. That, coupled with their obvious sincerity and unchallenged professional integrity, made them two of the most influential witnesses in the trial.

In relatively few hours of testimony, Michael Baden convincingly demolished the coroner's version of how intense the struggle that preceded the deaths of Nicole Brown and Ron Goldman must have been. Similarly, he offered what was clearly a more accurate assessment of how long it took them to die of their awful wounds. Finally, with winning candor, he made it obvious to the jurors that the facts on the ground would just not support the prosecution's luridly detailed reconstruction of the murders' actual sequence.

As we now know, there was evidence inside the coroner's office to support Baden's interpretation of those facts, though it was concealed from us at the time by the prosecutors. They always insisted, for example, that the reason Lakshmanan testified rather than his deputy, Irwin Goldin—who actually performed the autopsies—was that Goldin had committed so many errors and had testified so badly at the preliminary hearing. Based on a deposition taken after the criminal trial from Goldin, we can see there were other reasons, as well. One of the more lurid facets of Lakshmanan's reconstruction was his contention that marks on Nicole Brown's back were created when her assailant placed his foot there before pulling back her hair and slashing her throat. Both Lakshmanan and another prosecution witness, FBI agent William Bodziak, testified that the alleged imprint matched that of a Bruno Magli shoe. Baden, by contrast, testified that this purported shoe print, in fact, was nothing more than lividity, or pooled blood in the dead woman's back. Goldin, as it now emerges, had told deputy district attorney Brian Kelberg, who examined Lakshmanan, precisely that. He told the prosecutor that there were no bruises on Nicole Brown's back and that, if they had been present at the time of autopsy, he would have photographed them. Under California law, Kelberg had a duty to inform the defense of the contrary opinion he had obtained from Goldin, when the shoe theory was presented by the two other prosecution witnesses, and he did not even inform us.

Later in the trial, Barry Scheck led Henry Lee through an analysis of all the forensic evidence, particularly the critical blood splatters, which held the jurors entranced. Henry's memorable use of a red-ink dropper to demonstrate how a such a splatter is, in fact, deposited was not only brilliant courtroom theater but also utterly persuasive in its simplicity. Lee gently educated the jury on precisely why the LAPD's slipshod collection and handling methods could render all subsequent evidentiary analysis—no matter how sophisticated—virtually useless. More important, he pointed out to them that the clear, logical sequence that ought to link crime scene, evidence collection, and analysis in any murder had curious gaps in this case. Impeccable scientist that he is, Lee resolutely refused to speculate on why those links were missing. There was no way for him to know. So he simply summed up his perplexity in a charmingly accented phrase that became a kind of coda for our case: "Something wrong here."

As it happened, this deeply learned man's simple phrase precisely captured the jurors' sentiments about the evidence the prosecution presented to them. And, as we discovered during our post-trial interviews with them, many of the panelists adopted "something wrong here" as their own.

Naturally gifted expert witnesses like Michael Baden and

Henry Lee are educators, and their opinions accompany jurors into their deliberations in much the same way that a favorite teacher's lessons remain with us throughout our lives. Who can forget Lee's memorable comparison of questionable evidence to finding a cockroach in a bowl of spaghetti—once you find it, you "don't have to keep eating to see if there are any more." Baden and Lee had told our jurors compelling chapters in the story we planned to lay out for them. But behind the scenes, a drama within a drama was playing itself out, and its conclusion would provide the most telling episode in the story of O. J. Simpson's defense. Its protagonist was the LAPD detective from central casting, and his role, appropriately enough, would be defined by a movie script. The detective, of course, was Mark Fuhrman— and there definitely was something wrong there.

THOUGH THEY LATER TWISTED THEMSELVES INTO KNOTS trying to minimize Fuhrman's centrality to their case, Simpson's prosecutors were never able to escape the fact that this man with the dubious past and deceitful present was, for all intents and purposes, "present at the creation." Initially, in fact, the district attorney's office regarded that as a plus for its side. Fuhrman, they believed, was a model witness—handsome, intelligent, articulate, and well dressed in suits from Carroll and Company, the same Beverly Hills clothier from whom O.J. purchased some of his business attire. Wonder of wonders, he even took the only completely legible crime-scene notes any of us had ever seen. Lee Bailey, in fact, always suspected that those perfectly coherent and sequential notes with their meticulous block letters also were a fraud, composed at some point later rather than on the couch of Nicole Brown's condominium in the dark early-morning hours of June 13, as Fuhrman testified. We were never able to pin that down. But weeks before I joined O. J. Simpson's defense team, other people—many of them inside the district attorney's office—were already alarmed about the detective's role in the case. What Simpson's prosecutors did, when that alarm was brought to their attention, speaks volumes about their desperation to win at any cost.

In fact, the first alarms within the district attorney's own staff were raised on July 19, 1994, shortly after O.J.'s preliminary hearing. That morning, Andy Purdy, a detective from the LAPD's Hollywood Division, came downtown to the Criminal Courts Building with a murder case he believed was ready for prosecution. The prosecutors who review the evidence and make such decisions are called "filing deputies." For obvious reasons, they spend more than the average amount of time talking with police officers. In the natural course of things, there's an exchange of news and gossip from their respective organizations. Friendships—some of them quite close—develop.

The two filing deputies reviewing Purdy's case that morning were Lucienne Coleman and Julie Sagoyjian. As it happened, Coleman and Purdy were old friends. She had formerly worked in the D.A.'s sex crimes unit, and Purdy had been the investigating officer on several of the cases she had prosecuted there. That morning, the *Los Angeles Times* had published a story on the contents of Fuhrman's disability suit and had noted the speculation over whether someone harboring that sort of racial animosity might also be capable of planting evidence, such as the glove. Before they even got down to business, Coleman, who at that point was skeptical of the story's contents, said to Purdy: "Jesus Christ, did you see this story on Fuhrman? Can you believe it?"

To her surprise, Detective Purdy replied not only that he knew Fuhrman but also that he "wouldn't put anything past him."

Purdy then went on to tell Coleman and Sagoyjian that, during the mid-1980s, he had worked with Fuhrman in the

LAPD's West Los Angeles Division. "He scared the hell out of me from the get-go," Purdy said. In fact, what he regarded as Fuhrman's routine abuse of suspects, manipulation of evidence, and disregard of LAPD policy, particularly on issues of race and gender, so unnerved Purdy that he began to keep a log of his colleague's activities. The purpose of that document, Purdy told Coleman, was to protect himself against the trouble he feared one day would grow out of the investigations on which he and Fuhrman jointly worked.

In 1985, Purdy married a woman who also happened to be Jewish. When he returned to work at the West Los Angeles station after his honeymoon, he opened his locker and discovered it had been broken into and vandalized. Among other things, swastikas had been painted on the inside. Suspicion immediately centered on Fuhrman, Purdy said, "because I knew he was a Nazi."

"You mean he's a right-winger?" an increasingly perplexed Coleman inquired.

"No, I mean he is a Nazi," Purdy replied.

According to Purdy, Fuhrman frequently talked with his colleagues about his collection of Nazi military paraphernalia, particularly medals and badges. Fuhrman, Purdy said, often displayed items from his collection on his desk. When his superiors ordered him to stop, he defiantly began secreting Nazi emblems on his person. For a time, he wore an actual Nazi swastika pin hidden beneath the lapel of his jacket. That, too, was eventually discovered by his senior officers, who once again told him to knock it off. According to Purdy, Fuhrman's affinity for Nazi material did not end with wartime artifacts. He often belabored other officers with ideas gleaned from contemporary white supremacist tracts and sometimes spoke of his plans to buy land in northern Idaho, near the Hayden Lake redoubt of the neo-Nazi Aryan Nation's religious and paramilitary sect.

Knowing all this, the outraged Purdy demanded that his vandalized locker be dusted for fingerprints. Fuhrman, the examination showed, was indeed the culprit. According to what Purdy told Coleman and Sagoyjian that day, however, the matter "was handled at the division level" so that no mention of the matter appeared in Fuhrman's "packet," as an LAPD officer's personnel records are called.

Over the next few days, Coleman, Sagoyjian, and another filing deputy named Ellen Burke were regaled with other Fuhrman stories by the numerous LAPD officers with whom they came in contact each day. Many of these stories centered around Fuhrman's frequent mention of Nicole Brown in conversations they had had with him, memories of which were triggered by the intensive news coverage that followed Jeffrey Toobin's *New Yorker* story.

One such officer, Detective Mark Arneson of the 77th Division, had told Coleman and another deputy D.A., Jeanette Bernstein, that he had personally spoken with two officers there who told him that Fuhrman had bragged to them of having an affair with Nicole Brown after meeting her when he responded to a call to the Simpsons' Rockingham estate during one of their domestic disputes. According to Arneson, Fuhrman had even made a point of describing to these officers what he called Nicole's "boob job."

Coleman, a serious prosecutor with a reputation for strict attention to legal ethics, was by then seriously concerned. She demanded that Arneson supply her with the names of the officers to whom Fuhrman had allegedly spoken. He refused to give them.

In the meantime, Deputy D.A. Ellen Burke had been told a similar story by Detective I. Daryl Maxwell, working out of the LAPD's Rampart Division. He, too, spoke of colleagues to whom Fuhrman had boasted of a previous sexual relationship with the murdered woman. When he was asked, Maxwell also refused to reveal the names of these other officers. The prosecutors, who were no strangers to the LAPD's invisible—but all but unbreakable—code of silence, were by then seriously disturbed.

Coleman, Sagoyjian, Bernstein, and Burke met and discussed all this information among themselves. They were mutually concerned about two things: If the information they had heard was true—and Coleman had no doubts about her friend Andy Purdy's veracity—then Simpson's defense attorneys might be legally entitled to it since it had exculpatory implications. Perhaps more important from their parochial perspective, if such stories were circulating freely within the police department, the press and defense were bound to hear them on their own. If that occurred, the filing deputies feared, Fuhrman's testimony might blow up in their colleagues' faces.

The group agreed, therefore, that Coleman, a good friend of both Bill Hodgman's and Marcia Clark's, ought to go and tell them what the other deputy D.A.'s had heard.

In the first week of August 1994, Coleman went to Clark's office in the Criminal Courts Building and put the whole matter before the Simpson prosecutors. She told them the stories about the locker and Nicole Simpson, naming Purdy, Arneson, and Maxwell as the sources. Marcia exploded: "Bullshit, bullshit, bullshit," she snarled at her stunned friend.

Hodgman took another view. The stories, he said, should be "checked out."

"Bill," Clark retorted, "this is just more of the bullshit the defense is trying to plant in this case." Clark then turned on Coleman and said, "I am damned sick and tired of other deputy D.A.'s coming to me and trying to get involved in my case for their own self-aggrandizement!"

Stung and offended, Coleman stood up and said to Hodgman, "Bill, you've been told. You can do what you want with it." With that, she stormed from Clark's office never to return. Coleman, in fact, was so angry and perplexed not only about the way Clark had treated her but also about the situation's implications for the district attorney's office that she discussed the issue with a number of colleagues over the next few days. From her standpoint, the matter seemed closed. But six months later, on February 13, 1995, Coleman, who was then on vacation, received a telephone call from Bill Hodgman, who had recovered from his illness and was functioning as case manager for the D.A.'s Simpson team. Hodgman said that one of Gil Garcetti's assistants, Sandy Buttita, had received calls from some of the other deputies with whom Coleman had spoken about Fuhrman. If Coleman did have information about the detective, Hodgman said matter-of-factly, the office wanted her to speak with investigators from the LAPD's Internal Affairs Division. Coleman, understandably confused, reminded Hodgman of their earlier conversation with Clark. He professed not to recall it. Coleman then agreed to speak with the police investigators as soon as possible.

In the meantime, Coleman phoned her friend Andy Purdy to warn him to expect a call from his department's Internal Affairs Division. Purdy, angry and frightened, told her he had already received one.

"Don't you understand," he said, "that talking about this could cost me my job?" Purdy's agitation increased when Lucienne told him she had also told others of the existence of his "Fuhrman log." Later that same evening, Purdy phoned Coleman and—in what she recalls as an acrimonious conclusion to their friendship—informed her that he not only would deny ever having told her of such a document but also that he had destroyed the only copy that very day.

Two days later, on February 15, Coleman was interviewed by a pair of Internal Affairs investigators. As she subsequently would recall, their exchange "was more of an interrogation than an interview. It was clear to me from the start that what they wanted was information that would take the department off the hook on this thing. They weren't interested in anything else." Over the next few days, Burke and Sagoyjian would have similar experiences. In fact, when each of them asked to be allowed to tape-record their interviews, the investigators, who were taping themselves, refused. When the officers promised to supply the women with copies of the "official transcripts" of their interviews, neither of them pressed the tape issue. But they never received copies of their statements. In the meantime, all the deputy D.A.'s involved were ordered by their office not to discuss the matter with anybody. By then, however, word of the whole business had leaked not only to at least one reporter but also to a member of our team, Shawn Chapman, the former public defender who had once tried a case against Coleman. Shawn delicately made contact with Lucienne, who clearly was conscience-stricken over the implications of the process into which she had been drawn. After months of personal anguish over the question, she later came forward and supplied us with a declaration of all the facts she knew. As a former prosecutor who understood only too well the risk she was taking with a career she loved, I have always felt a special admiration for Lucienne Coleman's courage.

ONCE WE BECAME AWARE OF THE INTERNAL AFFAIRS IN-vestigation into the allegations against Fuhrman, we moved quietly to assert our client's legal right to obtain the results on discovery. The documents—parts of which were potentially subject to the privacy statutes that protect certain personnel records in California—were turned over to Judge Ito, who would redact them so that we obtained only that "relevant" information to which we were strictly entitled. When the reports were ultimately released to us by the court, we were astounded. The interviews with Coleman, Burke, and Sagoyjian bore only their names and those of the investigating officers. Everything else had been whited out by Ito. The interviews with Arneson and Maxwell contained only their denials, including Maxwell's assertion that Ellen Burke was "a liar." Purdy's interrogation— certainly the most critical of the documents we sought—was entirely blank.

It all seemed like another frustrating dead end. Fuhrman, it seemed, would remain beyond our reach. Then, on July 7, the day after the prosecution rested, Providence once again extended us its hand. That day, Pat McKenna—Lee Bailey's investigator— received a call from someone who said he'd heard something from one of his clients that might interest O. J. Simpson's lawyers. The client was a film producer who had recently discussed a potential project with a screenwriter, Laura Hart McKinny, who for some time had been working on a script about the conflict between male and female officers inside the Los Angeles Police Department. Despite years of effort, Hart McKinny had never actually had a script produced, but one of the things that interested the client was that she had spent hour upon hour tape-recording interviews with a male LAPD detective who was serving as her technical consultant.

The detective's name was Mark Fuhrman.

The caller went on to acquaint McKenna with what he knew of the tapes' contents. Pat's hastily scrawled out notes of their conversation read like this: "Plant Evidence. Get Niggers. So. Africa—Niggers—apartheid. Laura Hart McKinny," and were followed by a phone number in North Carolina, where the writer taught at a state film school.

McKenna called the number. Laura Hart McKinny answered. She seemed unsurprised to hear from us. She told McKenna she would telephone her own attorneys in Los Angeles and have them get in touch with us. That night, I spoke with her young lawyers, Matthew Schwartz and Ron Regwan, who have an entertainment law practice in Century City. As it turned out, they had been shopping Hart McKinny's tapes around town, attempting to determine their commercial value, and were concerned about maintaining the confidentiality of the material in which they believed their client had a potentially significant financial interest. We discussed how that might be accomplished if we obtained it through subpoena. Most of all, I wanted to know whether the potential benefit to O. J. Simpson was worth the distraction from our other tasks now that we were about to begin mounting our own case.

"Is this stuff really going to help us?" I inquired of the agreeable young Mr. Schwartz.

"Oh, Mr. Cochran," he replied, "we think these tapes would be well worth your while."

"Really?" I asked.

"Sir, they're explosive," Regwan said.

If all Messrs. Schwartz and Regwan's counsel is equally wise, their clients are very well advised indeed.

JUDGE ITO ISSUED THE SUBPOENA WE REQUESTED, AND I prepared to fly to North Carolina to ask that a local court enforce it. But before I left, another—far less pleasant—issue involving tape recordings arose. For some time, several of us had noticed that Bob Shapiro would periodically interrupt meetings or conversations with abrupt tangential statements that frequently sounded rehearsed. It was hard to know what to make of them, and I shrugged them off as a kind of minor irritation.

Then, one day, Shapiro, Simpson, Bailey, and I were conferring in the lockup before court. One of Bob's pants pockets gapped markedly, and, when I stared down into it, I saw the red light of a running microcassette recorder.

I angrily pulled Bob aside. "What are you doing?" I demanded, pointing down to the recorder.

"Oh," Shapiro responded in evident confusion. "I must have turned that on by mistake."

I immediately went out and recounted the incident to the other lawyers and Simpson, who had a similar experience to report. According to our client, not long before, Bob sat down across the table from him in one of the private booths in the jail's attorney room and said: "O.J., I think it would be helpful if you could really open up and share some of your deepest thoughts with me."

"The whole thing was just plain weird, Johnnie," Simpson said to me.

"What did you tell him?" I asked.

"Nothing," O.J. replied. "It was weird."

There was nothing to do but proceed with caution and wonder just how many of our other conversations had somehow ended up on our colleague's recorder.

Later that same day, Shapiro—to whom I had assigned fewer witnesses with each passing month—stumbled through a particularly poor examination for which he appeared inexplicably unprepared. As my co-counsel fumbled around with the papers before him on the podium, Simpson leaned over to me and whispered insistently: "This has got to stop."

On Friday, July 28, 1995, after a night on the red-eye from Los Angeles, F. Lee Bailey and I walked into a courtroom in Winston-Salem, North Carolina, to request that Judge William Wood, Jr., act on behalf of his state and enforce Judge Ito's subpoena of Laura Hart McKinny's tape-recorded conversations with Mark Fuhrman. We had also retained local counsel Robert Craig. It was the first day of O.J.'s trial I had missed. There was a mob scene at the courthouse. Once more, I began to sense just how widely the preoccupation with the Simpson trial had spread. Every available seat in Judge Wood's court, including those in the jury box, was filled, not just with regular spectators but with local judges and lawyers who had put their own business aside for the morning to catch a glimpse of us.

Almost immediately, we went back into Wood's chambers to listen to the tapes. It is hard to describe the atmosphere in those cramped chambers as we sat transfixed—each for our own reasons—by the sound of a disembodied Mark Fuhrman spewing out hatred and filth until the room's very air became fetid and heavy with his venom.

Despite what he had sworn under Lee's cross-examination, the word "nigger" seemed to pass from Fuhrman's lips as naturally as breath. More than that, there were stories of suspects beaten to a pulp, of confessions extracted under torture, of evidence planted, of cases fabricated, and of racial harassment. There were accounts of his disgust with interracial relationships and vicious slurs against women, Latinos, Jews, and gays. Perhaps most telling, there was an assessment—recorded in June 1995—of his own importance to the prosecution of O. J. Simpson.

"I'm the key witness in the trial of the century," he bragged. "If I go down, the glove goes out. And their case goes bye-bye."

Well, I thought to myself, even this miscreant isn't wrong about everything.

At about that point, Judge Wood apparently had had enough.

"Well, well," he said, "this is not a very nice fellow. He certainly has a dirty mouth, doesn't he? I've heard enough. Let's go out and deal with it, put it on the record."

Wood took the bench, then stunned everyone in the room with his ruling: "The subpoena will be denied," he said. "This detective was obviously playing a role. It was all for a screen-play." I do not know what Wood's views of racial matters may be; I am willing to give him the benefit of the doubt. I decided to take his ruling as just another reminder that the Mark Fuhrmans of the world survive, at least in part, because of other people's desire to avoid, even suppress, the distasteful, the hurtful, the troublesome, and the inconvenient. I'd spent a lifetime fighting otherwise well-meaning people's squeamishness, and I had no intention of surrendering now.

I turned to Lee Bailey, who looked as if he was about to choke on his outrage. "Never fear, my brother," I assured him, "this will not stand."

As soon as I could get to a phone, I called Ken Spaulding, a fine North Carolina lawyer I knew, and asked him to begin the appeals process. He was joined by Joe Cheshire, Kenny Fishman, and key staff from Bailey's Boston office. Eight days later, the North Carolina Court of Appeals unanimously ordered enforce-ment of Judge Ito's subpoena.

Back in Los Angeles, the task of actually transcribing the hours of tape-recorded conversations fell to Carmen Qualls, one of our firm's most valuable staff members. Carmen, with the help of the very able Toni Adams, put in several all-nighters to transcribe the Fuhrman tapes. Unfailingly competent, Carmen had assumed the duties of tailoring our office operations to the demands of the Simpson case. She maintained our war room and acted as administrative assistant for our team's members, some of whom were far from home. Not least, she arranged the nightly catered meals that made it possible for all of us to return from court and then work together until sleep overtook us. Among the highlights of Carmen's culinary endeavors were the numerous meals she arranged to have prepared for us by Magic Johnson's personal chef, Carol Quigless.

It was a sobered Carmen, however, who finally presented me with the transcripts of Fuhrman's remarks. Far from naive or sheltered, she nonetheless looked unusually weary, almost shaken. I asked whether she'd had any particular difficulty teasing the words from interviews frequently conducted in noisy restaurants. No, she said, though Laura Hart McKinny's almost unnaturally soft voice had been a bit of a problem. What about Fuhrman? I asked. In North Carolina, I had heard only some of the sixty-one-plus hate-laced excerpts we now knew the tapes contained. Had he dropped his voice when he spat his venom in public places?

"No," Carmen said almost sadly, "he'd get excited. That's how I could tell something was coming. If anything, that stuff was clearer than the rest. You know how your voice lifts when you're excited? That's how he would be when he would . . ." Carmen's voice and gaze trailed off as she handed me the last of the transcripts and left.

I sat there turning page after page. It was like looking at a snake: You don't really want to, but somehow it seems too dangerous to look away. It all was appalling, but two excerpts hit me with a deep and personal force. In one of them, Fuhrman talked about how his training officers had instructed him to disarm, then shoot, difficult suspects. "It's basically murder," he said proudly. "That is what they taught me then. That's too violent now. What have we become?"

Then he launched into what amounted to a nostalgic elegy for the choke hold, whose loss he bitterly resented and seemed to feel in a personal sense.

"You know why we stopped the choke?" he asked rhetorically. "We stopped the choke because a bunch of niggers have a bunch of these organizations in the south end and because all these niggers were choked out and killed ... Personally, I probably personally choked out between—oh, probably a hundred and fifty people, maybe two hundred."

I thought of Herb Avery and James Thomas Mincey and those other dead young men for whose families I had been able to do nothing at all. Then, suddenly, there was this: "I hope they never tear down the old Seventy-seventh Division station," Fuhrman laughed. "They ought to declare the place a historical landmark. You'd never be able to replace the smell of all the dead niggers we killed in there."

The officers who shot Johnie Choyce's son had come from that station, and so had so many others in the abuse cases I had futilely pursued in the desolate years before Ron Settles. They ought to build a monument there, I thought, a monument to Fuhrman's hateful arrogance, which finally has handed me something sharp enough to pierce the veil of silence behind which all the Mark Fuhrmans have been hiding all these years.

This time, I said to the Philistine, "I have you, and, like the lion and the bear, I will not let you go."

OVER THE NEXT FEW WEEKS, O. J. SIMPSON'S INCREAS-ingly desperate prosecutors attempted a series of maneuvers to prevent our jurors from hearing the evidence of Fuhrman's bias. At one point Marcia Clark announced that her office would attempt to have Judge Ito removed from the case because in one excerpt, Fuhrman, who had served under Captain Peggy York in West Los Angeles, could be heard making a series of derogatory remarks about the abilities and appearance of Ito's wife. It was a deeply painful event on all counts for Ito, who is not only a conscientious judge but also an unusually devoted and affectionate husband.

The next day, the prosecutors withdrew their threat and allowed another judge to rule on the relevance to our proceedings of Fuhrman's slurs about Peggy York. They were not, the other judge ruled, of any relevance to our case.

With the jury absent, we made an offer of proof for Ito of the sixty-one excerpts from the Fuhrman tapes we believed the men and women deciding O. J. Simpson's fate deserved to hear. Two days later, Ito ruled that we could play just two for them. Later he would rule that we would be allowed to call as witnesses not only Laura Hart McKinny but also two other women—Kathleen Bell and Natalie Singer, both white—and one man—Roderic Hodge—who is black, to testify to similar slurs and epithets the detective had spoken in their presence. All of it, of course, contradicted Fuhrman's sworn testimony of five months earlier.

The members of the defense team, with the exception of Robert Shapiro, were working at my office as we were out of court on that late August day. When we received a call from the press asking us how we felt about Judge Ito's ruling regarding the Fuhrman tapes, I quickly called the court clerk, Deirdre Robertson, and asked her to fax the ruling to us. Upon its receipt, we read the ruling and were stunned and disappointed. Members of the press had gathered in large numbers in the parking lot of our office building and asked us to speak to them regarding this latest ruling. Within minutes of receiving the ruling, all of us went to the parking lot as advocates for Mr. Simpson, and I spoke on behalf of the group, expressing our disappointment and belief that the ruling was, among other things, cruel and unfair. This observation was born of the moment's passion. In court the next morning or so, I advised Judge Ito that my comments to the press were not directed to him personally and that I did not mean to personally impugn him or his position.

On September 5, 1995, the jury heard those few excerpts from the Fuhrman tapes. The next day, out of their presence, we recalled Fuhrman to the stand. The jurors had been sent out because Fuhrman's attorney, former LAPD officer Darryl Mounger, had announced his client's intention to assert his right against self-incrimination under the Fifth Amendment of the United States Constitution. Under our system, which correctly safeguards the rights of the Fuhrmans as surely as it does any other person put in jeopardy of liberty or life by the power of the state, you may not call a witness for the sole purpose of forcing him to assert his privilege against self-incrimination. Somehow, at that moment, it did not matter to me that the jurors were not present. I had labored for this through all those long, lonely, frustrating, angry years. For all that time, the Philistine—supremely confident in his unassailable power—had laughed, while I fretted powerlessly against the terrible hurt he had dealt so many.

The atmosphere in the courtroom was so tense, even Ito looked uncomfortable. Darden had refused to enter the courtroom. Marcia Clark looked away as Mark Fuhrman, ashen, somehow shrunken, walked into court that day accompanied by his bodyguards. I thought back to the Book of Samuel, which had offered me strength and comfort on that night so many years ago when I had begun this long journey alone there in the kitchen of the little house in Leimert Park.

David said to the Philistine, "You come against me with sword and spear and javelin, but I come against you in the name of the Lord Almighty, the God of the armies of Israel, whom you have defied."

"Did you plant evidence?" Fuhrman was asked, and he responded by asserting his right against self-incrimination. I thought of Johnie Choyce, of James Thomas Mincey, of Herb Avery, of Murphy and Katie Pierson, of little Patty Díaz, and all those others who had suffered at the hands of this man and those far too many others who were like him.

> Reaching into his bag and taking out a stone, he slung it. . . ." So David triumphed over the Philistine with a sling and a stone; without a sword in his hand he struck down the Philistine and killed him.

"Thank you, Lord," I breathed in silent prayer as Fuhrman slunk from the stand, the prosecutors who scant months before had treated him as their champion now refusing even to return his gaze.

"Thank you, Lord, for this life's victory. Thank you for the gift of discernment, for the strength to know that the truth, indeed, is mightier than sword or stone. Thank you, Lord for this victory."

Still, I walked from the courtroom that day thinking there was one more battle to win—and that one belonged to O. J. Simpson.

14

From Seeds of Doubt, Justice Flowers

IN SILENCE, MARK FUHRMAN HAD SPOKEN MORE CAN-
didly than he ever had before.

On *Nightline* that evening, my friend Leslie Abramson, who
worked as one of ABC's legal analysts during the trial, summed
up the impact of the day's events on the prosecution: "Marcia
Clark clutched an asp to her bosom when she put Mark
Fuhrman on the stand," she told Ted Koppel, "and her snake
just bit her."

But another set of surprise witnesses and a crucial tactical
decision still lay between us and final argument. The witnesses—
a pair of former alleged Mafia bone crushers now lurking in the
shadows of the federal witness protection program—were a
couple of comic-opera characters, though their testimony's

import was deadly serious. According to statements we had received, the witnesses—brothers named Craig and Larry Fiato—had passed an afternoon waiting to testify in another case by drinking beer and chatting with their LAPD "baby-sitter," Detective Phil Vannatter. According to these two characters, Vannatter had told them that he and the other detectives had gone to O. J. Simpson's Rockingham estate on the morning after Nicole Brown's and Ronald Goldman's murders because they suspected our client was the culprit. In other words, Vannatter had lied twice under oath about the LAPD's rush to judgment in our case and, equally important, about the reason for the warrantless search of the Rockingham grounds.

On Tuesday, September 19, 1995, we recalled Vannatter to the stand, but he persisted in his deceit. Moments later, as the courtroom cameras were turned off to protect the identities of the government's two professional informants, the Fiato brothers made their entrance. In a way, it was a pity the cameras had gone dark because this was the trial's most cinematic moment. If Fuhrman was central casting's notion of the good cop, these were the bad guys—Larry, burly, mustachioed, and clad in a checked vest over a black shirt; Craig, also known as "Tony the Animal," a gravel-voiced character with snow-white hair, a black goatee, gold hoop earrings, and lizard-skin boots.

There was nothing remotely amusing about their testimony, however. According to Larry, Vannatter had told him during a meeting in January that "Mr. Simpson was a suspect." The detective's partner, Tom Lange, was also present during that conversation, Larry Fiato said. After a great deal of sparring, Craig Fiato was sworn in and testified that during a subsequent encounter, Vannatter had told him that "the husband is always the suspect."

With that, we knew we had fixed in the jurors' minds a critical chapter in our story—the Los Angeles Police Department's rush to judge O. J. Simpson guilty of two brutal murders.

There was a final decision to be made: Should our client take the stand in his own defense, as he and most of the rest of us always assumed he would? If O.J. testified, we knew Marcia Clark would cross-examine him.

In a strategy memo written earlier in the trial, Lee Bailey had summed up the possibilities inherent in that situation this way:

A. If the jury *believes* him, acquittal is assured.
B. If the jury *likes* him, acquittal is probable.
Y. If the jury *dislikes* him, the case is in trouble.
Z. If the jury thinks he is *lying*, all is lost.

"O.J., like every other honest but inexperienced witness who is new to litigation, will need guidance and advice before being sworn."

I wanted more detail on what the risks and benefits were at that moment in the trial.

Shortly thereafter, Jo-Ellan Dimitrius convened the last of the focus groups we employed at various points throughout the trial. Like the others, this one was comprised of a panel of people who had closely followed the trial and whose demographic attributes matched those of the jury. The session began with a straight-forward question: "Based on what you have read, seen, or heard about the O. J. Simpson case, how would you vote regarding Mr. Simpson's guilt or innocence if you had to vote today?"

Seventy percent of the focus group members said they would vote "not guilty."

We then staged mock final arguments for each side, antici-pating not only what we thought we might say, but also what we were fairly sure Clark and Darden would argue. "Based on the presentations you have heard today," the group was then asked, "how would you vote regarding Mr. Simpson's guilt or inno-cence if you had to vote today?"

At that point, the margin for acquittal rose to 85 percent.

After answering that question individually, the panelists were given the opportunity to engage in mock deliberations on their own. We then inquired: "Now that you have had a chance to discuss this case with others in your group, how would you vote regarding Mr. Simpson's guilt or innocence if you had to vote today?"

Once again, the "not guilty" votes climbed—this time to a stunning 90.9 percent.

The focus group was also asked to rate the attorneys involved in the trial on a variety of criteria, ranging from clarity of presentation to honesty. Each of us was then assigned a composite score based on a numerical scale that ran from a low of 1 to a high of 9. My score, 7.66, was the highest; Barry Scheck and Peter Neufeld tied for second at 7.59. In fact, the entire defense team scored above the prosecutors. Marcia Clark came in at 5.92, while Chris Darden was rated a 5.37. Perhaps most telling, Brian Kelberg, the deputy D.A. who had presented much of the prosecution's critical forensic evidence to the jury, ranked next to last among the fifteen lawyers rated by the panel. His score was a dismal 4.60.

If the results of Jo-Ellan's focus group accurately reflected the feelings of O.J.'s real jury, as we believed they did, then the prosecution's position was hopeless—unless, of course, we gave them an opportunity to recover. Marcia clearly was worn and depressed, but I never doubted that however badly she may have been beaten up, she was the kind of adversary who could get up off the canvas and come back to knock you out. A lengthy cross-examination of O. J. Simpson would give her the opportunity to do just that. Moreover, there was one other critical fact to be taken into account: From the beginning of the trial, one after another of our sequestered jurors had fallen by the wayside. We were down to just twelve jurors and two alternates. If O.J. took the stand, we estimated he would be up there for at least several weeks, perhaps more. The jury, obviously restive and disgruntled with the trial's slow pace, would never remain intact. A mistrial was the last thing we defense lawyers wanted; our client wanted it even less. The prosecution, on the other hand, seemed to want a mistrial. Why not? Their situation was desperate, and a second trial always is easier for the state, which has seen the entire defense case.

We decided that O. J. Simpson would waive his right to testify. On Friday, September 22, 1995, our client stood to offer that waiver and, understandably unable to restrain himself, he added something more. "Good morning, Your Honor," he said. "As much as I would like to address some of the misrepresentations about myself, and my Nicole, and our life together, I am mindful of the mood and the stamina of this jury. I have confidence—a lot more it seems than Miss Clark has—in their integrity and that they will find as the record stands now, that I did not, could not, and would not have committed this crime."

Minutes later, 361 days after we had begun picking the twelve people to whom we would soon submit the question of our client's fate, the defense rested.

M Y PREPARATIONS FOR FINAL ARGUMENT HAD BEGUN months before, during jury selection. So had those of Barry Scheck, who would present the portion of our argument dealing with the scientific and forensic evidence. I had shared final argument only once before in my career—and then with some reluctance. In this instance, I did so without hesitation. As he had proven over the previous year of turmoil and bitter conflict, Scheck is a defense lawyer's defense lawyer. My confidence in him was unreserved. He and Peter Neufeld withdrew over the next four days to ready their presentation.

The heart of the prosecution's forensic case was the blood evidence and the DNA analysis that had been run on it. Basically, Barry would summarize what we believed the testimony had already demonstrated. The D.A.'s blood evidence divided itself into two categories: The samples obtained from the socks found in O.J.'s bedroom at Rockingham and off the back gate at Bundy, we would argue, were the product of tampering. The socks appeared to have been placed at the foot of the habitually neat Simpson's bed to create the impression that he had left in a hurry, as Vannatter would allege in his search warrant affidavit. Dennis Fung, who collected the socks, saw no blood on them; neither did the three criminalists who examined them in the LAPD lab on June 19. In fact, no blood was detected on them until weeks later. Similarly, the blood sample was collected from the gate weeks after the crime, and then yielded not only improbably high concentrations of DNA similar to Simpson's, but also the preservative EDTA. The small quantities of relevant blood recovered elsewhere at Bundy, Rockingham, and from the Bronco, Barry would argue, either were the product of cross-contamination caused by the LAPD's sloppy collection and lab techniques or were linked to the quantity of blood we had shown was missing from the reference sample taken from O.J. following his initial interrogation.

While Scheck and Neufeld were planning the forensic portion of the close, I went to work compiling the twenty-eight-page outline from which I would deliver my own argument. Among the things with which I would deal were the prosecution's time line and also with what we had come to think of as our "problem" witnesses, one of whom had testified, two of whom had not. The time-line evidence presented by the prosecution had turned on the notion that the murders had occurred at 10:15 P.M. We had far more credible evidence, including the testimony of a young couple who had strolled past Nicole Brown's condo without seeing the bodies shortly after 10:25, that the murders occurred no earlier than 10:30 and perhaps later. In that time frame, O.J., whose airport limo driver saw him at 10:55, could not have committed the murders, then returned to Rockingham to create the thumps Kato Kaelin claimed to hear at approximately 10:40 to 10:45, as the prosecution alleged.

Our two witnesses promised in my opening statement and then never presented—Mary Anne Gerchas and Rosa Lopez—were another matter. We had had to forgo Gerchas's testimony because her criminal prosecution by the D.A.'s office rendered her possibly suspect in the eyes of the jury. So, too, Rosa Lopez, the Salvadoran maid who worked next door to Simpson's home and saw his Bronco during the crucial time period, was a problem. The prosecutors had beaten her up badly during her videotaped cross-examination, but I always believed in her veracity. Our focus group members did not, however, so we decided not to call her. On the other hand, I had elected to call Nicole's neighbor, Robert Heidstra, who had heard a commotion near Nicole's condo at 10:40 to 10:45, because that testimony supported our theory of the time line. I knew the prosecutors would elicit the fact that he also had seen a white sport utility vehicle similar to O. J. Simpson's Bronco in the area that night, which Heidstra saw turn south on Bundy, going in a direction away from Simpson's house on Rockingham. The latter fact could be explained by the abundance of such automobiles in the vicinity. I felt that his testimony on the time line was worth the risk.

As part of that process, we also brought in another Los Angeles criminal defense lawyer, Charles Lindner, a frequent writer on legal topics. We asked him to employ that skill to give us some fresh, perhaps simplified ways of restating our story to the jury. Lindner happens to be Jewish and, like so many people of his generation, lost much of his extended family in the Holocaust. As it happened, however, his major contribution to my subsequent argument was the analogy that raised a storm of controversy. Other members of the team contributed suggestions for phrases I might use. Scholarly Gerry Uelmen, for example, was the author of our memorable motto: "If it doesn't fit, you must acquit." Most important, I asked each member of the team—except Scheck and Neufeld, who were preoccupied with their own assignment—to submit, based on the evidence, a list of fifteen questions I could put directly to Marcia Clark. Each of them responded in his or her characteristically individual fashion.

But, taken together, their lists catalogued just how thickly the seeds of reasonable doubt had been sown throughout the trial:

Gerry Uelmen submitted eight:

1. Why was the Bronco released to the LAPD impound garage if there was evidence still in it?

2. Why didn't you let us hear the statement O.J. made to detectives after his arrest?

3. Why didn't you call the coroner who did the autopsies?

4. Why aren't there any bruises or marks on O.J. Simpson's body?

5. Why does the most DNA come from the bloodstains that showed up for the first time weeks after the murders?

6. Why did Mark Fuhrman lie to us?

7. Why did Phil Vannatter lie to us?

8. How come the gloves don't fit?

Alan Dershowitz faxed his queries from Harvard:

1. How do you explain the Rockingham glove still being damp with blood at 6:00 A.M., if it had been dropped there at 10:45 P.M. on a dry night?

2. What exactly is the state's theory as to how the glove got there? Why was there no blood near it?

3. Why did Fuhrman not tell the truth about time of photo showing him pointing at glove?

4. Why was Fuhrman alone outside crime scene for 18 minutes? Isn't it equally reasonable that the real killer dropped second glove outside of crime scene than behind O.J.'s house?

5. Why did Fuhrman, who was already off the case, insist on going to O.J.'s house, when others knew how to get there?

6. Why did Fuhrman, Vannatter, and their commander try to lie about whether O.J. was a suspect when they went to his house? What was that intended to cover-up? (Show video of Vannatter answering that O.J. was no more a suspect than Bob Shapiro—and ask whether any reasonable person could believe that!)

7. Why did no one see the blood on the gate until days after the crime? And why did *that* blood, which was supposedly exposed to the weather, etc., contain EDTA and higher concentrations of DNA than blood removed right after crime?

8. Is it merely coincidence that the amount of missing blood—according to Peratis's original sworn testimony—is unaccounted for *unless* it was later added to socks, gate, etc.?

9. How do you explain multiple problems with socks: Sequence of photos? No one saw blood? Transfer patterns? Isn't all this at least equally consistent with (Dr. Henry Lee's) "Something wrong?"

10. Should the jury still convict if it believes evidence may have been tampered with?

11. In light of knife wounds, shoe prints, etc., isn't it at least equally reasonable that more than one killer was involved? If state is wrong about its one-killer theory, isn't it at least equally reasonable that it is also wrong about *who* did it?

12. In light of glove not fitting and not shrinking (Herb MacDonell experiment), is it not at least equally reasonable that O.J. never owned them?

13. If the killer was covered with blood—as he had to be—how do you explain absence of large amount of blood either on way to car (if killer changed before getting into car) on in Bronco (if it were O.J. and he got into Bronco before changing)?

Bob Kardashian's list was brief:

1. How did the glove get to Rockingham?

2. Why no blood on Rockingham door knob/stairway/carpet in bedroom?

3. How could Allan Park not hear Bronco pull up to Rockingham?

4. Where are bloody clothes and weapon?

5. Why no bruises on O.J.?

6. What proves that O.J. ever owned Bruno Magli shoes?

7. What did Fuhrman do for 2½ hours while at Bundy?

8. Why were so many defense witnesses rejected by the prosecution?

9. Why four LAPD necessary to notify someone who isn't even the next of kin?

Bob Shapiro's questions were very much to the point:

1. Why did no one secure the Bronco at 7:00 A.M. pursuant to Vannatter's order?

2. Why did Vannatter bring blood 25 miles to Rockingham?

3. The glove doesn't fit.

4. Why did Fung test 11 of 12 items at Rockingham and not test the sock?

5. Where are the clothes?

6. Where is the knife?

7. Why would O.J. leave the children he loves to find their mother murdered?

8. Why did the only four homicide detectives leave Bundy without investigating and go to notify O.J. after two waited in the middle of the street for 2½ hours?

9. Why is there so little blood, if any, in the Bronco?

10. Why is there no blood trail to the glove?

11. Why did no one see blood on the socks for two months?

12. Why would O.J., if he was involved and didn't want to be observed, not go around the back of his residence?

13. Why should O.J. knock three times on Kato's window?

14. Why didn't four of the LAPD notify the coroner for ten hours?

15. Why, in a high profile case, would LAPD send out a trainee criminologist?

16. Why would O.J. talk to the police without a lawyer if he had something to hide?

17. Why would O.J. give a voluntary blood sample?

18. Why would O.J. bring one glove back and leave one at the crime scene?

19. O.J. had a great life, fame, fortune, great kids, a great mother to raise the kids, access to women throughout the world, a model girl-friend—kill Nicole?

20. Why did O.J. not have any scratches on him?

21. Socks—no dirt on the socks, etc.

Bob Blasier, as precise as always, submitted exactly the fifteen questions requested—and every one demanded an answer:

1. Why did the blood show up on the sock almost two months after a careful search for evidence, and why, as demonstrated by Dr. Lee and Professor MacDonell, was the blood applied when there was no foot in it?

2. Why was Mark Fuhrman—a detective who had been pushed off the case—the person who went by himself to the Bronco, over the fence, to interrogate Kato, and to "discover" the glove in the "thump-thump-thump" area?

3. Why was the glove still moist when Fuhrman found it if Mr. Simpson had dropped it seven hours earlier? And agent Bodziak told you blood dries very rapidly?

4. If Mark Fuhrman would speak so openly about his intense geno-cidal racism to a relative stranger such as Kathleen Bell, how many of his co-workers, the other detectives in the case, were also aware that he lied when he denied using the "N" word, and failed to come forward?

5. Why did you not call a single police officer to rebut police pho-tographer Rokahr's testimony that Detective Fuhrman was pointing at the glove *before* Fuhrman went to Rockingham?

6. If the glove had been dropped on the walkway at Rockingham ten minutes after the murder, why is there no blood or fibre on south

walkway or on the leaves the glove was resting on? Why is there no blood on the 150 feet of narrow walkway or on the stucco wall abutting it?

7. For what purpose was Vannatter carrying Mr. Simpson's blood in his pocket for three hours at a distance of twenty-five miles, instead of booking it down the hall at Parker Center?

8. Why did Deputy District Attorney Hank Goldberg, in a desperate attempt to cover up for the missing 1.5 ml of Mr. Simpson's blood, secretly go out to the home of police nurse Thano Peratis without notice to the defense and get him to contradict his previous sworn testimony at both the grand jury and the preliminary hearing?

9. Why, if according to Clark he walked into his own house wearing the murder clothes and shoes, is there not only any soil or so much as a smear or a drop of blood associated with the victims on the floor, the white carpeting, the door knobs, the light switches, and his bedding?

10. If Mr. Simpson just killed Mr. Goldman in a bloody battle involving more than two dozen knife wounds when Mr. Goldman remained standing and struggling for several minutes, how come there is less than $7/10$ of a drop consistent with Mr. Goldman found in the Bronco?

11. Why, following a bitter struggle with Mr. Goldman, were there no bruises or marks on O. J. Simpson's body?

12. Why do bloodstains with the most DNA not show up until weeks after the murder?

13. Why did Mark Fuhrman lie to us?

14. Why did Phil Vannatter lie to us?

15. Given Professor MacDonell's testimony that the gloves would not have shrunk no matter how much blood was smeared on them, and given that they never shrank from June 21st, 1994, until now despite having been repeatedly frozen and thawed, how come the gloves don't fit?

Lee Bailey's questions were followed by a personal note, which reflects the bond that had grown between us:

1. What reason did Mr. Simpson have to go to Nicole's home and kill her?

2. Would Mr. Simpson—whose face was well known, especially in that neighborhood—have chosen to kill Nicole in a lighted area near a public street, where a passer-by might have come at any time?

3. Would Mr. O. J. Simpson—or any other rational human being—kill the mother of his children while they are close at hand, likely to awaken at any time and come upon the scene?

4. Mr. Bodziak of the FBI has told you that a killer wearing Bruno Magli shoes left the crime scene and walked to the alley, then returned to the crime scene for some reason and walked to the alley a second time. Assuming that to be true, would Mr. Simpson—of all people— have risked a trip back to the scene with a dog howling and witnesses likely to come any minute?

5. Has the prosecution totally failed to show that Mark Fuhrman did not have the opportunity—during the three hours he spent at Bundy that morning—to spot and conceal in a readily available plastic bag the right hand glove?

6. Why was Mark Fuhrman—a detective who had been pushed off the case—the person who went by himself: (A) To the Bronco (B) Over the fence (C) To interrogate Kato (D) To "find" the glove in the "thump-thump-thump" area?

7. What was Mark Fuhrman really doing for fifteen minutes all alone outside the Simpson house that morning? Was he planting evidence which he alone could testify to, thus insuring that he would remain on the case?

8. Why was the glove still moist when Fuhrman found it if Mr. Simpson had dropped it seven hours before? As Agent Bodziak told you, blood dries "very rapidly."

9. Assuming the murders began at 10:35 P.M., as the evidence shows beyond any doubt—when and how could Mr. Simpson have accomplished them?

10. How could any human being who had just killed the mother of his children act as calm and relaxed as Mr. Simpson did—according to every witness who testified—for hours after the act?

11. If the police were really impartial, why didn't they ask Mr. Simpson to try on the glove on June 13, when he was being totally cooperative with them? It wouldn't have fit then any better than it did here.

12. For what purpose was Vannatter carrying Mr. Simpson's blood around in his pocket?

13. If Mr. Simpson had knifed two people to death in a bloody battle, why was only $7/10$ of one drop of blood found in the Bronco?

14. Why did the sock show up almost two months after a careful search for evidence, and why was the blood on it applied when there was no foot in it?

Then I'd say, "For Ms. Clark's convenience—should she decide to deal with these very troublesome questions—I am leaving a written list of them here when I conclude."

> With all Godspeed, my brother, sally forth into the firestorm
> and vanquish the evil foe. Let the force be with you.
> —Obi-Wan Kenobi

The evening of Monday, September 25, as I pulled together the last threads of my argument in my head, I received a call from Bob Shapiro. His antipathy to Scheck had grown as the trial progressed, and he made a last desperate plea that he, rather than Barry, deliver the balance of our argument to the jury. "He's too in-your-face, Johnnie," Bob said to me. "He turns people off. The judge doesn't like him, and I don't think the jury does either. I think I should argue."

"Bob," I replied, not bothering to keep the weariness out of my voice, "the focus group doesn't agree with you and, more important, neither do I. That jury loves Barry. He's going to argue."

That settled, I headed for bed to get what sleep I could.

I rose on the morning of Wednesday, September 27, and thought, This is the day I have waited for all my life.

• • •

335

SEPTEMBER 27, 1995: FINAL ARGUMENT IN THE CASE OF the *People of California v. Orenthal James Simpson.*

All that morning, I sat and listened as Marcia Clark hammered rhetorical nails into what she—and much of the nation— hoped would be my client's coffin.

Finally, she was done. We broke for lunch. I was up next.

I spent the next hour in a world of my own. Months before, I had confided my impression of our jury to that reporter, and nothing had happened since to change my mind: "These are good people," I said then. "These are my people. I know their hearts and they know mine. And when the time comes, that's how I'm going to speak to them—heart to heart."

I had so much in my heart that day: O. J. Simpson's future and so many other things—how we Americans live and how we understand each other as we do. If I was going to do justice to all of that, I knew I would have to go deeply within myself, to the place where we walk by faith and not by sight. I needed to be alone, away from my colleagues milling about, away from their banter and advice, away from O.J., who loved to talk and give advice. Over the course of this long and tumultuous trial, I had frequently been amused by and, nearly as often, impressed by his insights into a system and process about which he previously had known next to nothing. But at that moment, I needed neither diversion nor another viewpoint. What counsel I required, I knew was elsewhere.

The jurors were at lunch, so I asked the bailiff if I could use the jury room to collect my thoughts. He agreed, and moments later I found myself alone in the room where those twelve jurors would shortly decide my client's fate. I couldn't help but notice the newspapers scattered about. They looked like lace, all the articles concerning our case carefully cut out by the sheriffs charged with maintaining our sequestered panel's isolation.

In the center of the room was a table surrounded by chairs and, against one wall, a gray couch with brown arms. I sank into it and stared out the window. Half a world would be watching the argument I was about to give, but I needed to close all that out. I looked south, past the tall buildings along Broadway, and pictured my childhood home on West Twenty-eighth Street, just a few miles away. And, as I have on all the important days of my life, I thought of my mother. Every Saturday during the sixteen months of O. J. Simpson's double murder trial, when I was in town, I had gone to her crypt to pray.

So, I closed my eyes and did just that. I thought of Joshua's admonition, which my father had reminded me of just the night before: "Do not fear, for I am with you. Do not look anxiously about you for I am your God. I will strengthen you. Surely I will help you."

Time passed unnoticed. Forty minutes later, when the bailiff gently knocked on the door and said the jury was on its way back, I was very, very relaxed.

AT PRECISELY I P.M., JUDGE ITO TOOK THE BENCH, CAST his owlish gaze toward the defense table, and—in a quiet but clear voice—said: "Mr. Cochran, you may now begin your final argument."

"Thank you very kindly, Your Honor," I said. I rose. A silence as deep as any I've ever experienced settled over that courtroom. Others subsequently have told me that they felt as if the four walls themselves might crumble under the tension.

I didn't feel it. Silence doesn't frighten me. A believer knows that silence is not an absence, but a presence—a cloud out of which, since time immemorial, God has spoken to those who will listen.

"Put your hands in His unchanging hand," my mother used to tell me, quoting her favorite from among the old hymns I first had heard echoing off the white clapboards of the Little Union Baptist Church.

So as I approached the lectern, I bowed my head ever so slightly and recalled, as I had at so many critical junctures in my life, the words of the Prophet Isaiah:

> But they that wait upon the Lord shall renew their strength.
> They shall mount up with wings as eagles;
> They shall run and not be weary
> They shall walk and not faint.

I was ready at last.

Good afternoon, ladies and gentlemen [I began]. The defendant, Mr. Orenthal James Simpson, is now afforded an opportunity to argue the case, but I'm not going to argue with you, ladies and gentlemen. What I'm going to do is discuss the reasonable inferences which I feel can be drawn from this evidence . . . Listen for a moment, will you, please. One of my favorite people in history is the great Frederick Douglass. He said shortly after the slaves were freed, "In a composite nation like ours, as before the law, there should be no rich, no poor, no high, no low, no white, no black, but common country, common citizenship, equal rights and a common destiny." This marvelous statement was made more than one hundred years ago. . . . Now, in this case, you're aware that we represent Mr. Orenthal James Simpson. The prosecution never calls him Mr. Orenthal James Simpson. They call him the defendant. I want to tell you right at the outset that Mr. Orenthal James Simpson, like all defendants, is presumed innocent. He's entitled to the same dignity and respect as all the rest of us. As he sits over there now, he's cloaked in a presumption of innocence. You will determine the facts and whether or not he's set free to walk out those doors or whether he spends the rest of his life in prison. But he's Orenthal James Simpson. He's not just the defendant, and we on the defense are proud, consider it a privilege to have been part of representing him in this exercise, this journey toward justice. . . .

This is not a case for the timid or the weak of heart. This is not a case for the naive. This is a case for courageous citizens who believe in the Constitution. And while I'm talking about the Constitution, think with me for a moment how many times you heard my learned adversary say the defense didn't prove, the defense didn't do this, the defense didn't do that. Remember back in voir dire? What did the judge tell us? We don't have to do anything. We don't have to prove anything. This is the prosecution's burden, and we can't let them turn the Constitution on its head. We can't let them get away from their burden. . . . They must prove beyond a reasonable doubt and to a moral certainty, and we will talk about what a reasonable doubt means. . . .

Let me ask each of you a question. Have you ever in your life been falsely accused of something? Ever had to sit there and take it and watch the proceedings and wait and wait and wait, all the while knowing that you didn't do it? . . . Now, last night, as I thought about the arguments of my colleagues, two words came to mind. I asked my wife this morning to get the dictionary out and look up two words. The two words were "speculative," and "cynical."

"Cynical" is described as contemptuously distrustful of human nature and motives, gloomy, distrustful view of life. And to "speculate"—to engage in conjecture and to surmise—is to take to be the truth on the basis of insufficient evidence. I mention those two definitions to you because I felt that much of what we heard yesterday and again this morning was speculative.

Understand this, ladies and gentlemen, that none of us in this courtroom were out at 875 Bundy on June 12, 1994 . . . so that everything we say to you is our best effort to piece together what took place in this case. . . . It is a sad fact that in American society, a large number of people are murdered each year. Violence unfortunately has become a way of life in America. And so when this sort of tragedy does in fact happen, it becomes the business of the police to step up and step in and to take charge of the matter. A good, efficient, competent, noncorrupt police department will carefully set about the business of investigating homicides. They won't rush to judgment. They won't be bound by an obsession to win at all costs. They will set about trying to apprehend the killer or killers and trying to protect the innocent from suspicion. . . .

Your verdict in this case will go far beyond the walls of Department 103 because your verdict talks about justice in America and it talks about the police and whether they're above the law and it looks at the police perhaps as though they haven't been looked at very recently. Remember, I told you this is not for the naive, the faint of heart or the timid. . . .

Continuing on, there's absolutely no evidence at all that Mr. Simpson ever tried to hide a knife or clothes or anything else on his property. You'll recall that Fuhrman—and when I get to Fuhrman, we'll be spending some time on him, as you might imagine. But one of the things he said was that he encountered cobwebs further down that walkway, indicating, if that part is true—and I don't vouch for him at all—there had been nobody down that pathway for quite some time.

And so, Ms. Clark talks about O.J. being very, very recognizable. She talks about O. J. Simpson getting dressed up to go commit these murders. Just before the break, I was thinking—I was thinking last night about this case and their theory and how it didn't make any sense and how it didn't fit and how something is wrong. . . .

It occurred to me how they were going to come here, stand up here, and tell you how O. J. Simpson was going to disguise himself. He was going to put on a knit cap and some dark clothes, and he was going to get in this white Bronco, this recognizable person, and go over and kill his wife. That's what they want you to believe. . . . Let me show you something. This is a knit cap. Let me put this knit cap on. You have seen me for a year. If I put this knit cap on, who am I? I'm still Johnnie Cochran with a knit cap. And if you looked at O. J. Simpson over there—and he has a rather large head—O. J. Simpson in a knit cap from two blocks away is still O. J. Simpson. It's no disguise. It's no disguise. It makes no sense. It doesn't fit. If it doesn't fit, you must acquit. . . .

"Good time, Your Honor?" I asked Judge Ito, inquiring about our break.

"All right," said the judge. "Ladies and gentlemen, we are going to take our midafternoon recess at this time. Remember all my admonitions. We'll stand in recess for fifteen . . ."

Twenty minutes later, I resumed my argument, moving methodically through my outline toward one of the sets of facts that pointed most directly toward evidence tampering. That involved the videotape the police had made of O.J.'s bedroom. It did not show the socks they later claimed to have recovered from the carpet at the foot of his bed, the sock upon which incriminating traces of blood were not detected until much, much later. At my signal, we began replaying that video.

> Watch with me now [I invited the jurors], I want you to watch the time counter and understand how important this is. . . . This is Mr. Willie Ford, the police photographer, going up into the bedroom. It's 4:13 on June 13th, 1994. . . . Look at the foot of the bed there, where the socks are supposed to be. You'll see no socks in this video. And you'll recall that Mr. Willie Ford testified about this. I asked him, "Well, where are the socks, Mr. Ford?" And he said, "I didn't see any socks."
>
> Now that's interesting, isn't it? These mysterious socks, these socks that no one sees any blood on until August fourth all of a sudden . . . These socks will be their undoing. It just doesn't fit. None of you can deny there are no socks at the foot of that bed at 4:13. Where, then, are the socks, this important piece of evidence?

With the video complete, I reminded them that the criminalists, Dennis Fung and Andrea Mazzola, had testified that they collected those socks between 4:30 and 4:40.

> Let's give them the benefit of the doubt. How could the socks be there at 4:35, when you just saw they're not there at 4:13. Who's fooling whom here? They're setting this man up, and you

can see it with your own eyes. You're not naive. No one is foolish here. . . .

Then we find out [these socks] have EDTA [the preservative injected into blood samples] on them . . . How could it be on there? Why didn't they see blood before that? There's a big fight here. Where is the dirt? How could Mr. Simpson have worn these [black dress] socks with a sweat outfit? Wait a minute. Now you don't have to be from the fashion police to know that . . . You wear those kinds of socks with a suit. Doesn't it make sense that those socks were in the laundry hamper from Saturday night, when Mr. Simpson went to a formal event? They went and took them out of the hamper and staged it there. . . . It just doesn't fit. When it doesn't fit, you must acquit.

Dr. Herbert MacDonell [a renowned expert on blood splatters who had testified on Simpson's behalf] came in here and told you that there was no splatter or spatter on these socks. These socks had compression transfer, and he used his hands to show you somebody took those socks and they put something on them.

I then went on to talk about the tiny amounts of blood the police claimed to have recovered from O. J. Simpson's Bronco and how even those blood drops were not seen by the employees of the police impound garage to which the vehicle was taken after the LAPD towed it away from Rockingham.

Dr. Baden says the perpetrator would be covered with blood. Your common sense tells you that the perpetrator would be covered with blood. . . . How does anyone drive away in that car with bloody clothes with no blood there on the seats, no blood anyplace else? Every police officer who came in talked about how bloody this scene was. . . . It doesn't make any sense. They can't explain it because Mr. Simpson was not in that car and didn't commit these murders. That's the reasonable and logical explanation. None other will do, and it's too late for them to change now these kinds of shifting theories. . . . So the prosecution then has no shoes, no weapon, no clothes. They don't have anything except these socks, which appear all of a sudden under these circumstances. . . .

Now, when you want to think about the depths to which people will go to try to win. . . . I'm going to give you an example. There was a witness in this case named Thano Peratis. This is a man, who's their man, who took O. J. Simpson's blood. He's been a nurse for a number of years. You saw him. He works for the city of Los Angeles. He says that when he took this blood from O. J. Simpson on June 13th, he took between 7.9 and 8.1 CC's of blood. . . . He's sworn to tell the truth both places. Pretty clear, isn't it? Pretty clear . . . Something's wrong here, something's sinister here, something's wrong because if we take their figures and assume they took 8 CC's of blood, there's 6.5 CC's accounted for. There is 1.5 CC's of this blood missing. There's some missing blood in this case. Where is it? . . .

Vannatter, the man who carries the blood. Fuhrman, the man who finds the glove . . . Now, Detective Vannatter has been a police officer for twenty-seven, twenty-eight years, experienced LAPD Robbery-Homicide man who was put on this case because of his experience . . . here you have Mr. Simpson cooperating fully, gives his blood, 8 CC's of blood, we now know . . . The blood is then turned over to Vannatter. He could have gone a couple of floors and booked the blood, as the manual requires. But he didn't do that, did he? . . .

What he does is, he goes way out in this area marked Brentwood Heights. It must be twenty, twenty-five, twenty-seven miles to go way out there carrying the blood in this unsealed gray envelope, supposedly. Why is he doing that? Why is Vannatter carrying Mr. Simpson's blood out there? Why is he doing that? Doesn't make any sense. Violates their own rules . . . Has he ever done it in any other case? No. Name another case where this has happened. . . . It gets even stranger, doesn't it, because supposedly after the blood is carried out to O. J. Simpson's residence, Vannatter gives the blood to Fung, according to what we heard, but Fung then uses some kind of a trash bag, a black trash bag, and gives it to Mazzola, but he doesn't tell her that it's blood. Isn't that bizarre? . . . Mazzola is asked, "Well, do you see—did you see when Vannatter gave the blood to Fung." And she says, "No. I'd sat down on the couch and I was closing my eyes on Mr. Simpson's couch at that moment. I wasn't looking at that moment." . . . Always looking the other way, not looking, doesn't want to be involved, covering for somebody . . . It doesn't fit. . . .

Then we come, before we end the day, to Detective Mark Fuhrman. This man is an unspeakable disgrace. He's been unmasked before the whole world for what he is, and that's hopefully positive. His misdeeds go far beyond this case because he speaks of culture that's not tolerable in America. But let's talk about this case. People worry about, this is not the case of Mark Fuhrman. Well, it's not the case of Mark Fuhrman. Mark Fuhrman is not in custody. . . . You know, they were talking yesterday in their argument about, "Well, gee, you think he would commit a felony?" What do you think it was when he was asked the question by F. Lee Bailey. . . .

But what I find particularly troubling is that they all knew about Mark Fuhrman and they weren't going to tell you. They tried to ease him by. Of all the witnesses who've testified in this case, how many were taken up to the grand jury room where they have this prep session to ask him all these questions. . . . So they knew. Make no mistake about it. And so when they try and prepare him . . . get him ready and make him seem like a choirboy and make him come in here and raise his right hand as though he's going to tell you the truth and give you a true story here, they knew he was a liar and a racist. . . . There's something about good versus evil. There's something about truth. That truth crushed to earth will rise again. You can always count on that. He's the one who says the Bronco was parked askew, and he sees some spot on the door [at Rockingham]. He makes all of the discoveries. . . .

He's got to be the big man because he's had it in for O.J. because of his views since '85. This is the man, he's the guy who climbs over the fence. He's the guy who goes in and talks to Kato

Kaelin while the other detectives are talking to the family. He's the guy who's shining a light in Kato Kaelin's eyes. . . . He's the guy who's off this case who's supposedly there to help this man, our client . . . who then goes out all by himself. Now he's worried about bodies or suspects or whatever. He doesn't even take out his gun. He goes around the side of the house, and lo and behold, he claims he finds this glove and he says the glove is still moist and sticky.

Why would it be moist and sticky unless he brought it over there and planted it there to make this case? And there is a Caucasian hair on that glove. This man cannot be trusted. He is central to the prosecution, and for them to say he's not important is untrue and you will not fall for it, because as guardians of justice here, we can't let it happen. . . .

We'll see you tomorrow . . . thank you, Your Honor.

I looked at my watch. It was 7:45 in the evening. Outside, in the courthouse hallway, the latest source of controversy to attach itself to the Simpson case was waiting for me. On that day and for sometime to come, my family and I were accompanied by bodyguards provided by the Nation of Islam. For some time, I had been receiving death threats and a bomb threats, some of them faxed directly into the courtroom. At some point, the street address of our house had been posted on the Internet. My daughter Tiffany, the television journalist in South Carolina, had begun receiving threats against her life, too vile and obscene to quote. At precisely that moment, the presiding judge of the criminal courts, James Bascue, denied my longtime friend and sometime bodyguard Henry Grayson—a former investigator for the district attorney's office—to carry his gun when he accompanied me into the courthouse. Bascue also refused us permission to use the secure underground parking lot beneath the Criminal Courts Building, forcing us to pass through the increasingly unruly crowds on the street outside. So, when the Muslims offered us the services of their trained Fruit of Islam security guards, we accepted. They not only watched over us in Los Angeles but also over Tiffany three thousand worrisome miles away. I do not agree with Louis Farrakhan's alleged views on Jews, Christians, women, or a large range of other topics. But when my family was in need, his people reached out to us with help. I accepted, and I remain grateful to the men who assisted us when the legal authorities would not.

I do not know how the other participants in our trial fared that night. I slept like a rock and awoke refreshed and confident, knowing exactly where I wanted to resume that morning. After a few brief words of recapitulation, I went back to the man who was "present at the creation" of the prosecution's case.

Let's continue where we left off then, with this man Fuhrman. He's said some very interesting things.

He tells you that Rokahr, the photographer, took this photograph [of him pointing to the glove] after seven o'clock in the morning. And the reason he tells you that is because he wants that photograph of him pointing at the glove taken after he supposedly finds the glove at Rockingham. . . . Rokahr then comes here near the end of the case . . . and says these photographs on this contact sheet are all taken while it is dark. . . . Now we know it is not seven o'clock. You see that photograph up there. That is Mark Fuhrman pointing. . . . But he is lying again. He is lying. . . . Remember there is a question he was asked about the gloves, and Lee Bailey asked him about. Well—he says, well—he is talking about gloves and he says "them." He never explained that. He says "them." Does that mean two gloves? He said, "I saw them." Is that two gloves? Why would you say "them"? . . .

These are the facts. I haven't made them up. This is what you heard in this case. This is what we have proved. Some of it came in late; some of it came in early, but our job here is to piece this together so that you can then see this, so when he refers to the glove as "them," that has never been cleared up for you and he can't. . . .

One of the things that has made this country so great is people's willingness to stand up and say, "That is wrong. I'm not going to be part of it. I'm not going to be part of the cover-up." That is what I'm asking you to do. Stop this cover-up. Stop this cover-up. If you don't stop it, then who? Do you think the police department is going to stop it? Do you think the D.A.'s office is going to stop it? Do you think we can stop it by ourselves? It has to be stopped by you.

. . . the jury instruction which you know about now says essentially that a witness willfully false . . . in one material part of his or her testimony is to be distrusted in others. You may reject the whole testimony of a witness who willfully has testified falsely to a material point unless from all the evidence you believe the probability of truth favors his or her testimony in other particulars . . . Why is this instruction so important? . . . First of all, both prosecutors have now agreed that we have convinced them beyond a reasonable doubt, that Mark Fuhrman is a lying, perjuring, genocidal racist, and he has testified falsely in this case on a number of scores. . . . When you go back in the jury room, some of you may want to say, "Well, gee, you know, boys will be boys." This is just like police talk. This is the way they talk. That is not acceptable as the consciences of this community if you adopt that attitude. That is why we have this, because nobody has the courage to say it is wrong.

You are empowered to say, "We are not going to take that anymore." I'm sure you will do the right thing about that . . . Lest you feel that a greater probability of truth lies in something else, then you may disregard this testimony. This applies not only to Fuhrman, it applies to Vannatter, and then you see what trouble their case is in. They can't explain to you why Vannatter carried that blood, because they were setting this man up, and that glove, anybody among you think that glove was just sitting there, just placed there, moist and sticky after six and a half hours? The testimony is it will be dried in three or four hours, according to MacDonell. We are not naive. You understand there is no blood on anything else. There is no blood trail. There is no hair and fiber. And you get the ridiculous explanation that Mr. Simpson was running into air conditioners on his own property. . . .

So when they take the law into their own hands, they become worse than the people who break the law, because they are the protectors of the law. Who then polices the police? You police the police. You police them by your verdict. . . .

Once more, I reprised for the jurors the testimony of all those witnesses who had come forward to testify concerning Fuhrman's racism, concluding with this:

And now we have it. There was another man not too long ago in the world who had those same views, who wanted to burn people, who had racist views and ultimately had power over the people in his country. People didn't care. People said, "He's just crazy. He's just a half-baked painter." They didn't do anything about it. This man, this—scourge—became one of the worst people in the history of this world. Adolf Hitler. Because people didn't care, or they didn't try to stop him. He had the power over his racism and his anti-religion. Nobody wanted to stop him, and it ended up in World War II, the conduct of this man. And so Fuhrman, Fuhrman wants to take all black people now and burn them or bomb them. That is genocidal racism. Is that ethnic purity? What is that? We are paying this man's salary to espouse these views? Do you think he only told Kathleen Bell, whom he just had met? Do you think he talked to his partners about it? Do you think his commanders knew about it? Do you think everybody knew about it and turned their heads? Nobody did anything about it.

Based upon converstions with several witnesses who have been inside Mark Fuhrman's home, I believe that he is a brown shirt–wearing Nazi who collects and proudly displays Nazi memorabilia. While this analogy was relevant, it was never my intention to offend anyone.

Things happen for a reason in your life. Maybe this is one of the reasons we are all gathered together this day, one year and two days after we met. Maybe there is a reason for your purpose. Maybe this is why you were selected. There is something in your background, in your character, that helps you understand this is wrong. Maybe you are the right people at the right time at the right place to say, "No more, we are not going to have this. This is wrong." What they've done to our client is wrong. You cannot believe these people. You can't trust the message. You can't trust the messengers. It is frightening. It is, quite frankly, frightening, and it is not enough for the prosecutors now to stand up and say, "Oh well, let's just back off." . . . This is . . . frightening. It is not just African Americans, it is white people who would associate or deign to go out with a black person or marry one. You are free in America to love whoever you want, so it infects all of us, doesn't it, this one rotten apple, and yet they cover for him.

Yet they cover for him . . .

I then surrendered the podium to Barry Scheck for the presentation of our argument on the scientific evidence, promising the jurors I would return for one more conversation with them. There was, however, one more courtroom hurdle to clear. Peter Neufeld had broken his glasses that morning and asked to sit next to the prosecutors, behind the podium, so he could monitor the critical points he had helped to prepare. When Ito declined permission, Neufeld said he felt that the decision was unfair and he moved closer to the podium. At the next recess, the judge held him in contempt, demanding an apology.

Peter declined, whispering to me that he was prepared to tell Ito "to come down and sit with the prosecutors, where he belonged."

"My brother," I said, "if you do that, you will spend the weekend in jail, while O. J. Simpson goes home a free man." Within a few moments we had smoothed things out. I apologized to Judge Ito and Peter remained free and out of contempt.

Later that day, when Barry concluded his damning summation of the forensic evidence, I resumed my position at the podium. I ran briefly through the major issues of reasonable doubt, which we believed we had raised concerning the people's case. Then I concluded:

> And I always think in a circular fashion, that you kind of end up where you started out. The truth is a wonderful commodity in this society. Some people can't stand the truth. But you know what. That notwithstanding, we still have to deal with truth in this society.
>
> Carlysle said that no lie can live forever. . . . I happen to really like the Book of Proverbs and in Proverbs it talks a lot about false witnesses. It says that a false witness shall not be unpunished and he that speaketh lies shall not escape. . . .
>
> And James Russell Lowell said it best about wrong and evil. He said that truth's forever on the scaffold, wrong forever on the throne, yet that scaffold sways the future, and beyond the dim unknown standeth God within the shadows, keeping watch above his own. . . .
>
> I will some day go on to other cases, no doubt as will Ms. Clark and Mr. Darden. Judge Ito will try another case someday, I hope, but this is O. J. Simpson's one day in court. By your decision, you control his very life in your hands. Treat it carefully. Treat it fairly. Be fair. Don't be part of this continuing cover-up. Do the right thing, remembering that if it doesn't fit, you must acquit, that if these messengers have lied to you, you can't trust their message, that this has been a search for truth. That no matter how bad it looks, if truth is out there on a scaffold and wrong is in here on the throne, when that scaffold sways the

future and beyond the dim unknown standeth the same God—for all people—keeping watch above his own.

He watches all of us. He will watch you in your decision.

As I walked back to the counsel table, my teammates rose to meet me. One by one they congratulated me, even Bob Shapiro. "That was the greatest final argument I've ever heard," he said.

O. J. Simpson and I looked into each other's eyes. "Thank you" was all he could say. There was nothing else I wanted to hear.

Chris Darden and Marcia Clark followed with their rebuttals. It was clear from their demeanor that they felt they had lost the jury. In fact, during the morning break, Marcia had asked one of the reporters to stay behind. "Do you think they'll even listen to me?" she had asked, gesturing toward the empty jury box.

"Well, they're listening to Johnnie," the reporter replied, "so I assume they'll listen to you. You'll have to give one hell of an argument, but I'm just a reporter and you don't really need me to tell you that." In fact, when Marcia finished her rebuttal and offered to leave up her most important chart so that the jurors could make notes, not a single one lifted her or his pencil.

At 4:08 P.M. September 29, 1995, Judge Lance Ito concluded his instructions, submitted the case to the jury, and placed O. J. Simpson's future in their hands. Three minutes later, a jury room buzzer sounded three times, signaling that a foreperson had been selected. The decision came so quickly that it unnerved us all.

"Maybe they've got a verdict and we can all go home," I quipped to the court. The laughter that followed broke what had been a day of almost unbearable tension for us all. The jurors were sent back to their hotel for the weekend; their deliberations would resume the following Monday. All of us expected that their consideration of the yearlong trial would certainly take days, perhaps weeks. Dale, our friends the Sunderlands, and I took the opportunity to slip out of town on a discreet visit to the Napa Valley in Northern California, where we planned to celebrate my October 2 birthday in peace and privacy.

On Monday, October 2, Carl Douglas was charged with baby-sitting the jury—that is, with going to court each day and standing by for the questions, which on murder cases panels almost inevitably ask. Bill Hodgman was designated as his prosecutorial counterpart, and both had brought ample paperwork to fill what they assumed would be a week or so of empty hours. At 11 A.M., the jury requested that testimony given by Allan Park, the limousine driver who had picked up O.J. on the night of the murders, be read back to them.

Carl went to lunch after telephoning Jan, our receptionist, and asking her to contact me and inform me of the request for a readback. He was slightly perplexed, as it was unusually early in the process for the jurors to ask for testimony. When he returned from lunch, he was even more troubled to learn that the jurors wished to hear only that part of Park's testimony dealing with the so-called shadowy figure coming out of the house. Carl objected; the jurors, he felt, should hear all of Park's testimony. Ito concurred.

For the next hour, the jury sat listening, then took a break. The bailiff who accompanied them into the jury room returned and reported, "They didn't want to hear all of the testimony."

At 2:05 the jury sent out a second note saying they did not need to hear any additional testimony. Carl, Judge Ito, Hodgman, and Chris Darden, who had come down for the reading, stood around chatting in a friendly fashion. Moments later, another note came out of the jury room. It read: "We have reached a decision, could you please send the instructions?"

Ito blanched, then showed it to Hodgman, who also paled, as Carl read it over his shoulder.

"Gee, Bill," Carl said. "You look the way I feel."

"Thanks a lot, Carl," Hodgman replied. "I have to go upstairs and tell my boss about this, so I'd better take this look off my face."

"Holy cow," Ito suddenly said as the full import of the note dawned on him. The jurors had copies of his instructions with them. Though they'd used the wrong term, what they were requesting were verdict forms. It was 2:20 P.M.

"Take these back to them," he said to his clerk, Deirdre Robertson, then to the others: "Stick around. If they come back with a verdict quickly, we're all going to be . . . Just stick around."

Carl bolted for the telephone and called Jan. "Find Johnnie," he said. "Don't ask me why. Find him. Wherever he is, find him."

Carl spent the next eight minutes in the lockup trying to calm O. J. Simpson, who naturally feared the worst. "Juice," Carl shouted, "it can't be guilty. It's only been three hours. I have had jurors in cases of gang bangers involved in shootings with an impeccable eyewitness take more than three hours to deliberate. This jury would not convict O. J. Simpson in three hours."

AT 2:28 P.M., THE BUZZER FROM THE JURY ROOM sounded three times, the signal that a verdict had been reached. Carl, quickly calculating that it would have taken far longer to fill out the forms for a guilty verdict, was the first to realize that O. J. Simpson had probably been acquitted.

Minutes later, I was on the phone to the courtroom, speaking from the Opus One Winery in Napa, where the ever-resourceful Jan had located us in the middle of a leisurely tour and tasting.

"No way," Carl said, "there's no way they could have filled out those forms in eight minutes' time and come back with a conviction." We had to break off our conversation as the jury returned to the court. "Watch them," I said. "Then call me back. I want every detail. Every move. I want to know everything."

Armanda Cooley, the foreperson, confirmed that they had reached a verdict. Ito ordered it sealed until the next morning to give us all time to gather.

I spoke with Carl again a few minutes later. "Well," he said, "eight minutes, Johnnie, but they didn't look at us. I didn't get a vibe. But, Johnnie, after nine months this is a professional jury. They've learned to mask their feelings. They're not going to give out clues."

But we both had been around the block more than once. The facts suggested only one thing, even if we wouldn't allow ourselves to say it aloud. The ride into the San Francisco airport and the flight home to Los Angeles passed in a blur. What I recall most is what Ron Sunderland said to me as we prepared to leave the winery that afternoon. He draped his arm around my shoulder and said, "Johnnie, whatever happens, Hattie is proud of you."

AT HOME THAT NIGHT, THERE WERE PHONE CALLS FROM every member of the team but one. Scheck, Neufeld, Uelmen, Blasier—we all kicked around the sequence of events and, shyly, allowed ourselves the same guarded optimism.

"Here's hoping," said Barry Scheck from his Brooklyn apartment.

I never heard from Bob Shapiro. As I later discovered, he had phoned Alan Dershowitz and instructed him to begin working on the appeal that would follow a conviction. In the meantime, he slipped off to record a television interview with Barbara Walters to be broadcast the following evening. In it, he accused the rest of us of "playing the race card from the bottom of the deck." It was a desperate act of contrition for a defense he then believed had failed.

On Tuesday, October 3, 1995, Dale's Uncle Elliot, as he had done so often during the trial, called and led us in prayer. At 9 A.M., we were back in Judge Ito's courtroom. Shortly thereafter, I was on the phone with Pastor Epps, praying. "Whatever happens, Johnnie," he said to me, "you are a man who has tried to do his job properly, to help as many people as possible. We're proud of you here."

"Thank you, Pastor," I said. "Thank you very much."

Throughout the night, we had all tried to tease the meaning from the previous day's events. But despite our best efforts, we remained excruciatingly uncertain of what was about to occur. We had discreetly probed the bailiffs concerning the jury's behavior the evening before. Nothing they said told us anything we didn't already know, which was nothing. O.J. had questioned his jailers in his fashion and carefully scrutinized their every move for any clue to his fate. Nothing they had done or said, however, was particularly reassuring. We remained tense; Simpson clearly was frightened. I know that some lawyers actually prepare their clients for a verdict, choreographing their possible responses in advance: "If it's guilty, we'll do this. If it's an acquittal, you do this, while I do that." I've never believed in the practice, and in this case it would have been useless, anyway. We all were too beset with doubts and uncertainty, too keyed up emotionally ever to follow through on whatever plan we made.

At 10:07 A.M., the jury's sealed verdict was handed to Ito to read. As he looked down at it in silence, we searched the jury's faces for clues. Shapiro leaned over and said to our client, half out of his mind with worry, "It's going to be bad news, O.J. I can tell by the look on Ito's face."

"Be quiet," I snapped.

Seconds later, as the words "not guilty" echoed through the courtroom and across the nation, I muttered, "Yes, yes," and allowed my head to slump over onto O. J. Simpson's shoulder. There is no better support than a man restored to liberty.

There was a hubbub of postverdict press conferences. I offered thanks to God and to all the members of our team. Then, almost before I knew it, we were in the underground parking garage beneath the Criminal Courts Building. On this day, as on the day of our final arguments, the van that would carry us back to our office was allowed to pick us up there. Carl, Shawn, and I were euphoric, but as we got off the elevator, I couldn't help thinking back to the evening following our summations. That night, we three—exhausted but optimistic—had gotten off in this very spot and encountered Marcia Clark and Chris Darden.

Marcia stood apart, out in one of the darkened garage's open spaces. On her finger was a brightly colored yo-yo, which she flung over and over at the pavement under her feet. She never looked at it. Her eyes were trained on something distant, something the rest of us could not see. Up and down went the yo-yo. I walked over, put my arms around her and said, "Marcia Clark, you are one heck of a lawyer."

As I stepped away, not a word passed her lips. But as the yo-yo resumed its endless rise and fall, our eyes met briefly. Then she looked away.

Darden stood slumped nearby, his eyes fixed on a spot somewhere between his feet. I walked over and put my arms around him, too. "Brother," I said, "it wasn't personal. But, hey, we tried one heck of a case, didn't we?" There was no response.

Today, there would be no repetition of those awkward encounters. The prosecutors were up on the eighteenth floor, sifting through the emotional ashes before a bank of television cameras. Behind closed doors, just a foot away, the champagne their bosses had laid out in anticipation of victory sank unnoticed into a pool of melting ice.

Our celebration was to come. The van arrived. As the others clambered in, I looked about the darkened garage. O. J. Simpson had asked for my help, and though neither of us could have imagined what that ultimately would mean, I had kept faith with his trust. Behind me, the van's door slammed. Henry Grayson gunned the engine, and we shot up the concrete ramp and, suddenly, into the sunlit street.

One day, I thought, Geronimo Pratt and I will make this trip together.

15

A Duty of
Conversation

THE ACQUITTAL OF O. J. SIMPSON TRIGGERED A DIS-
cord which continues to roil through our nation. When the
outcry that followed the verdict rose with such force, many of
my friends and colleagues advised me that the best course of
action was to take a low profile.

"You are a lawyer," they said to me. "You've done your job.
Now let the professional talking heads, the guys with the word
processors, fight this thing out. You've got the glory. Why take
the lumps?"

On one level, that certainly was sound advice. I had—and
have—other cases to try, other clients who need my help. An
attorney in that position can have worse things said of him than,
"Well, I don't much like him or particularly care for what he did

in that case. But if I ever get in trouble, I'm calling Johnnie Cochran." And yet, some deep part of me insisted that daring, not prudence, was the virtue required by the moment. That thought crystallized with greatest clarity when I read one national columnist's remark that "Johnnie Cochran is a good lawyer, but a bad citizen."

Now, on one level, only a fool would allow himself to be defined by op-ed-page intellectuals who never have had a thought so complex that it could not be contained in 750 words. But it is also true that no one living in this country at this time can afford to dismiss the duties of citizenship. My dear father, who as a schoolboy in a segregated Louisiana high school was so eloquent his classmates dubbed him "Demosthenes," has several times quoted to me the Greek orator's famous aphorism: "There will be justice in Athens when those who are not injured are as outraged as those who are." In fact, the Athenian notion of citizenship informed the thinking of our own Founding Fathers. One of its key components was the insistence that all the city's citizens owed each other a duty of conversation, by which they meant a willingness to come together regularly and discuss their mutual interests.

There may never have been a time when we Americans so desperately needed to acknowledge precisely that duty to each other.

I believe that we Americans should vow two things: We owe each other a duty of honest conversation about *all* those things that unite and divide us, *and* a promise that we will open ourselves to the possibility that, in reasoning together, we may change each other for the better.

Since O. J. Simpson's acquittal, I have spoken to professional, church, and school audiences in eight countries, twenty-eight states, and more than fifty cities. I have found the people I met, whatever their race, religion, or ethnicity, remarkably open to the kind of dialogue the op-ed-page pundits insist has vanished from our national life. To those pundits who continue to insist that we have lost not only the will to discuss the problem of race in America, but also the very vocabulary with which to conduct such a discussion, I can only say that we will not find the words in silence. We must speak with one another about these critical issues, even if our speech is halting and its implications, at times, are uncomfortable. As I have said to so many of those audiences since the trial: "We should not run and hide. We should acknowledge the divide. We should work together to make things better."

The most interesting part of all my encounters has been the dialogue that occurs in the question-and-answer sessions I always try to have following my talks, wherever they are. Clearly, the verdict in the Simpson case was a stunning—even painful—event for many white Americans; its aftermath has hit many African Americans with similar force. Yet through all these months, in all these places, all these people and I have found nothing about the case that we could not discuss with one another. Certain questions have arisen over and over, and here are the thoughts to which they have led me:

Did you play the "race card" to win O.J.'s case?

No, we did not. In fact, I find that phrase distasteful, since it trivializes not only the criminal justice system, but also the most important social issue in out society, the question of racial equality. But if some people insist in comparing a double murder trial to a card game, then they ought to be honest enough to admit that we played the history and credibility cards. And, in my mind at least, that is not a distinction without a difference. "Race card," of course, is a metaphor and open to interpretation, but what I take it to mean—not unreasonably, I think—is this: As an African American advocate, I used some form of unspoken communication to arouse the unexamined attitudes, blind prejudices, and instinctual predispositions of our jury, which was made up mostly of blacks, who by nature are prey to their animal passions and easily led.

Professor Wilcox, who wrote the encyclopedia entry on race I read so long ago, would be proud. What do we have here but a slightly more polite reproduction of his definition of "the negro," with his propensity for mindless atrocity?

The defense team believed, in general, that African Americans would make particularly good jurors in this case because our defense rose and fell on our ability to present evidence of police misconduct. Our challenge, which we met, was to demonstrate that the Los Angeles Police Department rushed to judgment in O. J. Simpson's case and that, when it reached its conclusion, some members of the department lied and manipulated evidence to ensure that everyone else would share their hasty conclusion. To give the evidence of such conduct a fair hearing, a person must at least be willing to entertain the possibility that some police officers do such things in some circumstances.

We Americans, regrettably, remain two nations. We live in different neighborhoods, attend different schools, pursue our separate pleasures, and, most notably, worship apart from one another. We also have very different experiences with many of our public institutions. In white neighborhoods in Los Angeles, for example, the police department is largely benevolent, a helpful presence. You call them when something goes wrong; they come quickly and are polite, helpful, and reassuring.

But, as the story we have shared together in this book amply demonstrates, the LAPD has for generations behaved much differently in the city's predominantly minority neighborhoods. There is a long history of abusive, unpunished, even officially sanctioned misconduct. Much of that has changed; more remains to be done. Still, that history has left African American Angelenos with a well-founded skepticism about police conduct. They know that for *some* officers it is not an aberration but a pattern of conduct. More important, they know that such things do happen. It is to them a source of sadness and even anger—but not of surprise. This knowledge, however, has not made black Angelenos reflexively bitter toward the LAPD. Quite the contrary: Anyone who thinks our African American residents are hostile to their police ought to attend one of the dozens of neighborhood watch meetings the department conducts throughout South Los Angeles on any given night of the week. There, in an atmosphere of friendly goodwill, the department and the people of those communities work constructively together to ensure the safety of their neighborhoods. If anything, African Americans, particularly those who belong to our city's large black middle class, are a classic law and order constituency and the LAPD increasingly relies on their support. But they also are realistic constituents; they know their police are not perfect. They know that the LAPD is an institution still struggling to shake off its legacy of bigotry and deceit. They know that, sometimes, that legacy is not a distasteful artifact, but a grim presence.

Blacks do not believe that is true all the time, but their collective experience allows them to entertain the possibility that it happens some of the time. In other words, if you can present them with credible, coherent evidence of police misconduct, they will not look away, shake their heads, and mutter, "No, that doesn't happen. There has to be some other explanation."

O. J. Simpson, like any other person accused of a crime, had an absolute right to have his fate decided by a jury of his peers, a jury whose experiences encompassed the entire history of Los Angeles and all its people. That is what he received, and, I believe, the verdict handed down on the charges against him reflected that fact.

In connection with this "race card" question, I also have to say something about the incident that was, for me, the most painful of the entire trial. That was the accusation that by comparing Mark Fuhrman to Adolf Hitler in my final argument, I trivialized the *Shoah* or Holocaust. I never intended to suggest that Fuhrman's perjury was morally—or in any sense—comparable to the genocidal crimes of the Third Reich. Fuhrman did express a desire to bomb and burn all black people, and even an admiration for the Nazis through his acquisition of their memorabilia. He was, as the tapes incontrovertibly demonstrated, also an anti-Semite. I never suggested nor do I believe, however, that Fuhrman and Hitler were the same. I have been to Yad Vashem. No one goes away from that unchanged.

But I do continue to believe that the authoritarian impulse that lurks in the Mark Fuhrmans in our police forces is essentially totalitarian. If it is allowed to flourish unchecked by decent people, it can eventually grow to proportions of Hitlerian horror. The policeman on the street is the most powerful person in the criminal justice system. If he is in the grip of some grim private impulse or carries with him some bigoted private agenda, he can—all on his own—take your life, beat you, and choose to lie about your guilt or innocence. If the rest of the system then elects to accept his word without question, you are utterly at his mercy.

In one of its most inspiring moral injunctions the Talmud tells us, "If you save one life, it is as if you had saved the entire world." The wisdom of that saying is, of course, its recognition of the generative potential inherent in each man and woman. When you save a single life, you protect for all humanity all that person will accomplish and all that his or her children may do for the world ahead. Conversely, when you snuff out a life, you also deny all humanity, for all time, all the good and constructive things that he—and *all* his descendants—might have accomplished. In that sense, the bad cop, the killer cop, whom I have encountered more times than I care to recall, is a tiny portion of that great evil, which if allowed to increase leads to Auschwitz, to the massacre of the Armenians, the Muslims in Bosnia, the Rwandans, and even more recently, the Kurds.

As distressing as the misunderstanding of my passing reference to Hitler was, I also was interested in how quickly it was seized upon and misconstrued by people who have no particular interest in the welfare and progress of either the African American or Jewish communities. They did seem to take a kind of malicious delight, however, in the opportunity to foment discord between two groups of Americans who share so many values and, so often, a common struggle.

And that brings us back to this question of the "race card." As Bill Cosby once quipped, "Who dealt the hand? Who really owns the deck?"

How can you defend people who do those terrible things?

I am an advocate. I have sworn an oath to defend our Constitution and our laws. As I have labored to keep faith with that oath, I have been inspired by the examples and words of many colleagues. But the words to which I have returned again and again were spoken not by another member of the bar but by Dr. Martin Luther King, Jr., during one of the addresses he gave in the months surrounding the heroic Birmingham organizing campaign. In that speech, Dr. King compared our Declaration of Independence to a "promissory note," a binding pledge that this nation would guarantee all men and women their inalienable rights. He said, "It is obvious today that America has defaulted on this promissory note insofar as her citizens of color are concerned. Instead of honoring this sacred obligation, America has given the Negro people a bad check, a check which has come back marked 'insufficient funds.' "

Dr. King's remarks were addressed specifically to the condition of African American people, but the principle he propounded was a general one. Our Declaration of Independence and our Constitution, with its Bill of Rights, are the greatest blueprint ever devised for the practical realization of human liberty and happiness. They are not a vision of some distant and idealized future but living documents to be lived out right now, in every house on every street in every town in every state across this country.

Now, it is true that I do not accept every case that comes through the office door. Our firm has consciously decided not to represent drug dealers. I still recall quite vividly the circumstances under which we reached that decision. At the time, I had successfully represented a man charged with murder. He remained in custody after his acquittal, however, because he also faced charges growing out of his alleged drug dealing. He asked me to represent him on that matter, as well. While I was weighing whether to accept the case, one of his associates delivered $600,000 in cash to my office. The size of this proposed retainer was impressive, but not half so impressive as its bulk, consisting—as they say in the crime reports—of bills in various denominations, mostly small. There were so many bills we had trouble even counting them. Ultimately, we had to enlist the help of a bank's mechanical counter. The currency filled our office safe, then spilled over into every cabinet in the place with a lock. At that time, it was the largest retainer we'd ever received in a criminal case.

But as a professional intimately involved in the life of my city's African American community, I felt compelled to stop and ask myself: Do I really want to profit in any fashion from an activity that has brought so much misery and death, one that is robbing the most vulnerable among us of their hope and their futures?

The answer, I decided, was no. We re-counted every penny of the proposed retainer and returned it to the client's associates. Had I been the only lawyer in town, my answer might have been a different one. But, given the size of the local bar and the amount of cash on hand, I had no doubt the client would find a capable attorney to defend him. And from that day to this, we've never handled another case where the client was charged with drug trafficking.

But the fact that a lawyer need not take *every* case does not give him license to avoid *any* case that is unpleasant or unpopular. As a lawyer, I am committed to the principle that our constitutional guarantees can have force only if we consider and protect all the rights of all our people one individual at a time. A criminal trial provides for just such a consideration. That is why we trust our lives and liberty to the people. We do it because we know that, once again, Dr. King was right: "Injustice anywhere is a threat to justice everywhere."

How did you keep the "Dream Team" together?

In some ways, that is the most fascinating question of all, and in a very important way it may speak most directly to the reason so many people have been willing to dismiss O. J. Simpson's defense as a "race card." Before the O. J. Simpson trial put me on television screens around the world, the only black attorney ever to occupy a continuing role on TV was the infamous Algonquin J. Calhoun on the old *Amos 'n' Andy* show. Vain, verbose, avaricious, charmingly deceitful, and fundamentally incompetent, he conformed comfortably to most of the prevailing stereotypes about black professionals in general and African American lawyers in particular. By contrast, our defense team looked like the real America: Its members were men and women, young and old, black and white; Catholics, Protestants, Jews, and agnostics.

We were Democrat and, in at least one instance, Republican. We came from different parts of the country and had grown up in families rich, poor, and in between. The unspoken assumption on the part of many people is that in such a situation, race must be a divisive issue and that a black participant must inevitably be a divisive figure. That assumption blinds those who hold it to what our team understood: I was the most experienced trial lawyer involved. I had won dozens of high-profile cases in the very courthouse in which we were going to appear. I had the experience of managing a good-sized law firm and coordinating the work of numerous attorneys cooperating on complex litigation. I had the trust and confidence of our client. Given that background, and the fact that nearly all our teammates were committed, talented, highly principled advocates, why wouldn't I be able to "hold them together"—unless, of course, one assumes that skin color disqualifies one from leadership.

Many of our fellow Americans do assume just that. That is why, despite the fact that we African Americans comprise 12 percent of our nation's population, only 4.2 percent of all physicians are black, only 3.3 percent of all lawyers, only 3.7 percent of all engineers, and barely 5 percent of all college professors. The overwhelming majority of professors, by the way, are disproportionately clustered in institutions with virtually all-black student bodies.

Clearly, the implication of this question troubles some people on another level. Americans have grown accustomed to accepting accomplished African Americans in a variety of essentially nonthreatening roles—as entertainers and athletes, for example. But constitutionalism is as close to an established church as we Americans have. The courts are, in that sense, a kind of civic temple and our lawyers and judges a sort of priesthood. The questions at stake in a courtroom are among those we Americans hold most sacred, and their resolution involves the real power of the state. To watch an African American advocate participate not only as an equal but also as a victor in that process is a profoundly disturbing experience for some people.

To them, it is hard to know what to say except: Get over it.

How do you really feel about O. J. Simpson?

When two people share the kind of experience O.J. and I did, they are bound to develop strong—sometimes contradictory—feelings concerning one another. But the feelings I have for O.J. actually are pretty straightforward: I like him, both as a client and as a man. When a client tells you he is innocent and asks you to defend that claim, there's an implied promise that he is being straight with you. O.J. always kept his word; he never lied to us. When he told us something about his case, it always checked out. I can't say the same for all my clients. He also was the most instinctively perceptive client I've ever represented. He came into the criminal justice system knowing virtually nothing about its intricacies. Yet, time and again, I was amazed by how shrewdly intelligent his analysis and advice could be. Under our system, criminal defendants must be mentally able to "cooperate in their own defense." O.J. was one of those rare clients who was not only able to, but did cooperate in trying his own case.

As a man, O. J. Simpson has spent a lifetime cultivating the image of a guy who is not only talented, but also genuinely personable. He succeeded not because he is a brilliant actor, but because he really is both talented and personable. We got to know each other under the most difficult circumstances imaginable. I thought he was a nice guy when we started and I still think so.

The only thing I regret about our relationship is the fact that I can only stand by and watch while this man, who was acquitted of all the charges filed against him, is prevented from resuming the life he, like every other American, is entitled to lead.

How do you feel about the prosecutors?

The contentiousness between the prosecutors and our team grew out of our sworn fidelity to the roles required of us by the adversarial system of justice. As far as I was concerned, nothing that passed between us was personal. It's worth remembering that I've also sat on their side of the courtroom. During my years in the district attorney's office, I didn't only supervise. I also tried cases, including murder cases. I know both the trials and the satisfactions on their side of the room. I have great respect for Bill Hodgman and Marcia Clark as professional prosecutors. Circumstantial evidence cases—and, at the end of the day, that's what the case against O. J. Simpson was—are always difficult. If some of the investigators who compile that evidence are sloppy, deceitful, and biased, as they were in this case, things become very difficult indeed. Bill and Marcia did the best they could with what they had, but it was not sufficient to meet the burden of proof imposed on the state by our Constitution. I bear Chris Darden no ill will. In fact, during the trial, on several occasions, I offered him advice regarding his role with Mark Fuhrman, and on a couple of occasions since the trial I have tried to reach out to him, even serving as one of the hosts and speakers at a reception in his honor in December 1995. Thus far, he has not responded in kind. I wish him well and, more than that, wisdom. Unresolved "two-ness" is a difficult burden for an African American professional to bear in this society. It can be embittering, and, in that connection, I must also say that I do resent the attacks on our jury Darden has made since the trial's conclusion. That brings us to the next question.

What do you think of the jury?

There is a distressing paradox in most of the attacks leveled against these fourteen people who gave so much of themselves to make our system's promise of due process a living reality in Judge Lance Ito's courtroom. Every other opinion rendered concerning this case and its outcome—including my own—is the product of the extraordinary amount of publicity and contention that attended this trial. To some extent, all our views have been shaped by the pundits, TV talk shows, newspaper supplements, radio panels, and, sadly, tabloid "exposés" that have surrounded this whole sequence of events. There are only fourteen people in this entire country who we know formed their opinions about the case against O. J. Simpson solely on the basis of the evidence legally presented to them in court. Those fourteen people are the twelve jurors and two alternates who spent more than a year sequestered from their friends, loved ones, and normal lives.

For just five dollars a day, they gave up everything and everyone to sit through months of tedious testimony so that one man they had never met could receive the justice to which he is entitled. That is precisely the sort of selflessness that Abraham Lincoln had in mind when he called jury service "the highest exercise of citizenship."

Judge Ito, who carefully monitored everything involving our jury, remarked to us on more than one occasion that he had never seen a more diligent, hardworking group of serious-minded people. I agree, as do all the other members of the defense team.

These fourteen good citizens deserve our gratitude and not our censure. If we withhold the one and shower these folks with contempt, accusations, and abuse, what message are we sending to future juries? How many of them, lacking the independence and courage of our panelists, will be intimidated out of the full exercise of their essential function as the conscience of our community? If any reform is needed in our criminal justice system, it is to improve the way we treat these citizen volunteers.

What do you think of Judge Lance Ito?

I knew and appreciated Lance Ito as a fellow prosecutor and, later, as a judge before whom I have always been delighted to appear. Though his background as a career prosecutor means we differ on many issues involved in the criminal justice system, we are of one mind when it comes to the sanctity of its basic principles. Judge Ito is a man of great principle and integrity and a better judge than many because of his willingness to temper the iron fist of justice with reason and compassion. Of course, I still have trouble with his allowing the dream testimony. But although he ruled against us far more than I obviously would have preferred, he fulfilled his duty in O. J. Simpson's case: He guaranteed a credible jury and, therefore, a credible verdict.

That's not as easy as it sounds. Judges not only are fallible human beings like the rest of us, but also are subject to an array of behind-the-scenes political pressures, which the public never sees. During my years in the district attorney's office, I was disturbed to see firsthand how high-level officials in the office used the threat of blanket affidavits to intimidate judges. In the Simpson trial, we witnessed an example of just how pervasive that practice has become in today's criminal justice system.

On the day the district attorney was threatening to demand that Ito disqualify himself on the theory that Fuhrman's tape-recorded remarks about the judge's wife had created a conflict of interest, we all prepared to go into chambers to discuss the issue.

As he slouched past Peter Neufeld, Chris Darden casually remarked, "We [prosecutors] own every judge in this building, and now we're going to own this one, too."

If we had the slightest doubt about that remark's implications, they became clear later when Darden seated himself in the judge's chambers and began to lecture him on his alleged mistreatment of Brian Kelberg and Marcia Clark. The implied quid pro quo was clear: Do as we demand or you're off the case.

In such an atmosphere, judicial independence is not a thing to be taken lightly.

Don't you think criminal defendants have too many rights in our system?

For thirty-three years I've been defending the principles of justice outlined in the Constitution. Today, some believe that our system of justice needs changing, not defending. While they sit and scan the morning headlines or watch the nightly news, they feel that the emphasis on the *criminal* in the criminal justice system is entirely misplaced. Criminals are eligible for justice, victims wind up forgotten. Or so they believe. What these individuals fail to acknowledge, perhaps don't want to believe, is that judges are human, police officers may lie, and innocent people are sometimes charged with crimes.

I am an advocate because I understand that while you may be able to guarantee that you won't commit a crime, you can't guarantee that you won't be charged with a crime. And if you were charged with a crime, or if you mother or your father or your sister or your brother were charged with a crime, wouldn't you want every protection afforded you by the Constitution? Or would you feel that you had too many rights? And if you stood wrongly accused, who's the victim then?

When I walk into a courtroom, I'm not merely defending the

individual who stands accused. I'm defending a legal system that guarantees the presumption of innocence and every individual's right to equal protection under the law. The only way that you or I can be assured of our right to a fair trial is if every citizen in the land is assured of his or her right to a fair trial. When one of us is denied justice, all of us are denied justice.

I'm sure, for example, that Mark Fuhrman's views on the Fifth Amendment's protections against self-incrimination changed drastically as he made his long, lonely last walk up to the witness stand. Fuhrman, by the way, was absolutely entitled to invoke his constitutional privilege. I hope never to see the day when Americans, whatever their views, are hauled into court and compelled to give evidence against themselves. That would be not only a legal disaster but a grotesque human tragedy.

I feel the same about those people who argue that we ought to make our jury system more "efficient" by eliminating attorney and judicial voir dire and simply empaneling the first twelve people selected at random. That's the sort of hardheaded academic proposal to which the late C. Wright Mills used to refer as "crackpot realism." What's cracked about it is that we live in a multicultural society in which some people really do harbor bias against one another. Rooting that out may be inefficient, but can anyone argue that it really isn't necessary? What if the defendant is black or Jewish and the first twelve people called spend most of their free time watching *Triumph of the Will* and painting swastikas on the shuls in the next neighborhood? Can you reasonably expect that a defendant will get a fair trial under those circumstances?

What's really going on here is a set of assumptions that go like this:

Since the police have already arrested our generic criminal defendant (hereafter referred to as the GCD) and since the government's prosecutors have already charged him with a crime, it's safe to assume that all these serious, sane people can't be wrong. We can just do the efficient thing and assume our GCD is guilty. And, since the GCD is guilty, he should be convicted as expeditiously as possible. Any twelve people will do for the job. It does not matter if the twelve people randomly selected have an unreasonable (even pathological) loathing for the GCD. In fact, that might even be preferable—all the better to convict him, my dear, which is the most efficient result of all.

Now imagine yourself or someone about whom you care as the GCD. You might appreciate some attention to your rights.

I have similar feelings about proposals to eliminate the exclusionary rule. Without the threat of serious sanctions for official violation of our Fourth Amendment protections against unreasonable searches and seizures, no citizen would be safe from unbridled police overreaching. However distasteful the thought, there are some law enforcement officers willing to corrupt the process to convict defendants they believe are guilty. Sometimes that corruption involves manufacturing evidence. The exclusionary rule protects us against that abuse. In the criminal justice system, our trials are a search for truth, but not, alas, an absolute truth. That, like perfection, is beyond our reach this side of the grave. We do seek an attainable legal truth. We pursue it by forcing people, whatever their power or position, to play by the rules, to respect our right to privacy, to respect the sanctity of our homes and consciences. As a society, we esteem those values every bit as much as the conviction of the guilty. If we really wanted to give ourselves over to the fruitless pursuit of imagined absolute truth, we should allow the police to beat or torture suspects and witnesses until they speak what is demanded of them. We should allow our police to go anywhere and search anyone or anything without warrant or probable cause.

I still don't think that would yield absolute truth, but I guarantee it would turn the Constitution on its head and give us a police state. I say that with some confidence because it already has been tried in other places.

Are you anti-police?

Not long after O. J. Simpson's acquittal, I was washing my hands in a men's room at O'Hare International Airport in Chicago when a burly, older white man approached me. He identified himself as a retired LAPD officer and then said to me: "You just had to do it, didn't you? You just had to embarrass us in front of the whole world."

"My brother," I said to him evenly, fighting back my rising anger, "I did not embarrass you or anyone in the department. You humiliated yourselves."

Today, the overwhelming majority of the officers in the Los Angeles Police Department, like the vast majority of their colleagues across this country, are good and decent people rendering an indispensable civic service at great risk and for little compensation. Those officers have all my support and respect, as they are entitled to receive from every one of us. But credibility attaches to the person and not the position. When the police and city officials across this country close their eyes to the existence of a Mark Fuhrman because it is the convenient and expedient thing to do, it is they who humiliate all the good cops whose badges the Fuhrmans are not worthy to wear.

What do you think of the media?

At about the midpoint in the Simpson trial, Carl Douglas and I left the courthouse for lunch one day. When we returned, the building had been closed off by one of the recurrent bomb scares through which we suffered. I needed to let Judge Ito, who was sealed off in his courtroom at that point, know where we were.

As Carl and I tried to decide what to do, one of the nearby reporters overheard us and invited me to use the phone in her organization's trailer. It was in the media center that had been set up across the street from the Criminal Courts Building and dubbed "Camp O.J."

I thanked her, followed her to the trailer, and sat down at a desk inside. As I dialed the phone, I looked up. There, thumb-tacked to the wall, was a copy of my mother's death certificate. I slammed down the phone and demanded, "What is that doing here?"

"Oh," the unembarrassed reporter said to me, "don't worry. We got a tip that your mother had died penniless in a welfare hotel in Las Vegas, and we just had to check it out."

I rose in silent disgust and left.

Nothing—not the tabloid talk shows that caricatured not only my case but also my personal life, not the photographers who hounded us at every turn—better sums up the excesses into which the Simpson frenzy drew the American media. I respect the First Amendment as deeply as I do every other part of our Bill of Rights. We do not require restrictions on our freedom of expression any more than we need to reform our criminal justice system. What we do require is the exercise of responsible citizen-ship by the participants in both systems. The O. J. Simpson trial ought to provide the American media with an opportunity for some searching discussion of where the line between the serious press and the tabloid media—both print and electronic—ought to be drawn. In our case it blurred, to the detriment of everyone involved. I will leave it to others more qualified and experienced in these matters to say precisely where that line ought to be inscribed, but it needs to be drawn firmly and clearly.

On the specific matter of cameras in the courtroom, I believe that the First Amendment and the public interest give them the right to be there. For all the soap opera quality our case assumed for some people, its televised proceedings were an invaluable civics lesson for many more. At one point, for example, a schoolteacher approached Dean Gerry Uelmen and me on the street one day and thanked us for what was happening in court.

"The young people in my class," she said, "actually have been talking about the Fourth Amendment. You've given the whole country a seminar on the Constitution and illegal search and seizure."

"Then at this point," laughed the self-deprecating Gerry, "the only people left in this country who don't understand the Fourth Amendment are Kathleen Powell and Lance Ito," the judges who had denied his motion to suppress the fruits of the LAPD's warrantless searches.

What were the most memorable moments in O. J. Simpson's trial?

As I look back over those months of turmoil and conflict, four events stand out in my mind. The first three were the turning points in our journey to justice:

First—and perhaps most important—was the day on which we finished picking our jurors. As proud as we trial lawyers are of our abilities, the fact is that none of our skills, however polished, and none of our evidence, however convincing, necessarily amounts to anything, if we don't have a jury that is willing to listen. In O.J.'s case, we got state-of-the-art social science advice from Jo-Ellan Dimitrius, and then took it to heart. In our voir dire, we acted on her findings and, as a result, we were fortunate enough to try our case to a jury willing and able to accurately assess our evidence.

Second, of course, was Chris Darden's disastrous decision to ask O.J. to try on the gloves recovered at Bundy and Rockingham. What can I say except, "If it doesn't fit, you must acquit." The truth is that the prosecutors never really recovered from that debacle.

Third, the day that Mark Fuhrman came into court and was forced to assert his Fifth Amendment privilege is, for me, unforgettable. After hearing the prosecution's key witness impeached with his own recorded voice, as Fuhrman was, seeing him squirming there in the witness box was one of the high points in my career as an attorney. More important, in the jury's mind the tapes crowned the mountain of reasonable doubt we asked them to climb.

Last, there was the day Judge Ito's clerk read the verdict and sent O. J. Simpson home a free man. The experience of securing another human being's liberty is not a thrill, but an honor. I have never felt that more deeply than the day we restored O.J. to his family.

Finally, there is this:

After all that's happened, do you really think that blacks and whites can still find common ground in this country?

If you have followed me all this way, on this journey to justice, then you know what my answer is. Yes, of course, but only if we want it. And we must want it not only because we have no choice but also because, as my wise father would say, "It's the right thing to do."

Our successful defense of O. J. Simpson was built on the unspoken faith we shared with one another that competence, character, and courage come in all colors. What was true of our team is true of the nation from which we came and whose ideals we endeavored to serve.

At this century's beginning, a great thinker, W. E. B. Du Bois, said that the "problem of the twentieth century is the problem of the color line." At its midpoint, a great poet, W. H. Auden, wrote, "We must love one another or die."

Both things are true, and they point the way forward for us all. We can neither deny our greatest problem nor avoid the solution that is inherent in all the creeds and philosophies that express our better nature. My own access to that solution is through my Christian faith. Its moral vocabulary is my own; others will find this solution in the phrases of their own traditions. I will hold dearly to those I first heard in the Little Union Baptist Church, when my mother took my hand in hers and we sang together the words of her favorite hymn, "Hold to God's Unchanging Hand":

> *Time is filled with swift transition,*
> *Naught of earth unmoved can stand.*
> *Build your hopes on things eternal,*
> *Hold to God's unchanging hand!*
>
> *When your journey is completed,*
> *If to God you have been true,*
> *Fair and bright the home in glory,*
> *Your enraptured soul will view!*
> *Build your hopes on things eternal,*
>
> *Hold to God's unchanging hand!*
> *Amen!*

ACKNOWLEDGMENTS

FIRST OF ALL, GIVING HONOR TO GOD, WHO IS WORTHY to be praised and without whom this project would have never been completed. There are so many others to thank for assisting me in writing *Journey to Justice*. Initially, I want to thank and also dedicate this book to my longtime mentor, friend, and adviser, Sydney M. Irmas, who departed this life on August 29, 1996. To my collaborator, the incomparable Tim Rutten, who did an extraordinary job in capturing my voice and all other aspects of this unfinished odyssey. I am eternally grateful for all of your magnificent work.

I also wish to express my deep appreciation to my client Elmer G. Pratt, who, although he still remains incarcerated for a crime that he did not commit, has remained steadfast in his encouragement and faith in me and in the justice system. I can only hope that justice will soon be done in his case.

I want to thank my literary agent, Russell Galen, for his vision and wisdom in helping to get this project off the ground.

To Linda Grey, the president of Ballantine Books, for her

strong support and encouragement throughout this endeavor. To my editor, Cheryl Woodruff, associate publisher of One World Books, who is simply the best, and without whom this project would never have been started or completed. To Beverly Robinson, One World's outstanding publicity director, for her steady hand in planning all media-related aspects of this project. To the wonderful staff at Ballantine Books who assisted Cheryl Woodruff in bringing this project to fruition, most especially Gary Brozek, Nora Reichard, Jeff Smith, and Leah Odze Epstein.

To my wonderful and devoted legal staff, including the irrepressible, diligent miracle worker Carmen Qualls, the efficient, genteel Eloise McGill, and my legal colleagues Carl Douglas, Shawn Snider Chapman, Eddie J. Harris, Eric G. Ferrer, Cameron Stewart, Brian Dunn, and Don Wilson. To Kamau Omowale and all the rest of my office personnel who have remained diligent and true and continue to operate at a high level of efficiency during the many months that I have been out of the office speaking around the country and writing this book.

To my family, especially my sisters Pearl Cochran Baker and Martha Jean Cochran Sherrard and my brother RaLonzo, and my friends and clients who have always been there for me, steadfast in their support, helping me to believe that all things are possible. Especially notable among my friends are Ron Sunderland, whom I have spoken to every day for the past thirty-three years; Ralph Wiley, for his contributions during the early part of this undertaking; Ted Alexander, who is my oldest friend; Congressman Julian Dixon, my longtime friend and mentor; and of course my stealth friend, who shall remain nameless but who is a pillar of support at all times.

Finally, I want to acknowledge the support of all of my ministers, from the inimitable Dr. C.A.W. Clark of Dallas, Texas, who was the first minister that I ever heard preach the Gospel at the Little Union Baptist Church in Shreveport, Louisiana, to Dr. Charles Hampton of Bethel Baptist Church in San Diego, California, the late Dr. J. Raymond Henderson, Dr. Thomas Kilgore, Jr., and my present pastor, Dr. William Saxe Epps, all of Second Baptist Church in Los Angeles, California.

Johnnie L. Cochran, Jr., lives in Los Angeles with his wife, Dale Mason, and his father, Johnnie L. Cochran, Sr.

Tim Rutten is an award-winning reporter for the *Los Angeles Times*. He lives in Los Angeles with his wife, Leslie Abramson, and their son, Aidan.